The Hamlyn Encyclopedia of
CRICKET

AUSTRALIA
1ST INNINGS 514
2ND INNINGS

ENGLAND
1ST INNINGS
2ND INNINGS

WICKETS   3

LAMB   9

GOWER   2

SUNDRIES   11

TOTAL 303

AUSTRALIA   V   ENGLAND

BOWLERS	WKTS	RUNS	BATSMEN	OUT B	RUNS	FALL OF WKTS
1 HUGHES		51	ATHEY	B 5	55	1 FOR 112
2 REID		28	BROAD	C 9 3	116	2 - 273
3 WAUGH	1	39	GATTING	C 3 5	100	3 - 283
4 BORDER		1	WHITAKER			4 -
5 SLEEP	2	57	RICHARDS			5 -
6 MATTHEWS		80	DE FREITAS			6 -
7 JONES			EMBUREY			7 -
8 BOON			EDMONDS			8 -
9 MARSH			DILLEY			9 -
RITCHIE			OVER №	91		OVERS RQD 98
DYER		UMPIRES	CRAFTER	RANDELL		

LIGHT   DRAUGHT   EXPORT   STATE XI   EXPORT   DRAUGHT   LIGHT

WEST END BEERS

The Hamlyn Encyclopedia of
CRICKET

Peter Wynne-Thomas and Peter Arnold

Foreword by
MIKE GATTING

Colour photography by
PATRICK EAGAR

HAMLYN

Photographic acknowledgements
All photographs in this book are by Patrick Eagar with the exception of
the following: Peter Arnold 42 bottom, 43 right; Nottinghamshire
County Cricket Club 7, 9, 10, 12, 13, 18, 23, 28, 33, 67, 72, 74, 80,
98, 115, 122 (all five), 125, 127, 129, 133, 141, 148, 149, 156, 162,
164 top, 168, 169 left and right, 170, 172, 173, 174 left and right,
175; The Photo Source, London 160; The Photo Source/Central Press,
London 20, 25, 43 left, 101, 120, 144-5, 165; The Photo Source/Fox,
London 29, 77 left; The Photo Source/Keystone, London 61, 79, 91,
105, 120, 147, 164 bottom.

Title page: *The Adelaide Oval, one of the most pleasant of Australian grounds*

Published by
The Hamlyn Publishing Group Limited
Bridge House, 69 London Road
Twickenham, Middlesex TW1 3SB, England
and distributed for them by
Octopus Distribution Services Limited
Rushden, Northamptonshire NN10 9RZ, England

First published in 1987

ISBN 0 600 55229 2

Printed in Italy

Foreword

I have had my ups and downs in cricket as much as most players – and in my case the ups are getting higher and the downs lower. Who would have thought that I would captain England in a victorious Ashes tour only a year after having a nose which looked and felt as if it had done 15 rounds with Mike Tyson? Cricket springs its surprises all the time, and after 12 years in the first-class game I realise I still haven't seen it all by a long way.

I expected to find a few more surprises in this encyclopedia, and I was not disappointed. Come on – do you know who are the reigning Olympic champions at cricket? I wonder how the spectators at Seoul in 1988 would take the sight of Marshall bowling to Gower, or Hadlee to Vengsarkar for an Olympic gold medal?

I enjoyed in particular the names of some of the old wandering clubs, the superb photographs of many of the grounds I have been lucky enough to play on and comparing the biographies of players I have known with those of the giants of the past. My favourite old-timer? The Aussie wicketkeeper in the very first Test, Blackham. Having had a nose job done by a Malcolm Marshall bouncer, I can sympathise with him losing most of his teeth. It must have been worse for him, because it was his own team that were responsible!

I got a lot of pleasure reading this book and I hope you do too.

Mike Gatting

A

Abandoned matches

The weather has caused three Test Matches to be abandoned without a ball being bowled. All three involved England v Australia and two of these – in 1890 and 1938 – were scheduled to be played at Old Trafford. The third should have taken place on Melbourne Cricket Ground in 1970/71; of the three only the last was replaced by another match being hastily arranged for a later date.

The worst season for weather in as much as it caused matches to be washed out totally was 1979, when no fewer than ten County Championship or other first-class games never started. In 1974 Hampshire looked certain to win the County Championship, but then found their last match totally rained off.

For some years in the 1920s County Championship matches which were very badly affected by the weather were not counted in the Championship table and the positions of the counties were based on a percentage of points to matches actually played.

Adelaide

The playing area at the Oval, Adelaide, is one of the largest, being 207 yards by 140 yards. Laid out in the 1860s, it was first used for first-class cricket in 1877/78 and is the headquarters of the South Australian Cricket Association, which has played in the Sheffield Shield since that competition was instituted in 1892/93. The first Test Match on the ground was England v Australia in 1884/85. The ground capacity is about 40,000 and it is the most pleasantly situated of Australia's Test venues.

Administration

The administration of cricket in England has grown in a very haphazard manner. The Laws (q.v.) were first written down in the early 18th century, and the first versions are now lost. The MCC have been the official arbitrators of the Laws since the beginning of the 19th century and still remain the holders of the world copyright in them.

The principal competition in England, the County Championship, was run more or less by gentlemen's agreement and the press until the first written regulations were drawn up in 1873, mainly to prevent cricketers playing for two counties in the same season and to enforce the definition of 'residential' qualification for a county. The MCC agreed to act as arbitrators in any disputes over this qualification, Surrey CCC having initiated the meetings which led to this agreement.

The next stage came in 1890, when the rules regarding the actual regulation of the County Championship were set up, and the officials of the major counties requested the MCC to administer the rules.

Until the 20th century, touring teams from England had no 'official' backing from either the first-class counties as a body or MCC and were either run by professional cricketers purely for financial gain or were holiday trips for well-to-do amateurs. The teams which represented England in Test Matches in England were chosen by the committee who ran the ground on which the match took place.

The MCC took over the running of major tours overseas in 1903/04, but only after A.C. MacLaren had tried and failed to raise his own team. In October 1898, the Board of Control for Test matches in England held its first meeting and later chose for the first time a group of selectors to pick the England team for the 1899 Tests. The MCC secretary acted as secretary to the Board. C.W. Alcock, the Surrey secretary, arranged the 1899 Australian fixture list, however, as he had done for many of the previous visits.

The ICC (Imperial Cricket Conference) was formed in 1909 and consisted of representatives of England, Australia and South Africa. The original purpose was to agree regulations for Test Matches. The Australian Board of Control had been set up in 1905 and the South African Cricket Association in 1890.

For domestic county cricket in England, the MCC set up the Advisory County Cricket Committee in 1904 and this remained in operation until the whole structure was altered in 1969. In that year the Cricket Council came into being to become the governing body of English cricket, with the Test and County Cricket Board as its arm governing those aspects and the National Cricket Association looking after the game below county level.

(*see also* Administrators, Australian Cricket Board of Control, International Cricket Conference, Marylebone Cricket Club, National Cricket Association, Test and County Cricket Board)

Administrators

Cricket at both county and national level is administered by a handful of paid officials and a large number of voluntary committees. The most farsighted and progressive of the 19th-century officials was C.W. Alcock, the secretary of Surrey, who organised the fixture programmes for many of the early Australian touring teams, as well as being the instigator and organiser of the first Test Match staged in England. It was hardly a coincidence that Surrey rose, during his secretaryship, from one of the weaker counties to being the Championship leaders.

Of the voluntary officials of the late 19th century, two who were to remain powerful figures until the 1930s were Lord Hawke and Lord Harris. The former transformed Yorkshire and changed the lot of the professional cricketer, whilst the latter was more concerned with the rules and regulations of the game. He made his name through a campaign to stamp out 'throwing', and he also tried to set up a county cricket organisation, which unfortunately failed, due perhaps to his absence in India during its formative years. Lord Harris was also a rigorous supporter of the rules regarding the qualification of county cricketers. One famous example was his objection to W.R. Hammond playing for Gloucestershire.

Succeeding Lord Harris as the most influential figure

behind the scenes was Pelham Warner. He was on the MCC committee for the best part of 60 years, was chairman of the Test Selection Committee more than once and during the Second World War ran the fixtures at Lord's. Sir Pelham Warner died in 1963 in his 90th year.

The mantle of Sir Pelham has rested in more recent years on G.O.B. Allen, like Warner a former England captain and chairman of the Test Selectors. Allen was also treasurer of MCC and a long-standing member of the committee.

Of the paid officials, the various secretaries of the MCC, notably F.E. Lacey, Col R.S. Rait Kerr, S.C. Griffith and J.A. Bailey, have been influential figures. The relatively new bodies, the Cricket Council, TCCB and NCA have all been served by some able officials: F.R. Brown, C.H. Palmer, F.G. Mann and D.B. Carr among them.

Whilst in England the authority of the MCC has never been seriously questioned and this authority has now passed to the Cricket Council, Australian administrators have not been so fortunate. The rivalry between the states, notably between Victoria and New South Wales, has made for difficulties on the Board of Control, who, too often, have been accused of being divorced from reality. The outstanding figure in Australian administration since the Second World War has been Sir Don Bradman. In England many of the famous English Test players have taken a major part in cricket administration, but by and large the same has not been the case in Australia, due no doubt to the instrinsic differences between the cricketing development of the two countries. (*see also* Administration)

Airedale and Wharfedale League

Based in Yorkshire, the League was founded in 1936 and its leading clubs of recent years have been Knaresborough, Otley and Ilkley. The League's knock-out competition is the Waddilove Cup and in 1985 Otley performed the 'double' by taking both League and Cup. One of the most outstanding performances ever achieved in the League was a century off 38 balls by Paul Smith for Menston v Horsforth in 1982. The golden jubilee of the League in 1986 was marked by a special match and dinner.

All-England Eleven

In 1846 William Clarke, the Nottinghamshire captain, conceived the idea of gathering together the leading cricketers in England and then touring the British Isles playing exhibition matches wherever it was financially viable to do so. The idea was a tremendous success and his team for many years had more invitations than they could fulfil. Since the team virtually represented the strength of England, most of their opponents fielded 22 players against the England Eleven.

In 1852 several professionals in the side rebelled against Clarke's autocratic ways and set up a rival team – the United All-England Eleven. After Clarke died in 1856, these two sides played annual matches against each other at Lord's and for some years they were the matches of the season. The All-England Eleven finally faded away in the 1880s.

All-rounders

The all-rounder is a cricketer who is worth his place in the eleven both as a batsman and as a bowler. As the game has developed, players at the first-class level have tended more and more to specialise and the number of cricketers who can be described as true all-rounders has decreased. The most accurate gauge of a player's all-round ability is the match 'double', since this is proof of being able to produce excellent performances with both bat and ball in the same circumstances.

Only three cricketers have achieved the 'double' of 100 runs and 10 wickets in a Test Match:

A.K. Davidson	44 & 80	5-135 & 6-87	Australia v West Indies (Brisbane) 1960/61
I.T. Botham	114	6-58 & 7-48	England v India (Bombay) 1979/80
Imran Khan	117	6-98 & 5-82	Pakistan v India (Faisalabad) 1982/83

At a slightly lower level, in first-class matches, only three players have performed the even more extraordinary feat of a century in an innings and all ten wickets in an innings in the same match:

V.E. Walker	108	10-74	England v Surrey (Oval) 1859

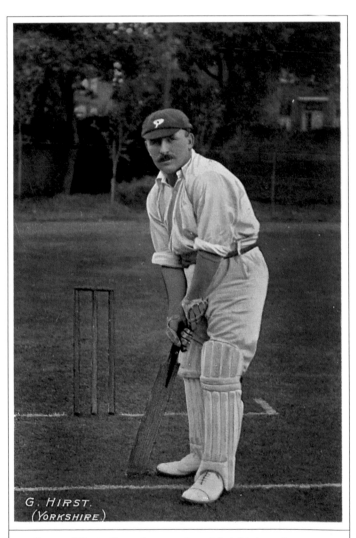

George Hirst, the only man in cricket history to score 2,000 runs and take 200 wickets in a season.

W.G. Grace	104	10-49	MCC v Oxford U (Oxford) 1886
F.A. Tarrant	182*	10-90	Maharajah of Cooch-Behar's XI v Lord Willingdon's XI (Poona) 1918/19

Two cricketers have scored centuries in each innings and taken ten wickets in the same match in first-class cricket:

G.H. Hirst	117* & 111	6-70 & 5-45	Yorkshire v Somerset (Bath) 1906
B.J.T. Bosanquet	103 & 100*	3-75 & 8-53	Middlesex v Sussex (Lord's) 1905

One player has made a double-century and taken 10 wickets in the same match in first-class cricket:

G. Giffen	217	9-96 & 7-70	South Australia v Victoria (Adelaide) 1891/92

The next measure of ability in English cricket used to be the season's 'double' of 1,000 runs and 100 wickets, with the greater feats of 2,000 runs and 200 wickets, or 2,000 runs and 100 wickets, as milestones for the outstanding players. Only one cricketer achieved 2,000 and 200: G.H. Hirst, 2,385 & 208, in 1906. J.H. Parks in 1937 hit 3,003 runs and took 101 wickets, whilst A.E. Trott twice scored over 1,000 runs and took over 200 wickets, a feat also achieved once by A.S. Kennedy.

Since the introduction of limited-overs cricket reduced the number of first-class matches in England, only one player has achieved the 1,000 runs and 100 wickets 'double': R.J. Hadlee in 1984.

Turning to career records, over 60 players have scored over 10,000 first-class runs and taken 1,000 first-class wickets. Only nine have gone on to the greater feat of 20,000 runs and 2,000 wickets:

	Runs	Avge	Wkts	Avge	Career
W.E. Astill (Leics)	22,731	22.55	2,431	23.76	1906-39
T.E. Bailey (Essex)	28,641	33.42	2,082	23.13	1945-67
W.G. Grace (Gloucs)	54,211	39.45	2,808	18.15	1865-1908
G.H. Hirst (Yorks)	36,356	34.13	2,742	18.73	1891-1929
R. Illingworth (Yorks, Leics)	24,134	28.06	2,072	20.28	1951-83
W. Rhodes (Yorks)	39,969	30.58	4,204	16.72	1898-1930
M.W. Tate (Sussex)	21,717	25.01	2,784	18.16	1912-37
F.J. Titmus (Middx, Surrey)	21,588	23.11	2,830	22.37	1949-82
F.E. Woolley (Kent)	58,959	40.77	2,066	19.87	1906-38

The above table obviously favours cricketers whose careers largely spanned the first 70 years of the 20th century. Turning to outstanding all-round Test careers, it will be noticed that all six players to hit 2,000 runs and take 200 wickets began their Test careers after 1950:

	Runs	Avge	Wkts	Avge	Career
I.T. Botham (England)	4,825	34.96	366	27.21	1977-86
R. Benaud (Australia)	2,201	24.45	248	27.03	1951-64
R.J. Hadlee (New Zealand)	2,397	25.77	334	22.51	1972-86
Imran Khan (Pakistan)	2,140	30.14	264	22.18	1971-86
Kapil Dev (India)	3,132	29.82	291	28.72	1978-86
G. St A. Sobers (West Indies)	8,032	57.78	235	34.03	1953-74

The names contained in the various sections above include all the very greatest all-rounders, except pre-1960 overseas cricketers, whose opportunities in Test and/or first-class cricket were very limited – such cricketers as Australia's W.W. Armstrong or K.R. Miller, the West Indian L.S. Constantine, the Indian C.K. Nayudu and, since South Africa has been excluded from Test cricket, E.J. Barlow, M.J. Procter and C.E.B. Rice.

Another class of all-rounder is the wicketkeeper-batsman. Twelve players have scored 10,000 runs and taken over 1,000 dismissals in the field, but only two have scored 30,000 runs and taken over 1,000 dismissals:

	Runs	Avge	Wkts	Avge	Career
L.E.G. Ames (Kent)	37,248	43.51	703	418	1926-51
J.M. Parks (Sussex, Som)	36,673	34.76	1,088	93	1949-76

Unfortunately there is no way of measuring the ability of fieldsmen in general, so it is not possible to draw up a list of all-rounders whose second ability is in the field. Fielding ability remains to be judged by the spectator.
(*see also* individual cricketers' entries)

Amateurs

In English cricket until 1963, there was a definite distinction in first-class matches between amateurs and professionals. On the more important grounds, the pavilions erected in late Victorian times had separate dressing rooms for the two classes and indeed separate entrances onto the field. For away fixtures the amateurs would travel first class and stay in top class hotels, whereas the professionals travelled third and stayed in less expensive establishments. It was almost obligatory that county teams were captained by an amateur and a great stir was created in traditional circles when a professional, Len Hutton, was chosen to lead England in 1952.

One of the fashionable contests at Lord's each year until 1963 was Gentlemen v Players. This match had been played since the early 19th century, but the Gentlemen did not have the strength to stand any reasonable chance of beating the Players until W.G. Grace came on the scene.

Grace in fact made a nonsense of the whole concept of the unpaid amateur for he, as a so-called amateur, was reputed to have made more money out of cricket than any of his professional contemporaries.

The leading Australian cricketers also cut right across the divide and though officially classed as amateurs on their tours to England were in fact paid more than English professionals. In matches outside England, apart from pre-1914 America and the West Indies, little distinction was made between paid and unpaid players.

In the mid-1980s in England the main place where such distinctions are found is in the local leagues, since some leagues maintain a rule that permits one or two paid players per team.

Ames, Leslie Ethelbert George

Born: 3 December 1905, Elham, Kent
Career: 593 *m*; 37,248 runs (av 43.61); 703 *ct*; 418 *st*
Tests: 47 *m*; 2,434 runs (av 40.56); 74 *ct*; 23 *st*

Ames was probably the world's outstanding wicketkeeper-batsman. He joined Kent as a batsman in 1923 but was advised to take up wicketkeeping. He made his Test debut in 1929, and was an England regular from 1931, beginning 50 years when, except for an eight-year break from 1959, a Kent keeper was usually England's first choice.

As a keeper Ames has a record number of stumpings, partly because he kept to A.P. Freeman, the prolific leg-spinner, for much of his time at Kent. As a batsman he scored more first-class runs than any keeper with 1,000 dismissals. His Test batting average is that of a batsman. He was England's keeper in the 1932-33 'bodyline' series.

After the Second World War he played for Kent as a batsman only, finally retiring in 1951. He was the first professional to become a Test selector, was manager of MCC tours, and became secretary, manager and president of Kent and an MCC committee member.

Analysis

Details of a bowler's performance in a match, usually shown as a set of four numbers, viz: 29.3-12-46-2, the sequence being number of overs bowled, number of maiden overs, number of runs conceded, number of wickets taken. In the example given the number of overs is 29.3, which is 29 complete overs and three balls of an incomplete over.

In a traditional-style scorebook the overs are set out ball-by-ball in the following manner:

$$\cdot\ \vdots\ \boxed{\mathrm{M}}\ \cdot\ \vdots$$

The term was first used in 1854.

Annuals

The standard cricket annual which publishes the full scores of all the important matches played during the English cricket season is Wisden Cricketers' Almanack. This annual first appeared in 1864 and has been issued every year since then, thus out-lasting a number of rival publications, mainly because it has always given detailed scores of matches. In recent years it has been expanded to include many of the first-class matches played overseas.

None of the other cricket-playing countries have an annual which extends back over 100 years. The present annuals for India, South Africa and New Zealand all began soon after the Second World War. The West Indies annual has been issued since 1970. Although there are various annuals for individual Australian states, a national Australian annual has never really taken root, though there have been a number of attempts to establish one.

Apart from Wisden, there are several other annuals published in England covering cricket on a national scale, the best-known being the Playfair Cricket Annual, *Daily Telegraph* Cricket Year Book, Benson & Hedges Cricket Year, and the ACS International Cricket Yearbook.

The majority of county cricket clubs, both first-class and minor, publish handbooks with the scores of their matches annually. Many cricket leagues in England also issue annuals, as do the cricket authorities in Ireland and Scotland.
(*see also* Reference books)

Appeal

A request by one of the fielding side for an umpire to decide whether a batsman is out. In the first known Laws of the game, Law 6 states: '[the umpires] are not to order any man out unless appealed to by one of ye players.' This concept (dated 1744) remains in the present day Law 27, which commences: 'The umpires shall not give a batsman out unless appealed to by the other side which shall be done prior to the bowler beginning his run-up or bowling action to deliver the next ball.'

One of the great Kent wicketkeepers, Leslie Ames was probably the world's leading wicketkeeper-batsman.

Argentina

Although they failed to win a single match in the 1986 ICC Trophy, Argentina have produced a number of notable cricketers and for the best part of 40 years were considered a first-class team. The first international match by Argentina was played in 1868 and in 1911/12 a fairly strong MCC side toured the country and played a series of three 'Tests', of which Argentina won the first. Similar tours took place between the wars, with the home country generally holding their own. The only first-class tour to England took place in 1932, when the visitors were styled 'South America', but mainly came from the Argentine.

After the Second World War it was a long time before the MCC decided to send a team to South America and by then, 1958/59, the standard of the game in the Argentine had dropped considerably. Two three-day games were played against the tourists, but MCC won both with ease.

Armstrong, Warwick Windridge

Born: 22 May 1879, Kyneton, Victoria, Australia
Died: 13 July 1947, Darling Point, NSW, Australia
Career: 269 m; 16,158 runs (av 46.83); 832 wkts (av 19.71)
Tests: 50 m; 2,863 runs (av 38.68); 87 wkts (av 33.59)
By the end of his career Armstrong weighed 20 stone, and was known as 'The Big Ship'. He was an attacking batsman with a determination which made him especially effective on

Australian captain and all-rounder Warwick Armstrong, who won eight successive Test Matches against England.

difficult wickets, and a leg-break bowler who had converted early from fast-medium.

He made his debut for Victoria in 1898/99, but was to play more often for Australian sides, making his Test debut in 1901/02. He toured England four times from 1902 to 1921, missing out, like other Australians, through being in dispute with the Board in 1912. He was a very successful all-rounder on each tour, performing the 'double' on the last three. He made his highest score, 303 not out, against Somerset at Bath in 1905.

Armstrong captained Australia against England in 1920/21 and 1921, winning eight consecutive Tests, so his career was marked by almost continuous success.

Art

The most commonly seen cricket illustrations are those which originally appeared in the weekly *Vanity Fair* magazine. These cartoons, which featured public figures from all walks of life, began appearing in 1869 as full-page illustrations, and between 1877 and 1913 31 cartoons were published of cricketers in cricketing dress. Other cricketers who had reached notoriety in other fields appeared in mufti. It is the ambition of collectors of cricketana to obtain a complete set of these cricketing cartoons, the early ones being by Carlo Pellegrini (who signed them Ape) and most of the rest by Sir Leslie Ward (Spy).

Of more artistic merit are the series of individual portraits done as lithographs by J.C. Anderson in the middle of the 19th century. These are to be found both plain and coloured.

A third set of portraits are by A. Chevallier Tayler, issued in 1905, and the 48 can be found either separately or bound in a single volume.

A recent set of paintings, copied from old photographs with the addition of 'Sunday School' type backgrounds, has been executed by Gerry Wright, but the best-known present-day artist who includes cricket fairly often in his work is Laurence Toynbee.

Two of the earliest paintings featuring cricket were by Francis Hayman. The first of his works was 'Cricket as played on the Artillery Ground' and the second 'Cricket played in Marylebone Fields'. Both date from the middle of the 18th century and are of high artistic merit, but have been copied so often and often so badly that many of the illustrations under these titles are very crude. Of equal interest are the sketches of contemporary players done by George Shepheard about 1790. These are on a single sheet which has 12 thumbnail sketches, nine of which are named.

The cartoonist Thomas Rowlandson produced his famous illustration of a women's match at Ball's Pond, Newington in 1811. In 1837 came the pencil drawings by G.F. Watts showing various batting strokes and done at the request of the notable cricketer, N. Felix. Watts later drew portraits of Fuller Pilch and Alfred Mynn. Felix himself produced the composite picture of the members of the All-England Eleven in 1847.

So far as photographs are concerned the earliest one of note is that of the 1859 England team leaving for North America. For many years the major producers of English team and individual cricket photographs were Hawkins & Co of Brighton, but G.W. Beldam set new standards in the Edwardian era with a great many pictures of cricketers in action. In the 1980s the best-known photographers in

England are Patrick Eagar, Ken Kelly, Adrian Murrell, Bill Smith and Bob Thomas.

Artificial pitches

The use of matting wickets, especially in South African cricket, goes back to the 1880s, and though turf replaced matting for Test and first-class matches in the 1930s, much club cricket there uses mats. Matting was also common on the Indian sub-continent, but is now seen mainly in minor matches. In Australia, whilst first-class cricket is played on turf, club matches have often been staged on matting stretched over concrete.

English cricketers at all levels have tended to look down their noses at artificial wickets. However, the cost of maintaining grass wickets has made some cricketing organisations think seriously about artificial wickets and in the 1960s and 1970s a number of manufacturers began to produce synthetic wickets. The most commonly used now in England is the Dunlop-Nottinghamshire pitch of 'synthetic grass'.

Ashes

When the Australians beat England at the Oval in 1882, an obituary notice for English cricket was published in the press. Sir Ivo Bligh, as captain of the English team which went out to Australia the following winter, stated that he would try to bring back the 'Ashes' of English cricket. His team duly beat Australia and a stump (or bail) was burnt, the ashes poured into a small urn and the whole presented to Ivo Bligh. The urn is permanently kept at Lord's, but since that year the Tests between England and Australia (with one or two odd exceptions) have been for the 'Ashes'.

Association football

Twelve Test cricketers have also won full England soccer caps: J. Arnold (1 match, 1933); A. Ducat (6, 1910-21); R.E. Foster (6, 1900-02); C.B. Fry (2, 1891-1901); L.H. Gay (4, 1891-94); W. Gunn (2, 1884); H.T.W. Hardinge (1, 1910); Hon A. Lyttelton (1, 1877); J.W.H. Makepeace (4, 1906-12); C.A. Milton (1, 1952); J. Sharp (2, 1903-05); W. Watson (4, 1950-51).

Three English Test grounds have also been the venue of international soccer matches: the Oval (10 matches, 1873-89); Bramall Lane (4 matches, 1897-1930); and Trent Bridge (2 matches, 1897-1909).

Assumed names

It was not uncommon prior to the First World War for county cricketers, who did not wish their identity known through the newspapers, to appear under assumed names – the main category appears to have been undergraduates who should have been at University. The most notorious example however was the captain of the 1880 Canadian side to England, who was an English army deserter. Unfortunately for him his real identity was discovered in mid-tour. He was arrested during the match with Leicestershire and subsequently served a spell in prison.

In earlier days it was regarded as not respectable in some quarters to play cricket with professionals and therefore a number of amateurs used aliases.

Auckland

The present Auckland ground at Eden Park was first used in 1912/13 and is the headquarters of Auckland Cricket Association. In the 1970s the ground was extensively modernised, but this was more on account of its function as a rugby field. The ground, which is rectangular, can hold 30,000 spectators. The first Test Match to be staged there was in 1929/30 between New Zealand and England. Prior to 1912/13, Auckland played on the Domain, where cricket had been played since 1860.

Australia

Recorded cricket in Australia began in the colony of New South Wales in 1803/04 and the first Australian cricket club was established in Sydney in 1826/27. The first major matches, however, involved Victoria and Van Diemen's Land (now Tasmania) and the original game between these two colonies was staged in Hobart in February 1851, only a few weeks after Victoria had been created.

Tasmanian cricket failed to improve during the 1860s and 1870s and the New South Wales v Victoria contest was soon established as the principal fixture of the Australia season.

South Australia gained first-class status in 1877/78 and Queensland joined the first-class teams in 1892/93, by which time there had been 13 English tours to the Antipodes. The original English side went out sponsored by the catering firm of Spiers and Pond in 1861/62, but found the opposition so weak that they opposed teams of 22 in all but one fixture: Victoria fielded only 18, but were defeated by an innings.

Charles Lawrence, the Surrey professional, and one of the tourists, accepted a post as coach to the leading club in Sydney, and two years later William Caffyn, who came out with the second English side, took a similar position in Melbourne. These two cricketers were responsible for the rapid rise in the standard of Australian cricket, so that when W.G. Grace took a side out in 1873/74 the visitors were beaten both by Victoria and New South Wales, though each home team still fielded 18 against 11. Victoria and New South Wales combined forces and attempted 15 against the English Eleven, but were defeated by 218 runs.

The first time 'Australia' went on to the field was on 15 March 1877 when they opposed James Lillywhite's England side in Melbourne in what is now regarded as the first Test Match (see separate entry for England v Australia Test series). In 1878 came the first overseas tour by a representative Australian team, the first match being against Southland at Invercargill in New Zealand in January 1878; the team, after touring New Zealand and playing matches in Australia, arrived in England where they had a programme of 37 matches of which 18 were won. Ten years earlier an Aborigines Team had toured England, but their games were not of a very serious nature.

The major domestic competition in Australia is the Sheffield Shield (q.v.), which began in 1892/93, involving New South Wales, Victoria and South Australia; Queensland joined in 1926/27, Western Australia in 1947/48 (winning the title in their first season), and Tasmania in 1977/78. The major limited-overs competition is the McDonald Cup (q.v.), which began (as the V&G Australasian Knock-Out Competition) in 1969/70.

Traditionally Australia are regarded as England's major cricketing rival, with the battle for the Ashes being of

LANCASHIRE C. C.

A. C. MacLAREN (Captain).

A. H. HORNBY

TYLDESLEY

HARRY.

L. O. S. POIDEVIN.

WORSLEY.

HUDDLESTON.

MAKEPEACE.

DEAN

SHARP.

H. D. STANNING.

The Lancashire side before the First World War. Harry Makepeace and Jack Sharp both played for Everton at soccer, and both played for England at both games.

The Australian team which toured England in 1886. Left to right, back: McIlwraith, Trumble, Jarvis, Bruce, Jones, Palmer, Spofforth. Front: Wardill, Blackham, Evans, Scott, Bonnor, Garrett, Giffen.

paramount importance, but since the mid-1970s internal problems have sapped the strength of Australian cricket, notably the Packer Affair and lately the rebel Australian team in South Africa, so that the great Australian sides under Armstrong and under Bradman are at present a distant golden memory of the country's more affluent days.

(*see also* the succeeding entries, England v Australia, and individual entries for states, cricketers, competitions and grounds)

Australia v India

Results: Played 42; Australia won 20; India won 8; Drawn 14

Kapil Dev led the Indian side on the 1985/86 tour to Australia, but failed to press home the Indians' obvious supremacy and each of the three Tests ended indecisively. The visitors could point to the inclement weather, but this was not the whole story. The scores in the first two innings of each Test show how much better the Indians were:

	India	Australia
First Test	520	318
Second Test	445	262
Third Test	600-4 dec	396

The nearest India got to success was at Melbourne in the second game, when at the end India needed only 67 runs and had eight wickets in hand. India's leading batsman was the veteran Gavaskar, who averaged 117.33, including two hundreds, and became the first Test cricketer to top 9,000 runs. It should be stated in all the praise which greeted the Indian batting, that 16 leading Australians had defected and gone on tour to South Africa, so the opposition bowling was not as strong as it might have been.

India have in fact won only a single series, this being against Kim Hughes' side in India in 1979/80. Here again the Australian camp was split and only the non-Packer players were available for selection.

At the request of the Australians, the Indian authorities arranged that that tour should begin on 1 September and two of the Tests were fixed for September. The experts seemed to forget that September was part of the monsoon season, though they were painfully reminded of the weather when rain ruined the chances of a definite result in both the First and Second Tests. India then caused a surprise by winning the Third Test at Kanpur, after trailing on their first innings, their victory being due to the bowling of Kapil Dev and Yadav, who between them removed Australia for only 125 runs in the final innings.

The Fourth and Fifth Tests ended in draws, but captain Gavaskar led the way to a resounding win in the final game. He hit 123 in India's total of 458 for 8 declared, then Dilip Doshi, Yadav and Kapil Dev bowled out the tourists for 160 and 198 – the margin was an innings and 100 runs.

When Gavaskar took his side over to Australia the following season, Packer and the Australian Board had buried the hatchet and therefore Australia were back at full strength with Greg Chappell in command. The sensational match of this series was played at Melbourne. Australia hit 419 in reply to the Indian first innings total of 237 and seemed to have the match sewn up. India then began their second innings with a stand of 165 by Gavaskar and Chauhan. Gavaskar was then given out lbw by umpire Whitehead. The Indian captain was so disgruntled with the decision that he ordered Chauhan to walk off the field with him. However, at the pavilion gate the Indian manager ordered Chauhan back to the crease. It was as well for India that he did so, because the tourists went on to win the game in the most unexpected way. Australia required just 143 for victory when they began the final innings, a task which should have been made easier since neither Kapil Dev nor Yadav was able to bowl initially owing to injury. However, Doshi and Ghavri reduced Australia to 24 for 3 at the close of play on the fourth day, and on the fifth morning Kapil Dev returned to take 5 for 28 and dismiss Australia for 83. The three-match series was therefore tied, as Australia had won the First Test (Greg Chappell made 204) and the Second had been drawn.

Australia v New Zealand

Results: Played 21; Australia won 9; New Zealand won 5; Drawn 7

New Zealand finally killed the tradition that they were a minor adjunct to their large neighbours in 1985/86. Two series of Tests were played. The first took place in Australia in November/December with the tour of John Coney's side for a rubber of three matches. In the First Test at Brisbane, Richard Hadlee set the scene on the opening day by taking 9 for 52 and dismissing Australia for 179. Reid and Martin Crowe then proceeded to hit individual hundreds and give the visitors a massive lead of 374. Allan Border and Greg Matthews made an attempt to retrieve a hopeless position, both hitting centuries, but Hadlee took another six wickets and New Zealand won by an innings. Australia came back in the Second Test, when Bob Holland's leg spin accounted for ten wickets and Australia won by four wickets, but Richard Hadlee took another 11 wickets in the Third and final Test to bring victory by six wickets and the fast bowler's tally for the series was a record 33 (average 12.15).

In February/March 1986 Border led the Australians for a second series, this time in New Zealand. At Wellington, in the First Test, a combination of rain and runs ensured a draw. The Second Test at Christchurch was also drawn. It was the spin of John Bracewell that won the Third Test – he took 10 for 106 – and thus gave New Zealand a second series win over Australia within the space of a single season.

The Australian-New Zealand Test series was a long time in coming to fruition. New South Wales opposed New Zealand in 1893/94 in New Zealand, then in 1898/99 New Zealand sent a side to Australia, playing Victoria and New South Wales. The first time Australia actually met New Zealand was in 1909/10, but the Australians, though led by Warwick Armstrong, were not representative. However, they won both matches. Arthur Sims' Australian side of 1913/14 also won both their games against New Zealand. The matches continued between the two wars, but it was not until 1945/46 that a meeting between the two countries was to be granted Test Match status: or rather the match played in 1945/46 was given Test Match status in 1948. It was a very brief affair with New Zealand dismissed for 42 and 54, Bill O'Reilly taking 8 for 33. The game took less than two days.

It was not until 1973/74 that the next Test took place. Bev Congdon and Ian Chappell fought two series in that season; three matches being played in each country, and it was in New Zealand in the second of the two series that New Zealand recorded their first Test win over Australia. This came in the Second Test at Christchurch, where Glenn Turner scored 101 out of 255 in the first innings and then made 110 not out when New Zealand needed 230 to win, taking his side to victory by five wickets. Richard Hadlee, with seven wickets, was New Zealand's most successful bowler, but he was ably assisted by his brother, Dayle, and Richard Collinge.

After this victory, Australia won the final match in the series with comparative ease, due to New Zealand's poor batting (Turner excepted).

Australia won the next two series, then under Geoff Howarth in 1981/82 a series was tied, a result which led to the New Zealand successes in 1985/86.

Australia v Pakistan

Results: Played 28; Australia won 11; Pakistan won 8; Drawn 9

Of the 11 series which have been played between the two countries, Pakistan have won three. The first series win in fact consisted of a single game and the Australians made no preparation for it. Under Ian Johnson in 1956, the side, which had toured England, had a brief holiday in Europe, then flew from Rome to Karachi, where they played the single Test, without playing any preliminary games at all, despite the fact that it was arranged to play the game on a matting wicket. Batting first, the Australians were dismissed for 80 by Fazal Mahmood, who took 6 for 34. Pakistan gained a first-innings lead of 119, and though Australia did somewhat better in their second innings, the medium paced deliveries of Fazal captured another seven wickets, giving him 13 for 114 in the match, and Pakistan strolled home by nine wickets.

Pakistan's second series success did not come until 1982/83, also in Pakistan. Australia's downfall was caused by the leg-spin of Abdul Qadir and the captaincy and all-round cricket of Imran Khan. Australia were under some disadvantage as both Greg Chappell and Lillee declined the tour.

In the First Test in Karachi Pakistan gained a first-innings lead of 135, but Australia could manage only 179 when they batted again and the home country won by nine wickets. The match was marred by the violent behaviour of the crowd and on two occasions the Australians left the field because of the rain of missiles aimed at the players.

Australia suffered an innings defeat in the Second Test at Faisalabad. Mansoor Akhtar and Zaheer Abbas hit hundreds in Pakistan's score of 501 for 6 declared, then Qadir dismissed Australia twice, taking 11 wickets in the match. Greg Ritchie was the only tourist to show much application against the spinners and took out his bat for 106. The Third Test at Lahore provided Pakistan with another nine-wicket win. Australia's middle order collapsed to Imran in the first innings, but some plucky tail end runs from Yardley and Lawson ensured a reasonable score. Pakistan, with hundreds from Mohsin Khan and Javed Miandad, gained a large lead and Imran dismissed Australia for 214 in their second innings. Pakistan therefore won the series three matches to nil.

The following season, 1983/84, Australia got their revenge, winning a five-match series by two games to nil. Pakistan were severely handicapped by the injury to Imran Khan, who could not play in the first three Tests and then was unable to bowl in the other two. The incapacity of Imran was that much worse, because their other front-line fast bowler was absent, Sarfraz having been banned from Test cricket because he criticised the selectors. Under these circumstances, the Australian batsmen (Qadir being unable to find his form) flourished. Yallop averaged 92.33, Border 85.80, Greg Chappell 72.80 and both Hughes and W.B. Phillips over 60. Australia won the First Test by an innings with

Rackemann taking 11 for 118. Rain saved Pakistan in the Second Test at Brisbane, but for the third game Pakistan flew out Sarfraz, and though he took only four wickets, he seemed to improve morale and Pakistan hit 624, with Mohsin Kahn, Qasim Omar and Javed Miandad making hundreds. It appeared that Australia were in danger of losing until Kim Hughes took them to safety with a brilliant 106. The Fourth Test was also drawn, but Australia won the Fifth with ease, Greg Chappell hitting 182 in his best style and Lillee taking eight wickets. Both these cricketers announced their retirement during the match.

Pakistan have yet to win a series in Australia – their only other victory being in 1979/80. Mushtaq Mohammad, however, tied two successive series in Australia in 1976/77 and 1978/79, Australia being handicapped during the latter by the absence of their leading cricketers with the Packer WSC.

Australia v South Africa
Results: Played 53; Australia won 29; South Africa won 11; Drawn 13

Although the series stretches back to 1902/03, it was not until 1952/53 that the South Africans really made any impression on their opponents, and in some ways the series which took place that season was the most remarkable between the two countries.

Jack Cheetham led a young South African side, which the

Australia playing West Indies at Perth, Second Test, 1975/76.
Roy Fredericks hooking Dennis Lillee for six.

press wrote off long before the series began. Indeed such was the feeling that the wisest heads suggested the tour ought to be cancelled, first because a crushing defeat would set South African cricket back years, and second because Australia had suffered a financial loss the previous season when West Indies came on tour, and public interest in the South African minnows was non-existent. The South African Board however stated that they were prepared to lose £10,000 on the trip, as they felt their young players required the experience. However, Cheetham's no-hopers surprised everybody with their performance.

Australia won the First Test by 96 runs due to some inspired bowling from their veteran Ray Lindwall, but in Melbourne South Africa, after being behind on their first innings, hit 388 in their second with Russell Endean making an undefeated 162. Hugh Tayfield then spun out Australia – he had figures of 6 for 84 and 7 for 81 – and South Africa gained their first Test victory over Australia since 1910/11.

The home side took matters more seriously for the Third Test and Neil Harvey gave one of the greatest batting exhibitions of his long career, staying six hours for 190. Lindwall and Miller bowled out the South Africans twice and Australia coasted home by an innings. The Fourth Test at Adelaide was a high-scoring draw, then came the Fifth Test at Melbourne. Harvey was again in fine fettle making 204 out of Australia's 520. South Africa replied with a solid 435, with no one reaching three figures. In Australia's second innings Fuller's fast deliveries soon removed both McDonald and Harvey, then the remainder of the batsmen struggled against the spin of Tayfield and Mansell. The result was that South Africa required 295 to win. As in the first innings all the leading batsmen responded and the tourists won by six wickets, thus drawing the series, two victories to each side. Although Tayfield was the leading figure, with 30 wickets in the series, South Africa's success was largely due to team spirit and brilliant fielding, plus the tactical sense of the captain, Jack Cheetham and the manager K.G. Viljoen.

Four series have been played since that historic tour and South Africa have had the whip hand in three of them. In the last series of all, in 1969/70, which was staged in South Africa, the home side beat Australia in all four Tests. The Australian tourists were led by Bill Lawry and they were overshadowed from the start. The First Test took place at Newlands, where a careful hundred by Eddie Barlow enabled South Africa to make 382. Australia collapsed in front of Peter Pollock and Mike Procter and, having a deficit of over 200, never recovered.

The Australians fared even worse in the Second Test at Durban, scoring only 157 in reply to South Africa's 622 for 9 declared. Graeme Pollock hit a new record of 274 and Barry Richards 140. South Africa won by an innings and plenty.

The two other Tests simply emphasised South Africa's strength. In the overall figures, Graeme Pollock and Barry Richards averaged over 70 with the bat, whilst Mike Procter and Peter Pollock were the principal wicket takers.

Joe Darling took the 1902 Australians to South Africa, after they had played a Test series against England, and this was the beginning of the matches between South Africa and Australia. Australia won the initial series by two matches to nil and then won by four matches to one when P.W. Sherwell's South Africans toured Australia in 1910/11.

South Africa took part in the 1912 Triangular series in England, when they failed, even against the star-shorn

Australians of the year. The all-conquering 1921 Australian side to England visited South Africa on the way home. South Africa narrowly escaped defeat in the first of the three Tests, but in the second they fought an honourable draw, due to the batting of Dave Nourse and C.N. Frank. Australia, however, won the Third Test comfortably, Ryder making a century and Macartney returning the best bowling figures.

In the two other series between the wars, Australia had matters very much their own way.

The 'rebel' Australians under Kim Hughes played three unofficial Tests in South Africa during 1985/86; the series was won by Clive Rice's South Africans by one match to nil. The leading batsman in the series was Graeme Pollock, who hit a century in the first match and fifties in each of the other games.

Australia v Sri Lanka
The only match between the two countries took place at Kandy in April 1983. Sri Lanka were completely outplayed. The Australians batted first and with hundreds from Kepler Wessels and David Hookes reached 514 for 4 and declared. Of the home side's batsmen only Ranatunga and Wettimuny coped with the spin of Yardley and Tom Hogan and Australia won by an innings and 38 runs.

Australia v West Indies
Results: Played 62; Australia won 27; West Indies won 19; Tied 1; Drawn 15
The outstanding match between the two sides must remain the famous tied Test at Brisbane in 1960/61. This was the first match of the five-match series by Frank Worrell's West Indian team in Australia. West Indies began with a score of 453, of which Gary Sobers hit 132 at a run a minute. Australia replied even more strongly with 505, due to an innings of 181 from Norman O'Neill and a much more commanding 92 from Bobby Simpson. Alan Davidson with 6 for 86 successfully held the West Indian total in their second innings to 284, which left the home country needing only 233 for victory. Wes Hall at his most aggressive reduced Australia to 57 for 5, but a later partnership by Davidson and the Australian captain, Richie Benaud, added a vital 134 and just 27 runs were required for an Australian victory with four wickets in hand. At this point Hall took the new ball. Davidson was then run out due to a brilliant throw from Solomon and when the final over started six runs were needed with three wickets left. A leg-bye was obtained from the first delivery. Benaud was caught at the wicket from the second. Meckiff played the third straight back to Hall, the bowler; the fourth ball resulted in a quick single, as did the fifth. Meckiff hit the sixth ball to leg and the batsmen, having run two, attempted a third (which would have given Australia the match) only to find Grout run out. So the scores were level and the last man, Kline, arrived to combat the two remaining deliveries. Kline hit the first to square-leg and with Meckiff backing up well set off for the winning run, but another exceptional throw by Solomon hit the stumps and the match was tied.

The rest of the series, although it could hardly surpass the tied Test, produced some exciting cricket. Australia won the Second Test, when Davidson skittled out West Indies for 181, giving his team a first-innings lead of 167. West Indies however fought back in the Third Test, Sobers hitting 168 and the wicketkeeper Alexander 108, in totals of 339 and 326, whilst Australia were dismissed relatively cheaply by the spinners Valentine and Gibbs.

The Fourth Test ended almost as dramatically as the First, when Kline, again the last Australian batsman, arrived at the wicket with 110 minutes play remaining and a mile behind. Somehow he survived, and Australia drew the match. Drama continued in the final Test, which Australia won by the narrow margin of two wickets.

When the tour started cricket in Australia had a sour reputation and it was due to the enterprise of the two captains, Benaud and Worrell, that this feeling was entirely obliterated. The bowler with the most wickets in the series was Alan Davidson with 33; Norman O'Neill and Rohan Kanhai each hit more than 500 runs.

Each of the nine series played since 1961 have been for the Frank Worrell Trophy. West Indies have had much the better of the recent encounters. The four West Indian sides since 1979/80 have been under the leadership of Clive Lloyd, who in those four rubbers has met with just two defeats, but claimed victory in nine matches. However, in 1975/76 Australia won the series by five matches to one. It was rather an odd series. In the first place the games were only arranged late in the day when the proposed Australian tour to South Africa was cancelled; in the second, West Indies possessed a team which on paper was the equal of Australia, yet were heavily defeated. It is true that the home side had Lillee and Thomson at their peak, but in Roberts and his colleagues the West Indies fast attack was scarcely threadbare. As it was Greg Chappell dominated everybody and everything, with, it must be said, much moral support from his brother Ian. Greg Chappell not only led Australia, but ended the series with a batting average of 117.00.

The next series, which took place in the West Indies, was little more than a farce. Virtually all the leading Australians were banned, having contracts with Packer's WSC, and the West Indian team was not untroubled, with Lloyd playing only in the first two matches and then Kallicharran leading his country in the three remaining Tests.

Before the Second World War the two sides met in only one series. This took place in Australia in 1930/31. For the West Indians much depended on the mercurial Learie Constantine. He performed well enough in the ordinary first-class matches, but failed miserably in the Tests, and West Indies had to rely almost entirely on Griffiths and Francis for their bowling. George Headley hit two Test hundreds, but topping the Test batting table was the captain G.C. Grant. Australia, of course, possessed Ponsford and Bradman – both averaged over 70 – and the most effective of their bowlers were the spinners, Clarrie Grimmett and Ironmonger. The former took 33 wickets and troubled nearly all the tourists. The West Indies have certainly altered their image since that path-finding trip.

Australian Cricket Board of Control

The Australian Cricket Board of Control (usually referred to as ACB) was founded in 1905 and is the representative body of cricket in Australia. Prior to the setting up of the Board, the Australasian Cricket Council was established in 1891, but was dissolved in 1900.
(*see also* Administrators)

Average
see Batsmen and Bowlers

B

b
An abbreviation for 'bowled' used in scorebooks and published scores: 'b Smith' means 'bowled by Smith'.

Bs
During the first 30 years of the 19th century, by odd coincidence many of the leading English cricketers had surnames commencing with the letter B. During this period the Bs played a number of matches against the Rest of England and were successful on several occasions. The Bs' greatest victory in the series came in 1817 when they won by 114 runs, the team being H. Bentley, J. Bowyer, W. Beldham, E.H. Budd, T. Beagley, J. Bray, Lord F. Beauclerk, John Bennett, J. Baker, B.A. Browne and J. Bentley.

In the game of 1810, however, the Bs had the misfortune to be dismissed for 6, which was, even for those days, an abysmal display and the lowest total ever recorded in England in a match of such importance.

Back up
Said of a fielder, who moves into position behind another fielder, normally the wicketkeeper, or bowler, when the ball hit by the batsman is being returned to the wicket; also said of a batsman at the non-striker's end, who is preparing for a possible run as the bowler delivers the ball. There are examples of the non-striking batsman being run out when he leaves the crease by the bowler, instead of delivering the ball, breaking the wicket. This, however, is regarded as ungentlemanly conduct and it is usual for a bowler to warn a batsman that he will be run out if he continues to leave the crease before the ball is delivered.

There are about 30 recorded instances of batsmen run out in this way in first-class cricket. The last known example in England was in 1972 when R.D. Jackman ran out R. Swetman, who was batting for Gloucestershire v Surrey at Bristol.

In 1947/48 W.A. Brown was twice run out at Sydney by M.H. Mankad of India, once in the Test Match.

The grim and forbidding Sydney Barnes was one of the most successful of all bowlers, and some say just about the best of all.

Bail

A piece of wood $4\frac{1}{8}$ inches long which spans the tops of two stumps, there being two bails to each set of three stumps, the stumps having grooves in the top to take the bails. In the original Laws of 1744 there was one bail 6 inches long. Two bails were introduced about 1786.

The furthest distance travelled by a bail after a batsman has been bowled in a first-class match is believed to be 67 yards 6 inches, when R.D. Burrows of Worcestershire dismissed W. Huddleston of Lancashire at Old Trafford in 1911; in any match, 83 yards 1 foot 9 inches, by A.O. Burrows at Hobart, Tasmania, in 1925/26.

Ball

The ball was originally to weigh between 5 and 6 oz, but no size was given in the 1744 Laws. It was not until 1838 that the Law specified the circumference, between 9 and $9\frac{1}{4}$ inches. The present Law lays down the weights and measurements as between $5\frac{1}{2}$ and $5\frac{3}{4}$ oz and between $8\frac{13}{16}$ and 9 inches.

The ball is made of cork parings and fine twine wound round a cork cube and covered in leather.

The Laws dictate how often a new ball can be introduced in the course of a match.

Bangalore

The Karnataka State Cricket Association Ground at Bangalore staged its first Test match only in 1974/75 when India played the West Indies. Cricket in Bangalore has a long history and Lord Hawke's team played a match in the city in 1892/93, as did the Oxford Authentics in 1902/03. When Mysore (now known as Karnataka) joined the Ranji Trophy in 1934/35, the Bangalore ground was considered the headquarters of that Cricket Association and has remained as such.

Bangladesh

Bangladesh did not do as well in the 1986 ICC Trophy as they had done in 1979, when they came second in their group with four victories.

Until 1973 the country was part of Pakistan and as such played domestic first-class cricket at Dacca (Dhaka). The MCC sent out touring teams in 1976/77 and again in 1978/79 and 1980/81, but although cricket remains popular, the standard is not improving.

No matches played by Bangladesh have been given first-class status, and the principal problems are a lack of fast bowlers and the easy-paced wickets on most Bangladesh grounds.

Barnes, Sydney Francis

Born: 19 April 1873, Smethwick, Staffordshire
Died: 26 December 1967, Chadsmoor, Staffordshire
Career: 133 *m*; 719 wkts (av 17.90)
Tests: 27 *m*; 189 wkts (av 16.43)
Barnes was an enigmatic figure, who although he tried county cricket twice, with Warwickshire and Lancashire, preferred league and minor counties cricket. Despite this lack of first-class exposure, he is often described as the greatest bowler cricket has seen. A right-arm bowler, his pace varied on both the fast and slow sides of medium, and he was a master of length and flight who turned the ball both ways.

Of gaunt appearance and unsmiling character, he was regarded as prickly, and treated with suspicion by the authorities. He went on four tours, three to Australia, but only ten of his 27 Tests were in England. His Test career ended with the First World War, with an astonishing 189 wickets, of which 49, a record for a series, came in four Tests in South Africa in 1913/14.

Barrington, Kenneth Frank

Born: 24 November 1930, Reading, Berkshire
Died: 14 March 1981, Bridgetown, Barbados
Career: 533 *m*; 31,714 runs (av 45.63); 273 wkts (av 32.62)
Tests: 82 *m*; 6,806 runs (av 58.67); 29 wkts (av 44.83)
Barrington joined Surrey in 1948, but did not make his debut until 1953, selection for England following in 1956. He was then a brilliant stroke-maker with a penchant for the off-drive. After scoring 0, 34 (top score) and 18 in two Tests, he was dropped, and completely altered his style, becoming an on-side player who eliminated risks from his batting. Restored to the England side four years later, he became their best and most reliable batsman, although he was once dropped for taking $7\frac{1}{4}$ hours over 137.

He was a member of the Surrey side for the last six of their seven consecutive Championships in the 1950s, but the Test arena was his natural one, and it is significant that his very high Test average much exceeds his career average. He also bowled occasional leg-breaks.

A mild heart attack ended his career in 1968, but with his experience, friendliness and humour he became an ideal manager/coach for England. He died after a second heart attack while assistant manager of the England touring party in the West Indies.

Bassetlaw League

Founded in 1904, the League has clubs from four counties: Derbyshire, Lincolnshire, Notts and Yorkshire, but is centred on Worksop. The principal sides in the leading divisions are Worksop, Chesterfield, Retford, Steetley, Bridon and the team entered by Notts CCC, consisting of promising colts. The knock-out competition is for the Tomlins Trophy.

Bat

Until the latter part of the 18th century, cricket bats were fashioned from a single piece of wood and shaped something like a hockey stick. This design was in order to cope with the ball being bowled literally along the ground. The idea of actually pitching the ball forced a change in the shape of the bat. The first regulation concerning a bat was introduced in 1771 by the committee of the Hambledon Club and published in the Laws in 1774. This stated that at its widest the bat should not exceed $4\frac{1}{4}$ inches. Thomas White was responsible for this rule, having come in with a bat the width of the stumps. In 1835 a regulation which limited the bat length to 38 inches was introduced. Cane-handled bats were first produced about 1853 and rubber covers for handles about 1880.

Cricket bat blades have been traditionally made from

The dashing young Ken Barrington in 1955, forcing a ball from Worcestershire's fast bowler Reg Perks through the gully.

willow – the Australian Test cricketer Dennis Lillee caused an upset by arriving at the wicket with an aluminium bat, so that the Laws have now been altered to include a statement saying the bats must be made of wood, though it is permissible to cover the blade with material for protection, strengthening or repair.

Bat-pad

A term introduced in the last 20 years to describe a fielding position close to the batsman in front of the wicket. Also used to describe a catch taken from a ball that the batsman has hit off his bat onto his pad(s).

Batsmen

The method which is commonly employed to compare the expertise of two or more batsmen is by calculating for each player what is called his batting average, a figure arrived at by dividing the total number of runs the batsman has scored by the total number of completed innings which he has played. To obtain any sort of worthwhile comparison, the figures used for all the batsmen must be taken from the same type of matches. Unless stated otherwise the averages which are published in daily newspapers, or the standard cricket reference books, are compiled from matches which are designated 'first-class'. Even within this class of match there is a wide scope ranging from an England v Australia Test match to Oxford University v Cambridge University. The conditions under which cricket is played also vary enormously from country to country and generation to generation. It is impossible to use batsmen's averages therefore to compare W.G. Grace with D.G. Bradman or G.A. Headley with Hanif Mohammad. All that can sensibly be done is to compare a given set of batsmen of the same generation and playing most of their cricket in one country.

Performances in Test cricket ought to provide a more accurate gauge, but only since the mid-1950s have there been enough Test matches to provide a meaningful average for more than a very limited number of players.

However, the simple 'average' for batsmen who have scored over 10,000 first-class runs shows one player so far in advance of the remainder as to leave no doubt of his superiority, at least in terms of 20th century cricketers. The following table gives first-class career figures for every player whose average exceeds 55.00 and 10,000 runs:

		M	I	NO	Runs	HS	Avge
D.G. Bradman	1927-48	234	338	43	28,067	452*	95.14
V.M. Merchant	1929-51	148	232	45	13,340	359*	71.33
W.H. Ponsford	1920-34	162	235	23	13,819	437	65.18
W.M. Woodfull	1921-34	174	245	39	13,388	284	64.99
A.L. Hassett	1932-53	216	322	32	16,890	232	58.24
V.S. Hazare	1934-66	239	369	46	18,754	316*	58.06
A.F. Kippax	1918-35	175	256	33	12,762	315*	57.22
G. Boycott	1962-86	690	1,014	162	48,426	261*	56.83
C.L. Walcott	1941-63	146	238	29	11,820	314*	56.55
K.S. Ranjitsinhji	1893-1920	307	500	62	24,692	285*	56.37
R.B. Simpson	1952-77	247	436	62	21,029	359	56.22
E. de C. Weekes	1944-64	152	241	24	12,010	304*	55.34
W.R. Hammond	1920-51	634	1,005	104	50,551	336*	56.10
L. Hutton	1934-60	513	814	91	40,140	364	55.51

Bradman's average is therefore about 30 runs above everyone except Merchant. It is interesting to remember that the press claimed during the famous 1932/33 'bodyline' series that the English bowlers had at last found Bradman's weakness. Checking the statistics for that series reveals that Bradman's average was 56 – even with that figure he would surpass all but half a dozen batsmen in the whole history of the game!

Using a single English season's record as a yardstick, Bradman is still at the head of the table. The following have averaged over 95 and scored 1,000 runs in a season:

		M	I	NO	Runs	HS	Avge
D.G. Bradman	1938	20	26	5	2,429	278	115.66
G. Boycott	1979	15	20	5	1,538	175*	102.53
G. Boycott	1971	21	30	5	2,503	233	100.12
D.G. Bradman	1930	27	36	6	2,960	334	98.66
H. Sutcliffe	1931	34	42	11	3,006	230	96.96

Reading the reminiscences of contemporary commentators produces an overall view of the greatest batsmen of pre-Bradman era. Fuller Pilch, whose main career was with Kent between 1836 and 1854 was described by the historian, Arthur Haygarth, as 'the best batsman that has ever yet appeared . . . his style of batting was very commanding, extremely forward, and he seemed to crush the best bowling by his long forward plunge before it had time to shoot or rise, or do mischief by catches.'

George Parr of Nottinghamshire was by general consent Pilch's successor. Hillyer, a bowling contemporary, noted: 'Parr was distinctly the premier bat of the 1850-60 decade, his hitting all round was simply splendid. Leg-hitting was then in vogue and Parr excelled in it.'

After Parr faded, three batsmen of equal stature briefly held the stage, Robert Carpenter and Tom Hayward of Cambridgeshire, and Richard Daft of Notts, but soon they were all surpassed by W.G. Grace, who by 1870, when he was in his early twenties, had risen to the top. In the 12 seasons 1869 to 1880 he headed the batting averages ten times. His most remarkable summer was 1871 when he hit 2,739 runs, average 78.25. This average had never been remotely approached up to that date.

In the middle of the 1880s, Wisden's Almanack commented of Arthur Shrewsbury, the Notts professional: 'Excepting of course W.G. Grace, it may be questioned if we have ever produced a more remarkable batsman. On sticky wickets he was, by mutual consent, without an equal in his best seasons, his defence being so strong and his patience so inexhaustible.'

Both Grace and Shrewsbury continued into the 20th century, but by then Ranjitsinhji and Fry had arrived. The former was the leading batsman in 1896, 1900 and 1904, and the latter in 1901, 1903, 1905, 1907, 1911 and 1912.

It is difficult to decide whether one particular batsman outshone all his contemporaries in the Edwardian era, but by the 1920s J.B. Hobbs had gained pride of place. He stood at the head of the averages in 1925, 1926, 1928 and 1929. It is sufficient to quote his England opening partner, Herbert Sutcliffe: 'I can say this without any doubt whatever that he was the most brilliant exponent of all time, and quite the best batsman of my generation on all types of wickets.'

In the 1930s, while Bradman was on his own, W.R. Hammond was the leading English batsman, his place being taken after the Second World War by Len Hutton, the Yorkshire opener. Between the retirement of Hutton and the

One of the most attractive sights on cricket grounds throughout the 1970s was Bishan Bedi tempting batsmen with his slow bowling.

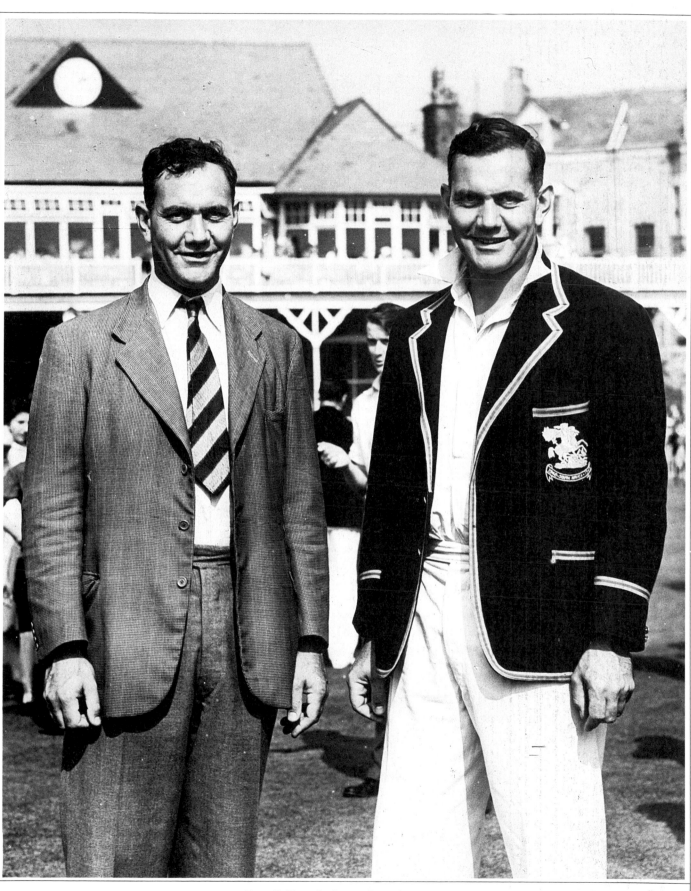

Eric (left) and Alec Bedser of Surrey;
Alec became a great England bowler.

supremacy of Geoff Boycott about 1970, once again there was no single outstanding English batsman. Peter May, Tom Graveney and Colin Cowdrey all had their admirers. In the 1980s the outstanding batsman in English county cricket has been Viv Richards, the Somerset and West Indian batsman.

Turning from England to other Test-playing countries, a similar assessment is much more difficult. The majority of overseas players until very recent years were amateurs whose careers in first-class cricket were much shorter in general than English cricketers', and who often had only a dozen or so innings in important matches in any one season. The name of George Headley stands out as the most noteworthy of pre-Second World War West Indian batsmen and he was succeeded after the war by Everton Weekes, followed by Gary Sobers in the 1960s.

Before the First World War, Victor Trumper takes pride of place among Australians. His obituary in Wisden's Almanack began: 'Of all the great Australian batsmen Victor Trumper was by general consent the best and most brilliant. No one else among the famous group, from Charles Bannerman thirty-nine years ago to Bardsley and Macartney at the present time, had quite such remarkable powers.'

Charles Macartney was perhaps Australia's greatest batsman following Trumper, but soon W.H. Ponsford arrived at the top briefly, before Bradman came. After Bradman retired Australia had several excellent players but none really head and shoulders over the rest. Bill Lawry and Norman O'Neill stand out in the early 1960s, and recently, Greg Chappell.

The two outstanding South Africans since the mid-1960s are Barry Richards, who also scored many runs for Hampshire and in World Series matches, and Graeme Pollock. In early years, Bruce Mitchell, Alan Melville and Dudley Nourse all led the field.

V.M. Merchant's record in Indian cricket is almost on a par with Bradman's in Australia. Sunil Gavaskar has been India's outstanding batsman since the mid-1960s. In Pakistan's history, Hanif Mohammad, Zaheer Abbas and Javed Miandad are names which stand out.

Although New Zealand produced C.S. Dempster and M.P. Donnelly before the Second World War, the first Kiwi batsman really to hit the headlines was Bert Sutcliffe, who was at his best in the late 1940s. Of more recent vintage is Glenn Turner, much of his cricket being played with Worcestershire.

The names which have been noted in this essay have gained their reputations by their ability to score runs, and not necessarily by their style. For some spectators, as for some batsmen, style and elegance are as important as runs. If it is difficult to compare the run-getting abilities of various batsmen, it is impossible to measure players in terms of elegance. That characteristic is in the eye of the beholder.

'Joe Guy sir; all ease and elegance, fit to play before Her Majesty in a drawing room.' Thus runs the description of a noted batsman of the 1840s and there have been many since. It would be foolish to try and make anything but a personal list, and that the reader can do for himself!
(see also individual cricketers' entries)

Bedfordshire

The present Bedfordshire Club was formed on 3 November 1899, but this merely replaced a previous club which had entered a side in the first year of the Minor Counties Championship in 1895. Bedfordshire's strongest team emerged in the 1970s when they won the Championship twice, being led by Jack Smith in both years, with Roger Cox and Roger Pearman as their leading batsmen and T.G.A. Morley as their principal bowler.

Bedi, Bishansingh Giansingh

Born: 25 September 1946, Amritsar, India
Career: 370 m; 1,560 wkts (av 21.69)
Tests: 67 m; 266 wkts (av 28.71)
Bishan Bedi was recognised on cricket grounds throughout the world by his beard and colourful *patka* (he is a Sikh), and his graceful and economical left-arm spin bowling action. He made his first-class debut aged 15 and his Test debut when 20.

Nobody bowled more balls for India, whom he captained in 22 of his 67 Tests, and he topped their wicket-takers' list until passed by Kapil Dev. He played six seasons in the 1970s for Northants.

Bedi was sometimes at odds with the Indian authorities, and was not afraid of controversy, as when he declared India's innings against West Indies in 1975/76 as a protest against intimidatory bowling.

Bedser, Alec Victor

Born: 4 July 1918, Reading, Berkshire
Career: 485 m; 1,924 wkts (av 20.41)
Tests: 51 m; 236 wkts (av 24.89)
One of twin brothers who made their debuts for Surrey in 1939, Bedser's career really blossomed immediately after the war, when he made his Test debut in the first post-war Test in England, in 1946. In his first two Tests he took 22 wickets, and he remained England's leading bowler for nine years.

A big man with big hands, Bedser was a tireless 'workhorse', who bowled a variety of fast-medium inswingers and leg-cutters. Bradman, whom he dismissed frequently, has said that in some conditions he was the most difficult bowler he faced. Bedser was particularly successful against Australia, when they were the world's strongest side, and had he not declined some overseas tours he would have increased his total of 236 Test wickets, which was in any case a record. He was also a regular throughout the seven consecutive years in the 1950s that Surrey won the Championship.

On retirement Bedser managed touring sides and was a long-serving selector, being chairman for 12 years to 1981.

Benaud, Richard

Born: 6 October 1930, Penrith, NSW, Australia
Career: 259 m; 11,719 runs (av 36.50); 945 wkts (av 24.73)
Tests: 63 m; 2,201 runs (av 24.45); 248 wkts (av 27.03)
Richie Benaud began his career for New South Wales as principally a batsman, ended it as principally a bowler, and in between was a leading Test Match all-rounder, the first to score 2,000 runs and take 200 wickets in Tests.

He was more than this, for he was also a brilliant fieldsman and probably the most astute of post-war Test captains. He captained Australia in 28 Tests, most notably during the superb home series against the West Indies in 1960/61,

One of the greatest of international captains, Australia's Richie Benaud later used his knowledge of the game to become one of its best commentators.

Jack Simmons bowling for Lancashire. In 1980 he was the first cricketer whose benefit exceeded £100,000.

which re-inspired Australian fervour in cricket. His greatest match was in England in 1961, when at Old Trafford he dismissed with his leg spinners Dexter, May, Close and Subba Row in five overs to turn impending defeat into an Ashes-retaining victory.

On retirement he became the best of the game's commentators, dispensing his impartial wisdom on both English and Australian television.

Benefits

Matches have been arranged for the 'benefit' of a particular player since early in the 19th century, if not before, but since the Second World War and more especially since the mid-1960s the concept of a county cricketer's 'Benefit Match' has changed dramatically. Events raising money for the beneficiary are now spread over a period of six months and can involve the best part of 100 different functions. The cricketer employs a professional 'fund-raiser' to plan the programme and organise the many activities, which are by no means all connected with cricket. Thus a well-known cricketer of the 1980s could expect to receive anything between £100,000 and £200,000. Following a House of Lords ruling in the 1920s, cricketers' benefits are free of income tax, but it remains to be seen how long this state of affairs will be maintained.

There was a time, however, when cricketers would think twice before accepting the offer of a county benefit. In the days when the benefit money was little more than the net profit from a single three-day county match, the cricketer, at least in theory, could end up by owing the club money if bad weather meant few spectators attended and the cricketer still had to pay all the overheads.

The first player reported to have received over £1,000 for his benefit was Alec Watson of Lancashire in 1885, when his net proceeds were £1,101 11s 1d. Cyril Washbrook, also of Lancashire, was the first to exceed £10,000, with £14,000 in 1948 and the first to receive over £100,000 was Jack Simmons, again of Lancashire, with £128,000 in 1980.

Benson & Hedges Cup

The competition, which is limited to 55 overs per team, is for the 17 English first-class counties plus three other sides, these currently being a Minor Counties XI, Combined Universities and Scotland. The teams play initially in four leagues of five sides each, then the two top teams in each league go through to a knock-out section, the final being staged at Lord's. The winners since the Cup was instituted in 1972 have been:

1972 Leicestershire	1977 Gloucestershire	1982 Somerset
1973 Kent	1978 Kent	1983 Middlesex
1974 Surrey	1979 Essex	1984 Lancashire
1975 Leicestershire	1980 Northamptonshire	1985 Leicestershire
1976 Kent	1981 Somerset	1986 Middlesex

The competition has seen several very exciting finals with the result coming in the 55th over of the second innings. In 1986 Kent seemed hopelessly behind when they needed 51 from the last five overs, but this incredibly narrowed to five off the final ball; Dilley could only hit two, so Middlesex won by two runs.

Berkshire

Having joined the Minor Counties Championship in 1896, Berkshire have competed in every competition since. They were at their peak in the 1920s, winning two of their three titles in 1924 and 1928. In the former year Robert Relf bowled the side to success in rather odd circumstances. A native of Berkshire, he had played for Sussex from 1905, but in 1923 had appeared for his native county. In 1924 he was chosen to play for Sussex v Surrey, but Surrey queried his qualification, so Relf left Sussex and played again for Berkshire, taking 55 wickets at 8.83. Another Berkshire notable of 1924 was A.P.F. Chapman, soon to leave for Kent and two years on to captain England in the famous 1926 game at the Oval.

Berkshire last won the title in 1953. The present county club was formed in March 1895.

Bermuda

Bermuda joined the International Cricket Conference in 1966 and appeared in the ICC Trophy Competition. In 1986, the team won seven out of eight matches in Group Two of the ICC Trophy and went through to the semi-finals, where they

The 1983 Benson & Hedges Cup final between the two leading sides of the 1980s.
Keith Fletcher of Essex caught at silly point by Clive Radley of Middlesex.

were completely outmanoeuvred by Zimbabwe and lost by ten wickets. In 1982 they reached the final of the competition only to meet Zimbabwe and lose; in the first competition in 1979 they lost in the semi-finals to Canada.

Cricket was firmly established in Bermuda by the middle of the 19th century, but it was not until 1891 that an overseas team came to the colony and then, not from England, but from Philadelphia. Likewise the first Bermudan team to go abroad went to the United States in 1905. The major touring team to visit Bermuda between the wars was Sir Julien Cahn's side in 1933; it was not until 1960 that a side from Bermuda toured England and further such tours took place in 1962 and 1978.

Betting
see Gambling

Big hits
C.I. Thornton, who played for Kent and Middlesex between 1867 and 1885, was described thus: 'in his day he was one of the biggest – if not actually the mightiest of all time – of hitters.' His longest measured hit in practice was 168 yards 2 feet, and in a match, in 1871, 152 yards. Contemporary with Thornton was the Australian, G.J. Bonnor, 'The Colonial Hercules', who stood 6 feet 6 inches and weighed 16 stone. Although there appeared to be no measurements for Bonnor's hits, in one game he hit the ball so high that he was running his third run when the ball was caught.

In 1968 Gary Sobers for Notts v Glamorgan hit six sixes off a six-ball over bowled by Malcolm Nash. The feat was equalled in India in 1984/85 by R.J. Shastri.

Of all the long hits, one which is often recalled was by Albert Trott at Lord's in 1899, when he hit a delivery from the Australian bowler, M.A. Noble, on to the pavilion roof.

Of the present-day cricketers, the best-known hitter is Ian Botham, who holds the record for the most sixes hit in a single English first-class season, having made 80 such hits in 1985.

Birmingham League
The Birmingham League was formed in 1888 and is reputed to be the oldest extant cricket league in England. Leading sides include Moseley, West Bromwich, Dartmouth, Walsall, Kidderminster, Stourbridge and a Warwickshire County Colts side. The League is the strongest in the Midlands and includes a number of former county cricketers.

Blackham, John McCarthy
Born: 11 May 1854, North Fitzroy, Victoria, Australia
Died: 28 December 1932, Melbourne, Australia
Career: 275 *m*; 6,395 runs (av 16.78); 273 *ct*; 180 *st*
Tests: 35 *m*; 800 runs (av 15.68); 36 *ct*; 24 *st*
Blackham was called the 'Prince of Wicketkeepers'. He played for Victoria for 21 seasons from 1874/75, and made his Test debut in the first Test of all, in 1876/77. At first he had a rival as keeper in the Test team in the captain, W.L. Murdoch, but quickly established his place. He became captain himself, and led the tourists to England in 1893. Blackham was in the first eight Australian touring teams to England.

Blackham influenced the style of wicketkeeping, cultivat-

The 'Prince of Wicketkeepers', J. McC. Blackham, Australia's keeper in 35 Test Matches, including the first ever played.

ing the neat, unobtrusive technique which such as Bob Taylor favoured in modern times, and developing the taking of the ball and whipping-off of the bails in one movement, which is now universal. His pioneering cost him dear – by the time he retired he had 'practically all his front teeth knocked out'.

Blind spot
The ideal spot on the ground where the bowler should pitch a ball so as to place the batsman in two minds as to whether to play a back stroke or a forward stroke. First mentioned in 1864.

Block
To stop the ball in a defensive manner, therefore not attempting to score a run. The 'block-hole' is the dent in the turf directly in front of the wicket where the batsman rests his bat prior to executing a stroke.

Bodyline captain Douglas Jardine presenting a cheque to his two destroyers, the Nottinghamshire and England fast bowlers Voce (left) and Larwood at Trent Bridge. The cheque resulted from a public subscription organised by Nottingham newspapers.

Bodyline

The term 'bodyline' was coined by the Australian press to describe the type of bowling which was used by England's fast bowlers, notably Larwood and Voce, during the 1932/33 tour of Australia.

During the 1920s, especially in Australia, bat completely dominated ball. Scoring reached new heights and Ponsford and then Bradman were piling record upon record. The captain of the English touring team, D.R. Jardine, decided that the only way to curb this run spree was by the use of what he called 'leg-theory'. In essence this meant bowling fast deliveries at the leg stump with a semi-circle of close fielders on the leg side. The batsman had to play the ball and any mishit would probably result in a catch on the leg-side.

Such a theory would work satisfactorily only if the team possessed an accurate fast bowler. In Larwood, England had such a bowler. Australia had several fast bowlers, but they were much too inaccurate to be effective.

The batsman's answer to leg-theory is the possession of an effective hook stroke. In the First Test of the 1932/33 series at Sydney, Bradman did not play, but Stan McCabe demonstrated, with an innings of 187 not out, that it was possible to use the hook to tame Larwood and Voce. Australia's openers, W.M. Woodfull and W.H. Ponsford, both prolific batsmen, were unable to cope with the fast deliveries, being dismissed for a total of 41 runs in their four innings. England won the match by an innings.

Australia won the Second Test, with Bradman making an unbeaten century in the second innings, but the wicket was much slower than usually encountered at Melbourne, and the Australian spin bowler, Bill O'Reilly, took ten wickets in the match. With the series now one match each, the interest in the Third Test at Adelaide was enormous. England batted first and made 341; Australia then collapsed to 51 for 4. Ponsford and Richardson then raised the total to 131, when the latter was bowled by Allen. The wicketkeeper, Oldfield, assisted Ponsford in another stand which realised 63 runs, then Oldfield was struck on the side of the head by a ball from Larwood. The injured batsman was taken from the field and played no further part in the match. Early in the same innings Larwood had hit the Australian captain, Woodfull, over the heart. This provoked the captain's comment that there were two sides playing and one was not playing cricket. The Australian Board of Control then sent a telegram to the MCC which stated that bodyline bowling was unsportmanlike and should cease at once. The Test at Adelaide continued and England won by 338 runs, but the atmosphere was becoming increasingly bitter. The MCC replied to the telegram saying they had complete confidence in the English captain, managers and team and deploring the description 'unsportsmanlike'. The Fourth and Fifth Tests were played without any serious injuries and with England winning the series by four matches to one. Larwood took 33 wickets at 19.51 runs each, easily the best record on either side.

Australian captain Allan Border off-driving against England at Adelaide in 1986/87. He is Australia's leading batsman of the 1980s.

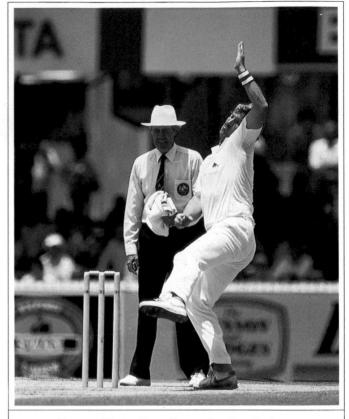

The world's leading all-rounder, Ian Botham, bowling at Perth in 1986/87. Botham passed Lillee's record aggregate of Test wickets in 1986.

During 1933 the West Indian touring team to England used leg-theory, but the softer English wickets did not really lend themselves to this type of bowling. In the winter of 1933/34 the MCC committee passed a resolution stating that any form of bowling which attacked the batsman was against the spirit of the game and a meeting of county captains agreed not to employ leg-theory. The Australians toured England in 1934. Jardine, Larwood and Voce were not chosen to play for England and according to their supporters had been deliberately cast aside. The Notts captain, A.W. Carr, ignored the gentlemen's agreement to outlaw leg-theory and one or two counties indicated that they would refuse to play Notts in 1935 if Carr continued in his attitude (Larwood and Voce were both Notts cricketers). The Notts Committee sacked Carr, but an extra-ordinary general meeting of the county members then threw out the committee and supported Carr. After further moves however the committee were reinstated and made a change of captaincy. The MCC then in effect changed the Laws so that the outlawing of leg-theory became official and umpires were empowered to act against it.

Many books have been written on this subject, which has also been expounded at length in the form of a televised serial, based on the lives of Jardine, Larwood and Bradman.

Bombay

The Brabourne Stadium in Bombay was built in 1936 as the showpiece of Indian cricket by the exclusive Cricket Club of India and the first Test Match was played there between India

and West Indies in 1948/49. The ground is capable of holding about 50,000 spectators. The stadium, which has some splendid facilities, including residential, has now fallen on hard times owing to a dispute between the Cricket Club of India and the Bombay Cricket Association, and the latter built a new ground, the Wankhede Stadium, about a mile away. Since 1974/75 Test Matches have been staged on the new ground.

First-class cricket in Bombay was originally played on the Gymkhana Ground, the venue of the annual Presidency Matches and it was on that ground that the first Bombay Test was played in 1933/34 when India played England.

Bombay Tournament

This competition, which for over 40 years was the principal first-class tournament in India, began in 1892/93 when the Europeans played the Parsis. In the early years it consisted usually of two matches between these two sides, one match being played in Bombay and the other in Poona. In 1907/08 the competition became triangular with the Hindus making a third side. The Muslims entered a team in 1912/13 and the Bombay Pentangular Tournament began in 1937/38 when 'The Rest' (mainly Eurasians and non-European Christians) entered a team. The last tournament was held in 1947/48.

Book cricket

Designed originally by schoolboys to give the master or

Australian fast bowler Geoff Lawson ducks a bouncer from England's Richard Ellison at Edgbaston in 1985 and loses his helmet.

prefect an impression of industrious work, whilst in fact filling in time. Each letter of the alphabet is designated as a number of runs, six, four, three, two or one, or a mode of dismissal. This simply converts a page of Latin, which the pupil appears to be studying with great diligence, into an interesting cricket match.

Border, Allan Robert

Born: 27 July 1955, Cremorne, NSW, Australia
Career: 194 *m*; 14,820 runs (av 53.69); 55 wkts (av 36.60)
Tests: 86 *m*; 6,672 runs (av 52.12); 16 wkts (av 41.12)
Captain of Queensland since 1983/84 and of Australia, Border is his country's most effective batsman. Left-handed and coming in usually at No.4, he headed the Test averages on both the 1981 and 1985 Australian tours to England. He has also toured the West Indies, India, Pakistan and Sri Lanka. He played one match for Gloucestershire in 1977 and then a season with Essex in 1986; his only double century was 200 for his native New South Wales against Queensland in 1979/80 – he joined the latter state the following season.

Botham, Ian Terence

Born: 24 November 1955, Heswall, Cheshire
Career: 290 *m*; 14,679 runs (av 35.20); 936 wkts (av 26.35)
Tests: 89 *m*; 4,825 runs (av 34.96); 366 wkts (av 27.21)
Botham is the leading cricketer of the 1980s; an outstanding all-rounder whose figures, partly because of the proliferation of Test cricket in recent times, dwarf all who went before him. A measure of his talent lies in the fact that, although he has taken more Test wickets than any other cricketer, the feats which will become legends concern his batting.

He made his debut for Somerset in 1974, and for England in 1977. Batting about No. 6, he became the hardest-hitting batsman in the game, the Jessop of his day, and his fast-medium swing bowling, particularly early in his career and when conditions were helpful, could be devastating.

His first singular Test performance came in 1978, when he scored 108 and took 8 for 34 against Pakistan at Lord's. He raced to 1,000 Test runs and 100 Test wickets in 21 Tests, the quickest (in terms of matches) ever, reached 2,000 and 200 in 42 tests, the third to do it (the youngest and quickest), and became the first to pass 3,000 and 300.

In 1979/80, in the Golden Jubilee Test in India, he became the first England player to score a century and take ten wickets in a Test.

His most famous match was at Headingley in 1981, when, despite his six wickets and top score of 50, England followed on against Australia, and at 135 for 7 were 500-1 against in the betting shop. Botham's 149 not out then won the match. This followed a pair at Lord's, when he was sacked as England captain after 12 Tests.

Botham has frequently been in trouble with the authorities, and was suspended in 1986 for two months after admissions of drug-taking. At the end of the season, after a shake-up at Somerset, he left the county in support of the sacked Viv Richards and Joel Garner to join Worcestershire.

Bouncer

A short-pitched fast delivery by the bowler which rises abnormally high from the ground. First used in print in 1928 and now in general use, rather than the word 'bumper'.

If in the opinion of the umpire the bowler uses 'bouncers' to intimidate the batsman, the law now states that the umpire should warn the bowler against using this delivery and no-ball him if he continues to do so, and direct the captain to take off the bowler.

Boundaries

The normal practice on cricket grounds is to award a batsman four runs for a hit which crosses the boundary lines, except when the ball clears the line without touching the ground, in which case the batsman obtains six runs.

The boundary is usually marked by a white line, rope, or series of markers and in county matches is about 75 yards from the wicket. Before permanent seating was a feature on cricket grounds there was no boundary and all hits were run out, the ring of spectators parting to allow the ball and the pursuing fielder to continue on their way. The first exceptions to this were made when the ball was stopped by a tent or the pavilion. In these cases an agreed number of runs were awarded. Boundary lines came into general use in the second half of the 19th century. Prior to this the boundary rope was used not to award batsmen runs, but merely to keep spectators off the playing area.

The most boundaries in a single first-class innings are 68 fours by P.A. Perrin in his score of 343 not out for Essex v Derbyshire at Chesterfield in 1904. In a minor match, G.T.S. Stevens hit 64 fours and 24 sixes at Neasden, London, in 1919.

Bowl

To deliver the ball to the batsman in a manner which is permitted under the Laws.
(*see also* Overarm, Roundarm and Underarm)

Bowled

The most satisfying (to the bowler) mode of dismissal of a batsman, a delivery from the bowler hitting the stumps and removing at least one bail.
(*see also* Played on)

Bowlers

see Fast bowlers, Medium-paced bowlers and Slow bowlers

Boycott, Geoffrey

Born: 21 October 1940, Fitzwilliam, Yorkshire
Career: 609 *m*; 48,426 runs (av 56.83)
Tests: 108 *m*; 8,114 runs (av 47.72)
In 1986 Boycott passed Graveney's aggregate of first-class runs to become the highest scorer of any player still living. He stands eighth in the all-time list – none of those above him has a higher average. These statistics would please him. His one fault, say his critics, was an over-riding obsession with his own figures to the detriment of the team.

He made his debut as an opening bat for Yorkshire in 1962, and for England in 1964. He wore spectacles, later changed to contact lenses. He worked and practised hard at his technique, and became the most reliable opener in the game.

Boycott did not always get the recognition he thought he deserved, and spent three years out of the Test team after being disappointed over the captaincy. His greatest moment came soon after his reinstatement, when he scored his 100th hundred in an Ashes match before his own supporters at Headingley. Later he overtook Gary Sobers' Test record aggregate of runs.

He captained Yorkshire, but was sacked because of his individualistic approach. When his contract was not renewed in 1983 he challenged the committee, and won the day, becoming a committee member himself and continuing as a player. However, his Yorkshire career appeared to be at an end when he was again discarded at the end of 1986.

Bradford League

The best-known of the Yorkshire leagues, the Bradford League was formed in 1903. During the two world wars the League attracted many Test cricketers. One of the oldest of the present member clubs is Pudsey St Lawrence, which produced Herbert Sutcliffe and Len Hutton. Many notable Yorkshire county players have been bred in the League over the years. Undercliffe, led by the former Leicestershire bowler Peter Booth, won the competition in 1986, with Hanging Heaton second. Winners the previous year, Pudsey St Lawrence had to be content with third place.

Bradman, Donald George

Born: 27 August 1908, Cootamundra, NSW, Australia
Career: 234 m; 28,067 runs (av 95.14)
Tests: 52 m; 6,996 runs (av 99.94)

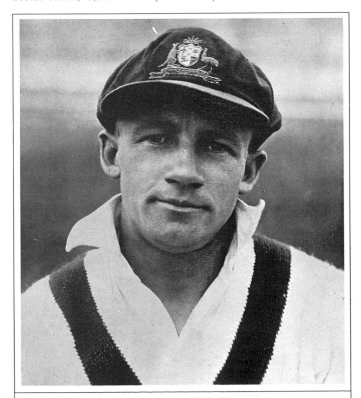

Don Bradman as he looked in the 1930s, when he was at the peak of his powers as the most successful batsman the game has ever seen.

Bradman's figures establish him as unquestionably the greatest batsman who ever lived. He made his debut for New South Wales (he later played for South Australia) in 1927/28, and from soon after his Test debut in 1928/29 it was obvious that he was a special player.

He was not regarded as an elegant batsman – his most typical stroke was a pull through mid-wicket – but his timing and mastery had its own style. On the easy Australian wickets from the late 1920s he dominated bowlers, and established a world record score of 452 not out against Queensland that stood for many years. The theory that he was less of a master on English wickets is false. On four tours he scored 9,837 runs at an average of over 96.

In the Test Match at Headingley in 1930, he was 309 not out at the end of the first day (he did not open!), and his final 334 was an Ashes record until beaten by Hutton.

Bradman captained Australia in 24 Tests, and was captain of the 1948 touring side which remained unbeaten. On retirement, he became a selector and chairman of the Board of Control, and was knighted in 1949.

Bramall Lane

This former Yorkshire cricket ground is the only venue in England where a Test Match has been staged and where cricket is now no longer played. The first important match to be played on the ground took place in 1855, when Yorkshire played Sussex, the ground having been opened that year by Sheffield Cricket Club. From 1862 the ground was also used for soccer, but Sheffield United Football Club, who now occupy the whole ground, did not come into existence until 1889. Ten years later the Sheffield United Cricket and Football Club formed a limited liability company and bought the freehold of the ground from the Norfolk Estate.

The ground saw its first Test Match when England played Australia there in 1902. Cricket however ceased in 1973, the final county game being against Lancashire on 4, 6 and 7 August 1973. The area used for cricket is now mainly occupied by a football stand.

Brazil

Regular cricket was established in Brazil in the 1870s, but it was not until the 1920s that the principal international match against the Argentine was first played. Some authorities have suggested that the Argentina v Brazil contests of the inter-war period ought to rank as first-class games, but this view is not held generally.

The MCC team which visited Brazil in 1958/59 completely outplayed the local side and no improvement was found when a second tour was made in 1964/65. Brazil is not a member of the ICC.

Bridgetown

The Kensington Oval in Bridgetown, Barbados, was the scene of the first Test Match ever staged in the West Indies, the match being against England in 1929/30. The ground, on which Barbados play their first-class matches, was laid out in the 19th century by the Pickwick Cricket Club. It can hold about 10,000 spectators.

Brisbane

The Woolloongabba Ground in Brisbane, usually referred to as the 'Gabba', has been used for Test cricket since 1931/32. It is also the home of the Queensland Cricket Association, but prior to this date the principal ground in Brisbane was the Exhibition Ground, and Brisbane saw its first Test there in 1928/29. It was on the Gabba in 1960/61 that the famous tied Test Match between Australia and West Indies was played.

Until the 1950s, the Gabba was not very well appointed, but in more recent years it has been considerably renovated and the facilities are now excellent.

Broad, Brian Christopher

Born: 29 September 1957, Bristol
Career: 171 m; 10,297 runs (av 36.38)
Tests: 10 m; 768 runs (av 48.00)

Chris Broad, a tall left-handed opening batsman, who crouches in his stance and uses the method of holding his bat well off the ground while awaiting the ball, began his career with Gloucestershire in 1979, but switched to Notts in 1984. Test Match recognition came that year against West Indies, but he was omitted after that season until the 1986/87 tour of Australia, when he was immediately the most successful batsman, scoring centuries in three successive Tests, to join Hobbs, Sutcliffe and Hammond as Englishmen to perform this feat against Australia.

Broadcasting

A running commentary on a cricket match was first broadcast by the BBC in 1927, when F.H. Gillingham reported from the Essex v New Zealand match, but the first

Geoffrey Boycott turns a ball to leg. In 1986 he became the highest scoring batsman in first-class cricket still living.

The Kensington Oval at Bridgetown, Barbados, with the Australian tourists batting in 1973.

Chris Broad, the most successful batsman of the Test series between England and Australia in 1986/87.

From up with the floodlights, the Channel 9 Television view of cricket at Perth, Western Australia.

*John Arlott, who made an art of the radio cricket commentary, at work in his last Test Match,
the Centenary Test at Lord's in 1980.*

commentator to make a name for himself in this new art was Howard Marshall, from 1935 onwards.

After the Second World War continuous commentaries on Test Matches became a standard feature of broadcasting with Rex Alston and John Arlott being the two most notable exponents and Jim Swanton providing summaries at close of play and innings' intervals. Various retired cricketers were gradually introduced into the teams of broadcasters. The BBC radio team has been for some years entitled 'Test Match Special' under the captaincy of the veteran broadcaster, Brian Johnston with at present Henry Blofield, Christopher Martin-Jenkins and Tony Lewis. The team also have a resident scorer, who is Bill Frindall.

A rival team provide commentaries for television. The first game ever to be televised was the Second Test at Lord's in 1938, but this broadcast could only be received in the London area. After closing down during the Second World War, the development of televised cricket was rather slow and not until the 1960s did it really take off nationally. Brian Johnston was one of the main TV presenters until his move to radio. In recent years the former Australian Test captain Richie Benaud has become one of the best-known commentators, together with the late Jim Laker. Until he retired in 1986, Peter West was a major figure in the broadcasts in the role of 'link-man'.

Many innovations in televised broadcasting came about with the advent of Packer's World Series cricket, notably the use of more cameras and various ideas to improve the sound effects.

Brothers

In English first-class cricket three families have provided seven cricketing brothers, namely:

The Fosters: B.S. (1902-12), G.N. (1903-31), H.K. (1894-1925), M.K. (1908-36), N.J.A. (1923), R.E. (1899-1912), W.L. (1899-1911)

The Studds: A.H. (1887-88), C.T. (1879-1903), E.J.C. (1878-85), G.B. (1879-86), H.W. (1890-98), J.E.K. (1878-85), R.A. (1895)

The Walker brothers: A. (1846-60), A.H. (1855-62), F. (1849-60), I.D. (1862-84), J. (1846-68), R.D. (1861-78), V.E. (1856-77)

On three occasions three brothers have played in a Test Match together: W.G., G.F. and E.M. Grace for England in 1880; Hanif, Mushtaq and Sadiq Mohammad for Pakistan in 1969/70; and A., G.G. and F. Hearne in the England v South Africa match in 1891/92, the last named playing for South Africa, the first two for England.

(see also Families)

Buckinghamshire

Having gained eight Minor Counties Championship titles spread between 1899 and 1969, Buckinghamshire have been one of the strongest of the counties in the competition. In fact in 1921 they were asked to become first-class, but declined due to lack of playing facilities. With five titles between the wars they were particularly well endowed in the 1920s, owing much to their slow-medium left-arm professional, Frank Edwards. He took 104 wickets for 9.99 runs each when the title was won in 1923, and over 1,000 wickets for the county in his career. The captain at this time was W.B. Franklin, who kept wicket and had a perfect understanding of Edwards' subtle variations. The county was formed in January 1891 and have competed in every Minor Counties competition, except the first in 1895.

Bumper

A term first used in print in 1859 – see Bouncer.

Butter-fingers

A term of derision used to describe a fieldsman who misses an easy catch. The expression appears in Dickens' 'Pickwick Papers', being used by Jingle to describe individuals who mis-fielded.

Bye

A run scored from a ball which passes the wicket untouched by the batsman. A bye, as such, was not defined in the Laws until the 1884 revision, but byes were recorded in the score details from the earliest known records: see Kent v All England in 1744, for example.

Byes are not credited to the batsmen, nor are they included in runs conceded by the bowlers.

The most byes conceded by a team in a first-class innings are 57 by Cambridge University v Yorkshire at Fenner's in 1884.

C

c

An abbreviation for 'caught' used in scorebooks and published scores: 'c Smith' means 'caught out by Smith'.

Calcutta

Calcutta Cricket Club was founded in 1792 and in some respects has been regarded as the Indian equivalent of the MCC. The club laid out the ground at Eden Gardens and this ground can now claim to be the oldest cricket ground in the world on which Test Matches are played. The first English side to tour India (Vernon's team of 1889/90) played its first two matches in India (having previously played in Ceylon) at Eden Gardens, but the first recognised first-class game there was not until 1917/18. Bengal have played first-class matches at Eden Gardens since the Ranji Trophy was founded and the first Test Match on the ground was in 1933/34 when India played England.

Concrete stands encircle the ground which has a capacity of over 80,000. Whilst no authenticated attendance figures exist it is believed that about 400,000 spectators have been present at one or two of the Tests staged in Calcutta in recent years and thus Eden Gardens can claim this as a record.

Cambridge

Fenner's Cricket Ground in Cambridge is the home of the University Cricket Club. The ground was first used in 1846, having been laid out by F.P. Fenner, a well-known local professional cricketer, and in 1848 the University began playing its matches there. The previous venue, which continued to be used for cricket, was Parker's Piece. The ground has always had a reputation as a good batting strip. The present pavilion is a recent building, which replaced one damaged during the Second World War.

Cambridge University

The first recorded match by Cambridge University was played against Eton in 1754 and the annual match against Oxford began in 1827. For many years the 'University Match' at Lord's was one of the events of the season and drew large crowds, but since the Second World War interest in the game has slowly dwindled. Cambridge play their home matches on the Fenner's Ground, which is notable for its batting wickets. By tradition Cambridge University is ranked first-class, though the days when the team could give a first-class county a decent match have gone.

Part of the huge crowd at Eden Gardens, Calcutta, for the Test Match with England in 1976/77. This ground can claim the largest attendance for a cricket match.

Cambridgeshire

Having three of the most famous professionals of the 1860s, Bob Carpenter, Tom Hayward and George Tarrant, Cambridgeshire competed in the County Championship from 1864 to 1871, but the County Club collapsed and the present club did not come into existence until 1891. They joined the Minor Counties Championship in 1898 and have played in all but two of the competitions since. They have won the title once, in 1963, under the leadership of M.A. Crouch, who had up till then been captain for 14 years. The reason for their success was however the arrival of Johnny Wardle, the former Yorkshire and England spinner, who took 55 wickets at 16.83 runs each. The left-hand batsman, Terry Hale, hit most runs, with 682, averaging 62.00.

Canada

Although the first match with the United States took place in 1844 and the first England tour in 1859 commenced its programme in Canada, the game never became as well established as in Philadelphia and New York. Many of the English teams which visited North America before the First World War played matches in Canada as well as the United States, but the former games were generally regarded as a minor section of the programme.

The Canadians made a disastrous first tour to England in 1880, when it was discovered in mid-season that their captain was an English army deserter, playing under an alias.

Kent playing Glamorgan at Kent's headquarters at Canterbury, with its famous old tree inside the boundary.

Fenner's, the lovely ground (with a batsman's wicket) where Cambridge University have played cricket since 1848.

The principal centre of cricket in Canada has been Toronto, but the game also flourished in British Colombia. The major tour to Canada between the wars was by MCC in 1937, when the visitors played 19 matches in a month at venues right across Canada. They lost only one match, at which stage they were described as 'in an advanced state of exhaustion and decrepitude'.

A similar tour was undertaken in 1951, when the MCC met with two defeats in 22 matches. In 1954 a Canadian team toured England and for the first and only time was granted first-class status. In the 1979 ICC Trophy Canada reached the final and were then beaten by Sri Lanka, but both finalists played in the Prudential World Cup. Canada lost all three of their matches, being beaten by Pakistan, England and Australia.

In the ICC tournaments of 1982 and 1986 Canada did not reach the final.

Cancelled matches
The match between West Indies and England scheduled for Georgetown, Guyana, in 1980/81 is the only Test Match which has been cancelled just a few days before it was to begin. The reason for the cancellation was that the Guyanan Government withdrew the visitor's permit which had been issued to the Surrey and England cricketer, Robin Jackman. The Guyanan Government took this action because of Jackman's cricketing connections with South Africa.

In 1968/69, the proposed English tour to South Africa was cancelled when South Africa refused to allow the touring side to include Basil d'Oliveira, the Cape Coloured cricketer, who had qualified for England by residence and played for Worcestershire. The South African tour to England in 1970 was cancelled by instructions from the British Government, as were other tours, to and from South Africa, by other authorities in the 1970s.

Canterbury, Kent
The St Lawrence Ground at Canterbury is one of the most picturesque of English county grounds. The headquarters of Kent County Cricket Club, it was laid out in 1847, with the first important match being Kent v England in August of that year. The annual Canterbury Cricket Week, in which Kent opposed an England team selected by MCC, and then the Gentlemen of Kent played a similarly selected amateur side, was combined with theatrical performances by the Old Stagers and was for many years one of the most important features of the cricket year. It still continues with Kent usually playing two inter-county matches during the week.

Cap
To award a player his cap has two meanings. In county cricket, a player is awarded his cap (usually by the County Committee) when he has performed well in the first eleven for some time and generally has secured a regular place in the eleven. In international cricket a player gains his cap on his debut for his country. At other levels of the game, the award varies between these two definitions.

Cape Town
The principal cricket ground in Cape Town is Newlands, which was opened in 1888, and the first first-class match, which was also the first Test Match, took place between South Africa and England there in 1888/89. The ground is the headquarters of Western Province Cricket Union, which stages its Currie Cup matches there. The ground is most pleasantly situated and the famous Table Mountain can be seen in the background.

Captains
The longest serving county captains have been W.G. Grace (Gloucestershire 1871-98) and Lord Hawke (Yorkshire 1883-1910); both reigned for 28 seasons. The most successful county captain was Stuart Surridge of Surrey, who led the county for five seasons (1952-56) and won the County Championship in each.

Clive Lloyd led West Indies in 74 Test Matches, which is a record for any country, and won 36 of those matches, another record.

England's captain for most Tests is Peter May with 41 and Australia's is Greg Chappell with 48.

Car cricket
Played by children on a tedious journey by road. Each vehicle counts a given number of runs, for example a double decker bus might be agreed as six, a lorry as four and a car as a single. A motorbike is usually agreed as a wicket.

Cardiff
For many years the principal cricket ground in the city was Cardiff Arms Park, which had been used by Cardiff Cricket Club since 1867 and was the main Glamorgan County ground, when that team gained first-class status in 1921. The cricket ground was next to the Welsh rugby ground and the first sign that cricket was on the way out came in 1934 when the old pavilion was demolished to make way for a double-decker rugby stand. Glamorgan finally moved from Cardiff Arms Park to the present ground at Sophia Gardens in 1967, the first match there being against Indians on 24, 25 and 26 May.

Carrying bat
This phrase is used when a batsman is not out at the end of an innings, and more particularly when one of the two opening batsmen is not out when all the ten wickets have fallen. In this latter form it is a feat which is one of the most difficult to achieve: there are in first-class cricket twice as many examples of batsmen scoring double centuries as carrying their bats through completed innings. In Test cricket the feat is even more rare, no batsman having achieved it on more than two occasions. Those performing the feat twice are L. Hutton for England against West Indies and Australia, W.M. Woodfull for Australia, twice against England, W.M. Lawry for Australia against India and England and Glenn Turner for New Zealand against England and West Indies.

Catch
The catching of the ball by a fieldsman, when it has been hit

by the batsman and before it touches the ground. Thus a batsman is 'caught out'.

Central Lancashire League
Founded in 1892, the League does not quite equal its neighbours, the Lancashire League, in the overall quality of its professionals, but nevertheless some very famous names can be found in its archives: Gary Sobers (Radcliffe), Jock Livingston (Royton), Cec Pepper (Rochdale), Charles Barnett (Rochdale), John Reid (Heywood), George Tribe (Milnrow), Frank Worrell (Radcliffe) and Basil d'Oliveira (Middleton) are some of the professionals. In 1986 Littleborough won the League with Ezra Moseley as professional and Vanburn Holder (Royton), Mohsin Khan (Walsden) and Madan Lal (Ashton) were other 1986 professionals.

Century
The score of 100 or more runs by an individual batsman, also used as half-century (50) and double century (200). The term was first used in print in 1876.

Chappell, Gregory Stephen
Born: 7 August 1948, Unley, South Australia
Career: 321 m; 24,535 runs (av 52.20); 291 wkts (av 29.95)
Tests: 87 m; 7,110 runs (av 53.86); 47 wkts (av 40.70)
Greg Chappell was the leading Australian batsman of the late 1970s and early 1980s. He scored more runs for Australia than any other player. He followed his brother Ian, and grandfather, Vic Richardson, as captain of Australia.

Chappell's first series as captain, in 1975/76, was his most successful. In the First Test against the West Indies he became the first Australian captain to score a century in each innings. The strong West Indians were beaten 5-1, Chappell scoring 702 runs, average 117.

A tall, very elegant batsman, Chappell made his debut in 1966/67 for South Australia, but later switched to Queensland. He played two seasons for Somerset, very successfully.

He made a century in his first and last Tests, and in the last took his Test catches to 122, a record for an outfielder.

Cheshire
For the second time in their history Cheshire won the Minor Counties Championship in 1985, under the leadership of Arthur Sutton, who was in his 27th year with the club – their only other win came in 1967. The reason for their 1985 victory was the all-round cricket of the Pakistani Test player, Mudassar Nazar, plus the batting of Ian Tansley and the bowling of Neil O'Brien.

Cheshire had a good side in the 1870s and 1880s, but it was unfortunate for the county that their club collapsed in the 1890s and was not revived until 1908. They joined the Minor Counties Championship the following year and have taken part ever since.

Chinaman
A ball delivered by a slow left-arm bowler, which breaks to the leg, instead of the more usual break to the off, of a right-handed batsman. One of the best-known exponents was the Australian Fleetwood-Smith. In Australia, the definition is usually given as the other way round: a left-arm bowler's ball which breaks to the off, instead of the expected leg.

Christchurch, New Zealand
The headquarters of Canterbury Cricket Association is at Lancaster Park, Christchurch, the ground having been opened in 1881/82 when Canterbury played the English touring team. The Test Match which was played there against England in 1929/30 was the first such game staged on New Zealand soil. The ground is also used for rugby football.

Cigarette cards
The first cards depicting cricketers were issued in New York and in Australia in the 1880s, but the first major series of 'Cricketers' was produced and printed in England by Wills and consisted of 50. In the early years of the 20th century many cricketing sets were issued by quite a number of firms. The most extensive series ever issued on cricketers appeared in 1908 by Taddy & Co and there are 238 known cards in this set; each county has either 14 or 15 representatives.

F & J Smith printed a series of 70 for the 1912 Triangular Tests, and this was the last set prior to the First World War. After the war the first cricketing series did not appear until 1923, when R & J Hill and Godfrey Phillips both published sets, the latter running to 224 cards. In 1926 John Player started their system of a set for each Australian Tour year, which continued until 1938.

Since the Second World War there have been no cigarette cards, but trade cards have continued to be issued by many firms and, in fact, there were many trade cards produced prior to 1939. It is estimated that there have been well in excess of 6,000 cigarette cards of cricketers and the same number of trade cards.

Club cricket
The first national knock-out competition for cricket clubs was the brainchild of Derrick Robins and was set up through the offices of *The Cricketer* in 1969. Over 350 clubs applied, but the entry was restricted to 256, and the first final, held at Edgbaston, was won by Hampstead, who beat Pocklington Pixies by 14 runs in a game of 40 overs per side. John Haig sponsored the Trophy from 1976 to 1982, since when William Younger have been the sponsors. The most successful club have been Scarborough, who have gained the title five times. In the 1986 final Stourbridge beat Weston-super-Mare by four wickets.

Collectors
As is demonstrated from the prices realised at auctions of cricketana (q.v.), the hobby of collecting cricketing items is very much alive. Well-known collectors of the present day include David Frith, Geoffrey Copinger, Tony Woodhouse, Bob Jones, D.B. Wells and many others. Some like Vic Lewis (ties) or Terry Taylor (autographs) follow one particular path.

The father of the cricket-collectors was A.L. Ford of Southgate, who bought his first book in 1853 and began

One of the main cricket grounds in Wales is
Glamorgan's Sophia Gardens, Cardiff, which replaced
the rugby ground at Cardiff Arms Park.

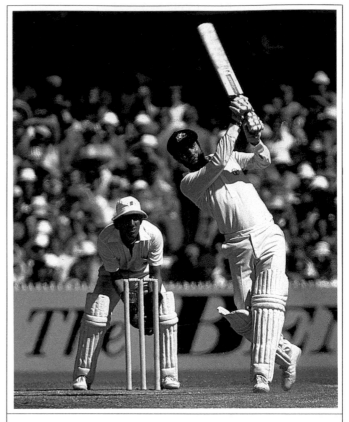

The leading Australian batsman of the 1970s,
Greg Chappell, whose Test aggregate is
Australia's highest.

A relic of British influence in the Greek islands, the cricket pitch in Corfu Town,
still in regular use by locals and visiting teams.

collecting in 1861. He appears to have had a head start on potential rivals and thus to have collected many rare items for a song. The other Victorian collectors, Charles Pratt Green of Malvern, A.J. Gaston of Brighton and Thomas Padwick of Redhill, began seriously in the 1880s, with A.D. Taylor and the Rev R.S. Holmes not far behind them. The historian F.S. Ashley-Cooper began building his famous collection before the turn of the century.

Of the collectors who began their hobby in the inter-world war period, some are of course still active, but the best known was J.W. Goldman of London and later of Egham. It was in fact Mr Goldman who wrote a series of articles in the 1930s on collecting cricketana and thus inspired many of the more modern collectors.

(*see also* Cricketana)

Colombo

Although Sri Lanka have only recently joined the ranks of Test-playing countries, there are already three cricket grounds in Colombo which have staged Test Matches, namely the P. Saravanamuttu Oval (first 1982/83), Sinhalese Sports Club (first 1984/85) and Colombo Cricket Club (first 1984/85).

Compton, Denis Charles Scott

Born: 23 May 1918, Hendon, Middlesex
Career: 515 *m*; 38,942 runs (av 51.85); 622 wkts (av 32.27)
Tests: 78 *m*; 5,807 runs (av 50.06); 25 wkts (av 56.40)
Compton was a brilliant right-hand batsman and occasional left-arm bowler. He was a natural ball-player from youth,

Denis Compton, one of the game's naturals, whose dazzling batting brightened the seasons after the Second World War.

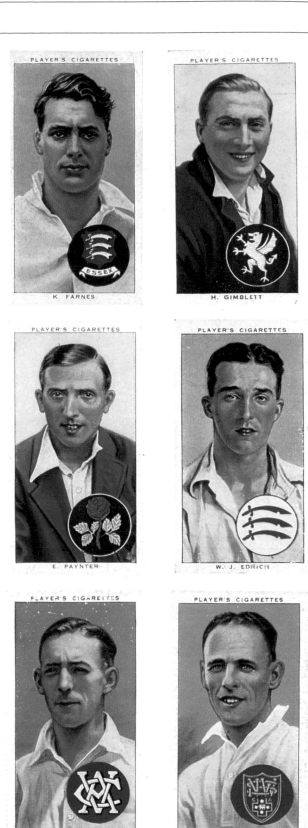

A selection of cigarette cards from the 'Cricketers' 1938' series of John Player and Sons. They show England players Ken Farnes, Harold Gimblett, Eddie Paynter and Bill Edrich and Australian tourists Lindsay Hassett and Jack Fingleton.

making his debut for Middlesex in 1936 when 18, and for Arsenal FC in the First Division the following winter.

He played for England when 19, being run out backing up for 65 in his first innings – in his next, against Australia the following year, he scored 102. In 1947, with his partner Bill Edrich just behind, he swept all before him. He scored 3,816 runs, average 90.85, and 18 centuries, both figures still records for a single season. In 1948/49 he scored 300 in 181 minutes for MCC v North-East Transvaal, the fastest-ever first-class triple century.

It was the cavalier manner of Compton's play which was so impressive. He was an entertainer, who played the game in a happy spirit, delighting with his unorthodox shots, particularly the sweep, which he made famous. He was a fighter, however, two of his best innings coming in adverse circumstances against Australia: 145 not out after coming back from being hit on the head by a bouncer at Old Trafford in 1948, and 184 in a lost cause at Trent Bridge in the same series.

He won a Cup winners' medal and wartime caps at soccer, but it was a soccer injury to his knee that made the latter half of his cricket career difficult. He missed most of the 1950 season after one of his operations, and was never quite the same again, although he made his highest Test score, 278 against Pakistan, in 1954.

Constantine, Learie Nicholas

Born: 21 September 1901, Diego Martin, Trinidad
Died: 1 July 1971, Hampstead, London
Career: 119 *m*; 4,475 runs (av 24.05); 439 wkts (av 20.25)
Tests: 18 *m*; 635 runs (av 19.24); 58 wkts (av 30.10)

Constantine's figures do not suggest that he was a great player, but it must be remembered that he played for West Indies from 1928, the year they were given Test status, and he was his team's outstanding all-rounder when they were usually being outplayed.

He made his debut for Trinidad in 1921/22, and toured England in 1923, before West Indies were a Test side. He returned three more times (although by 1933 he was already in England playing league cricket for Rochdale). He also toured Australia.

He was an effective fast bowler, and a dazzling hard-hitting middle-order batsman. But he was also possibly the best fielder the game has ever seen, with a dynamic presence which inspired his team-mates. After retirement he became High Commissioner for Trinidad and Tobago and was created a life peer in 1969.

Corfu

The largest of the Ionian Islands, Corfu has had cricketing connections from the days when the islands belonged to Britain. Several English club sides go annually to Corfu to play matches against the local teams, of which there are three, and an Anglo-Corfiot Cricket Association exists to promote cricket in Corfu.

Cornwall

Having been formed in 1894, the present Cornish club joined the Minor Counties Championship in 1904, but on the whole they have not enjoyed a great deal of good fortune until more recent times, being second in the competition in 1974 and 1976. They owed their position in those years mainly to Dave Halfyard, who had played first-class cricket for Kent and Notts. In 1974 he took 74 wickets at 9.71 each, including all ten wickets in an innings against Dorset at Penzance. Cornwall then challenged Oxfordshire for the 1974 title, but the latter seemed only interested in a draw and Halfyard became so frustrated that in one over he delivered a ball underarm, then three donkey-drops. Cornwall's other main bowler, Laity, bowled left-arm instead of his normal right-arm style.

Country house cricket

Many of the large country houses in the days before the First World War had their own private cricket grounds and staged a 'cricket week', when the home side stayed in the house for the week and three other teams came down, each for a two-day match. A typical such house was Frensham Hill, the home of Mr and Mrs Charrington, when the usual teams to be invited were the I Zingari, the Free Foresters and the Aldershot Command.

After the First World War, the number of houses with cricket grounds diminished considerably, Hubert Martineau's at Holyport near Maidenhead and Sir Walter Lawrence's at Hyde Hall, Sawbridgeworth, being probably the best of those which survived.

The Second World War finally ended the country house cricket weeks, with their accompanying house parties, but a few houses still have grounds which are used.

County Championship

The modern Olympic Games began in 1896; the Football League in 1888; the First Test was played in 1877. All are accepted, definitive dates from which those who take an interest in such matters can compile the best, worst, longest, shortest and every other 'record' which the growing quiz addict population need in their reference books.

The County Championship will not conform to a nice mathematical formula. In the 1890s, the experts proclaimed 1875 as the definitive season for the start of the Championship; within a few years this had shifted to 1873, on the grounds that in 1873 it was agreed that a player was allowed to represent only one team in any one season. Prior to that year a player was qualified for the county of his birth and the county of his residence and if these differed, he could choose match by match which to represent.

In the 1950s, the noted cricket statistician, Roy Webber, suddenly published a list of 'County Champions' which showed some dramatic changes to the list which had been printed year after year since the 1890s. Using his accountant's mind he had tidied up the competitions which had taken place in the 1870s and discovered that the authorities at the time had made 'mistakes'.

Mr Webber's revelations caused the leading cricket historian of the day, Rowland Bowen, to go in search of the true facts. He emerged with the convincing argument that Webber was misguided, and furthermore the most suitable date to start the Championship was 1864; there being a complete list of County Champions proclaimed annually in the contemporary press from that year, and that as overarm bowling was legalised in the same year, it could be regarded as the start of 'modern' cricket.

Bowen's treatise, which appeared in the 1963 edition of Wisden Cricketers' Almanack, gained general acceptance, but the mathematicians did not slumber for long, and in the middle of the 1980s, in some annuals, the list of County Champions was chopped back to 1890, using the argument that it was only in that season that the counties themselves controlled the method by which the title should be decided. Statistically speaking, 1890 is a most agreeable starting date because it removes all the Webber v Bowen controversy, which not only revolved around who was Champion when, but also which counties took part in the Championship. Mathematicians have been concerned over the standing of Hampshire and Somerset prior to 1890, also the rather odd position of Derbyshire in 1874, brought about by the idea that in the 1870s the rule 'least matches lost' decided the champions, and there are several other anomalies which refuse to fit a set grid.

The first time a county was acclaimed 'Champion County' was in 1827 when Sussex were awarded the title. From then until the 1860s the 'Championship' operated in the same way as a present day boxing title – in other words the County remained 'Champions' until beaten. Since only a handful of matches took place annually and only three or four counties were capable of making a realistic challenge, this system, albeit totally invented by the press, remained satisfactory. In the late 1850s and early 1860s several new county clubs of good standing were founded, or established on a firmer footing, and it was necessary for the press to devise some sort of rudimentary league system. Every county however did not play the same number of matches, or indeed the same opponents, so that while 'least matches lost' was suggested as the way to decide the best county, it had to be used with judgement, so that a county could not simply play and beat two of the weakest of the counties and then claim the title on the grounds that they had lost fewest matches. Mathematicians have tried to invent annual league tables showing counties in order of merit in the 1860s and 1870s, but these tables are meaningless, for the reason just given.

The list of Champions therefore should be divided into three parts: pre-1864; 1864 to 1889; 1890 to date, and such a list appears at the close of this essay.

The early Championship revolved around Sussex, Kent and Surrey, with Kent being predominant through most of the 1830s and 1840s due in large measure to Alfred Mynn and Fuller Pilch. In 1853 Notts became the first northern county to threaten the South, but having no proper county organisation they could not maintain a regular challenge and Surrey held the stage during most of the 1850s. The Surrey stars of the 1850s were Caesar, Caffyn, Lockyer and Martingell. Surrey faded as the 1860s progressed and Notts, under better management, swept to the fore. In George Parr they possessed the best batsman, and they could call upon a succession of noteworthy bowlers – Jackson, Wootton, Jemmy Shaw and Alfred Shaw. In 1870, however, the Grace family created Gloucestershire. They tied for the title in 1873 and reached their high water mark in 1877, when seven out of eight matches were won.

Gloucestershire were originally a completely amateur side and this proved their weakness; by 1880 they had been overtaken by the more permanent professional sides, notably Nottinghamshire and Lancashire. In the 1880s there were 11 counties whose matches were taken into consideration when the Championship title was decided and the league system based on 'least matches lost' became more rigid. In 1883 Nottinghamshire won only four of 12 matches, whereas Surrey won ten out of 20 and Lancashire six out of 12, but Nottinghamshire were awarded the title on 'least matches lost'. This caused some upset in the Surrey camp, and when a similar pattern was repeated in 1885 and 1886, the protests grew louder. The editor of Wisden then invented his own system, which he operated first in 1888, when he also announced that only eight counties were first-class: Gloucestershire, Kent, Lancashire, Middlesex, Nottinghamshire, Surrey, Sussex and Yorkshire. To his acute embarrassment, however, the following year three of the eight tied for first place. The counties themselves then stepped in and created a new league system. Up to this point the MCC had had nothing to do with the 'County Championship', but in 1895, when it was expanded to include Derbyshire, Essex, Hampshire, Leicestershire and Warwickshire (Somerset had returned in 1891), MCC were asked to take control of the competition and agreed to do so.

Nottinghamshire had been the dominant county through the 1880s, even if they tended to win the title through avoiding defeat rather than winning matches; in 1887 Surrey took over at the top and remained there until 1895, except for a poor summer in 1893. In the three years 1892 to 1894, for the only time in the history of the competition, each county played all opponents home and away. The expansion in 1895 killed this ideal, and not until 1929 did counties all play the same number of games, so before then a system of percentages had to be used to calculate which county could claim to be the Champions.

The counties promoted in 1895, plus Worcestershire in 1899, Northamptonshire in 1905 and Glamorgan in 1921, by and large remained second class in all but name right up to the Second World War. Warwickshire and Derbyshire did win one title each, but it was most unusual for the younger counties to play any major part in the Championship title race. Yorkshire were generally front runners with Lancashire, Nottinghamshire, Kent, Surrey and Middlesex at different times succeeding in challenging Yorkshire. The ignominy of bottom place was usually fought out between Northamptonshire and Glamorgan, with Worcestershire and Leicestershire also competing.

After the Second World War, Nottinghamshire and Kent of the old counties fell on hard times, but Yorkshire, Surrey and Middlesex continued to maintain leading positions – Surrey had their record-breaking run in the 1950s. The rule allowing immediate registration of overseas players arrived in the winter of 1967/8 and finally the old order changed. Each county's position in the league table became much more variable, but in the 1980s Middlesex and Essex were very much front runners.

The system for calculating the points in the County Championship table has changed several times over the years, sometimes two or three times in successive seasons. Since 1981 the system has been 16 points for a win, plus bonus points to be won on the first 100 overs of each side's first innings as follows: for the batting side, 1 point for scoring 150-199, 2 points for 200-249, 3 points for 250-299 and 4 points for 300 plus; for the bowling side, 1 point for capturing 3 or 4 wickets, 2 points for 5 or 6 wickets, 3 points for 7 or 8 wickets and 4 points for 9 or 10 wickets.

Table of Champions

1827 Sussex	1894 Surrey
1828 Kent	1895 Surrey
1830 Surrey	1896 Yorkshire
1831 Surrey	1897 Lancashire
1833 Sussex	1898 Yorkshire
1837 Kent	1899 Surrey
1838 Kent	1900 Yorkshire
1839 Kent	1901 Yorkshire
1841 Kent	1902 Yorkshire
1842 Kent	1903 Middlesex
1843 Kent	1904 Lancashire
1845 Sussex	1905 Yorkshire
1847 Kent	1906 Kent
1848 Sussex	1907 Nottinghamshire
1849 Kent	1908 Yorkshire
1850 Surrey	1909 Kent
1851 Surrey	1910 Kent
1853 Notts	1911 Warwickshire
1854 Surrey	1912 Yorkshire
1855 Sussex	1913 Kent
1856 Surrey	1914 Surrey
1857 Surrey	1919 Yorkshire
1858 Surrey	1920 Middlesex
1862 Nottinghamshire	1921 Middlesex
	1922 Yorkshire
1864 Surrey	1923 Yorkshire
1865 Nottinghamshire	1924 Yorkshire
1866 Middlesex	1925 Yorkshire
1867 Yorkshire	1926 Lancashire
1868 Nottinghamshire	1927 Lancashire
1869 Nottinghamshire	1928 Lancashire
Yorkshire	1929 Nottinghamshire
1870 Yorkshire	1930 Lancashire
1871 Nottinghamshire	1931 Yorkshire
1872 Nottinghamshire	1932 Yorkshire
1873 Gloucestershire	1933 Yorkshire
Nottinghamshire	1934 Lancashire
1874 Gloucestershire	1935 Yorkshire
1875 Nottinghamshire	1936 Derbyshire
1876 Gloucestershire	1937 Yorkshire
1877 Gloucestershire	1938 Yorkshire
1878 Undecided	1939 Yorkshire
1879 Nottinghamshire	1946 Yorkshire
Lancashire	1947 Middlesex
1880 Nottinghamshire	1948 Glamorgan
1881 Lancashire	1949 Middlesex
1882 Nottinghamshire	Yorkshire
1883 Nottinghamshire	1950 Lancashire
1884 Nottinghamshire	Surrey
1885 Nottinghamshire	1951 Warwickshire
1886 Nottinghamshire	1952 Surrey
1887 Surrey	1953 Surrey
1888 Surrey	1954 Surrey
1889 Lancashire	1955 Surrey
Nottinghamshire	1956 Surrey
Surrey	1957 Surrey
	1958 Surrey
1890 Surrey	1959 Yorkshire
1891 Surrey	1960 Yorkshire
1892 Surrey	1961 Hampshire
1893 Yorkshire	1962 Yorkshire

1963 Yorkshire	1976 Middlesex
1964 Worcestershire	1977 Middlesex
1965 Worcestershire	Kent
1966 Yorkshire	1978 Kent
1967 Yorkshire	1979 Essex
1968 Yorkshire	1980 Middlesex
1969 Glamorgan	1981 Nottinghamshire
1970 Kent	1982 Middlesex
1971 Surrey	1983 Essex
1972 Warwickshire	1984 Essex
1973 Hampshire	1985 Middlesex
1974 Worcestershire	1986 Essex
1975 Leicestershire	

Cover

A fielding position on the off side between point and mid-off, but deeper. A fieldsman in this area is described as 'in the covers'. The position is also referred to as cover-point. 'Extra-cover' is a fielding position between cover and mid-off and 'deep extra-cover' is out on the boundary behind extra-cover.

Covering the wicket

One subject on which cricket experts differ, and quite heated arguments are generated, is the subject of the covering of wickets against the weather. The argument for is that covering wickets reduces delays due to weather to a minimum and thus encourages spectators to risk their money, and against that the more wickets are covered the less encouragement is given to bowlers, especially slow bowlers, who can exploit damp wickets.

The present Law 11 allows complete covering of the pitch before a match starts, but not during a match 'unless by prior arrangement or regulation'.

Until 1884, the decision whether to cover the pitch was left to the ground authorities and tarpaulins were used on some of the major grounds. In 1884 covering of pitches during matches was made illegal and it was not until the 1920s that this was altered, but then covering was made optional. It was not until 1960, however, that in a Test match in England pitches were totally covered after the match had begun.

For the 1959 season compulsory covering of wickets in County Championship matches was introduced, i.e. on each night of the match and as soon as the weather caused a break in play, as well as before the match. This virtual total covering except when play is taking place, was somewhat relaxed in 1963.

The problem of the best way to deal with the matter remains unresolved.

Cowdrey, Michael Colin

Born: 24 December 1932, Ootacamund, India
Career: 692 *m*; 42,719 runs (av 42.89)
Tests: 114 *m*; 7,624 runs (av 44.06)
Cowdrey was a schoolboy prodigy, playing for Tonbridge School at Lord's when 13, the youngest to appear in such an important match. He went on to play over 400 matches for Kent, and in a record 114 Test Matches, a total since passed by Gavaskar.

He was in some ways a commanding batsman. He was generous in build, and the weight and timing of his drives sent

Colin Cowdrey batting on England's 1974/75 tour of Australia, when he was flown out as reinforcement to face Lillee and Thomson.

Martin Crowe emerged as New Zealand's leading batsman of the late 1980s, and joined Somerset for the 1987 season.

the ball effortlessly to the boundary. He was classically correct in his strokes. However, sometimes he seemed too good-natured to dominate the attack, and would fall into periods of fiddling introspection.

Cowdrey captained England, but not on a tour to Australia, which was his ambition. His highest innings was 307 for MCC against South Australia in Adelaide, but the best probably 102 out of an all-out 191 for England against Australia at Melbourne in 1954/55.

Crease

The lines marked in whitewash adjacent to the wicket. The 'bowling crease' runs through and parallel with the three stumps and it extends 4 feet each side of the stumps, being a total of 8 feet 8 inches in length. The 'return creases' are short lines at each end of the bowling crease and at right angles to it. The 'popping crease' is a line parallel to the bowling crease and 4 feet in front of it, being the forward limit of the batsman's ground.

Cricketana

The first articles on cricketana seem to be those by J.W. Goldman in *The Cricketer* during the 1930s; L.E.S. Gutteridge,

the manager of Epworth's secondhand bookshop in London, wrote a most interesting series on the same subject in *The Cricketer* of 1959, and those who wish to learn more on cricketana might well look up those articles.

Cricketana is literally anything appertaining to the game, which anyone might find collectable. Some of the major fine arts auction houses have in recent years taken to organising sales devoted entirely to cricketana and the prices for quite modest items have risen steeply. China, pictures, bats, caps, ties, autographs and, of course, books are the principal items involved.

(*see also* Collectors)

Crowe, Martin David

Born: 22 September 1962, Auckland, New Zealand
Career: 121 *m*; 8,270 runs (av 49.52); 102 wkts (av 31.80)
Tests: 32 *m*; 1,807 runs (av 38.44); 12 wkts (av 46.58)
Younger brother of Jeff Crowe, who also represents New Zealand, Martin Crowe made his Test debut in 1981/82, having first played for Auckland two years earlier. A talented middle-order right-hand batsman, he toured England in 1983 and 1986, topping the Test batting averages on the latter tour. He made his debut for Somerset in 1984 and had

an exceptional first season, hitting 1,870 runs (average 53.42) and being the county's leading batsman. He is also a useful seam bowler. There was a great deal of controversy when the Somerset committee chose him as their overseas player for 1987 instead of the combined talents of the two West Indians, Joel Garner and Viv Richards.

Crumbling wicket

A wicket on which the soil is breaking up due to lack of moisture. This looseness can assist the spin bowlers and also make for variable bounce. It is a condition normally met on the final day of a three-day match when the weather has been dry.

Cumberland

The county did not compete regularly in the Minor Counties Championship until 1955, being for many years without any proper county organisation (the present club was formed in 1948). They finally achieved their first title in 1986, due to the bowling of David Halliwell and the batting of Dean Hodgson. John Moyes was captain of the county on this historic occasion – the title was won in the play-off match at Worcester by two wickets. This welcome success came after 30 difficult years, when the county were often at the foot of the table and more than once had to recruit a player from the spectators in order to complete the eleven.

Currie Cup

Sir Donald Currie, the shipping magnate, announced at a banquet which was held just before the first English side left home to tour South Africa, that he proposed to give a challenge cup to the South African team which gave the best performance against the English touring team.

Kimberley beat the English side by ten wickets and therefore took the Cup. C. Aubrey Smith, the captain of that 1888/89 touring side, remained in Johannesburg after the tour finished, and in 1890 suggested that Transvaal might be good enough to beat Kimberley and thus take the trophy. He therefore took a Transvaal side to Kimberley and won the first Currie Cup tournament by beating Kimberley with six wickets in hand. The following year Kimberley managed to retrieve the title. In 1892 Western Province sent a team and beat both Transvaal and Griqualand West (i.e. Kimberley). The competition further expanded in March 1894 when Eastern Province and Natal joined the hunt. The four challengers played a competition between themselves, the winner then challenging Western Province. Natal thus played Western Province, but the latter won by an innings.

A league system was introduced in 1906/07, by which time Orange Free State had been added to the competing teams. Transvaal, however, won, with five wins out of five matches.

By 1986, Transvaal had won the Cup outright 21 times and tied four times, Natal had won 18, and tied twice, Western Province had won 13 and tied twice and Kimberley (Griqualand West) had won once.

In 1951/52 the competition was divided into Sections A and B; in 1960/61 the Sections were amalgamated, but in 1962/63 reinstated. For one season only, Section B was in two parts, one for Section A second teams and the other for first teams.

Since 1977/78 Section B teams have played for the Castle Bowl. The competition was not usually staged when a touring team playing Test Matches visited South Africa.

Cut

A stroke used by a batsman to deal with a ball somewhat short of a length and on the off side of the wicket, the ball being struck with the bat horizontal and square with the wicket. Also known as an off-cut.

D

Daisy-cutter

A fast under-arm delivery which travels just above ground level. Alfred Walker, the Middlesex amateur of the 1850s, was described as 'delivering good old-fashioned unsophisticated daisy-cutters.' Seen nowadays only in unregulated children's cricket.

Declarations

The first captain to declare an innings closed in first-class cricket was John Shuter of Surrey at 3.30 pm on the last day of the match (8 June 1889), when Surrey had made 338 for 7 – Surrey's opponents, Gloucestershire, were then dismissed for 92.

There was a spate of freak declarations in 1931, when captains tried to obtain maximum points for an outright win, when much of the playing time had been washed out. The first such declaration was at Bramall Lane when Gloucestershire's captain declared after one ball and the Yorkshire captain followed suit; Gloucestershire's second innings then commenced.

On the first day of the Second Test at Lord's against New Zealand in 1949, the England captain, F.G. Mann, declared England's first innings closed at 6.05 pm, and New Zealand then batted for 15 minutes scoring 20 for 0. After the close of play it was realised that Mann's declaration was illegal, as an experimental law which at the time allowed a declaration on the first day of a three-day match did not apply to the Test series. As New Zealand made no objections, the game was continued as normal on the second day.

DeFreitas, Phillip Anthony Jason

Born: 18 February 1966, Scotts Head, Dominica
Career: 36 *m*; 762 runs (av 20.59); 121 wkts (av 23.75)
Tests: 4 *m*; 77 runs (av 19.25); 9 wkts (av 49.56)

DeFreitas played his first cricket on the beaches of Dominica, but when he was nine his parents moved to Willesden, London. He impressed in club cricket, and chose an offer from Leicestershire rather than Middlesex, making his debut in 1985, and playing in nine first-class matches. In 1986 he impressed with 94 wickets, average 23.05, and 645 runs, average 23.04; won the Britannic Assurance 'Player of the Season' award and earned selection for the touring party for Australia. A tall, slim right-arm fast-medium bowler and middle-order batsman, he made his Test debut in the First Test at Brisbane, the fourth youngest, after Close, Compton and Dilley, to play for England in an Ashes Test.

Delhi

First used for Test cricket when India played the West Indies in 1948/49, the Feroz Shah Kotla Ground in Delhi is the headquarters of the Delhi and District Cricket Association, which was founded in 1932 and joined the Ranji Trophy competition in 1934/35. The ground is not up to the standard of the other major Test venues in India, but is the best ground in the capital.

Denmark

With two cricketers – Ole Mortensen (Derbyshire) and Soren Henriksen (Lancashire) – playing for first-class counties in the mid-1980s, Denmark must be regarded as the strongest continental cricketing country, though they were beaten by five wickets in the semi-finals of the 1986 ICC Trophy by Holland.

The first organised competition in Denmark started in 1890, but it was not until after the First World War that English touring teams visited the country with any frequency. Denmark's principal international opponents are Holland, and matches between the two countries began in 1955. The country joined the ICC in 1966 and won its group in the first ICC Trophy competition of 1979, but were beaten in the semi-finals by Sri Lanka.

Deodhar Trophy

Instituted in 1973/74, the Deodhar Trophy is the principal limited-overs competition in India. The five Duleep Trophy zone teams compete on a knock-out basis with the matches limited to 50 overs per side. The winners have been as follows:

1973/74 South	1978/79 South	1983/84 West
1974/75 South	1979/80 West	1984/85 West
1975/76 West	1980/81 South	1985/86 West
1976/77 Central	1981/82 South	
1977/78 North	1982/83 West	

Derbyshire

A county whose traditional strength is their pace bowling, Derbyshire have had to fight hard to survive as a first-class team. More often than not the batting has been their weakness. In the mid-1930s, Derbyshire's cricket reached a standard higher than at any time in their history, and for some six seasons the team were the equal of any in England, actually winning the Championship in 1936. Seven of this famous eleven obtained Test honours at a time when Tests were nothing like as frequent as they are now, and an England cap was therefore that much more prized. Denis Smith and Stan Worthington were the principal batsmen of the 1930s, George Pope and Les Townsend the all-rounders with Tommy Mitchell as a leg-spinner and Bill Copson the fiery fast bowler; behind the wicket was Harry Elliott. All seven were born and bred in the county, but at other times, like so many of the counties with small populations, Derbyshire have had to import players to remain competitive.

In 1871, through the bowling of Mycroft (whose name Conan Doyle borrowed for Sherlock Holmes' brother) and Flint, the county were raised to first-class status, but in the 1880s several leading Derbyshire players defected to more prosperous parts and the journalists struck Derbyshire from the first-class list. The team returned to the Championship in 1895, but remained for the most part among the also-rans until the 1930s. After the Second World War, a fine pair of opening bowlers, Cliff Gladwin and Les Jackson, made the 1950s fairly successful, but as their powers declined so did the county. Eddie Barlow, the South African all-rounder, took Derbyshire to the final of the Benson & Hedges Cup in 1978 and three years later, Barry Wood, late of Lancashire, led the county to their first one-day title, when Northants were beaten, with the scores tied, in the NatWest final. Peter Kirsten of South Africa was the leading batsman in those years with John Wright of New Zealand, but the county could boast two home-grown England cricketers, Mike Hendrick, the accurate pace bowler, and Geoff Miller, the all-rounder, as well as the wicketkeeper from next door, Bob Taylor.

The county's main ground is on the old racecourse at Derby, a spot which until very recently was renowned for its spartan conditions, and a much more pleasant venue is at Queen's Park, Chesterfield, which the county have used regularly since 1898. Several other grounds have been used for first-class matches, including that at Buxton, which is still visited on occasion and the Ilkeston ground, for long the site of the annual battle with Nottinghamshire.

Devon

The county applied unsuccessfully for entry into the first-class competition in 1948, but in fact their record in the Minor Counties Championship has never been more than a modest one and they have won the title only once; this was in 1978. Their two principal bowlers that year were A.W. Allin (who tired of first-class cricket after a single summer with Glamorgan, when he topped their bowling averages) and D.I. Yeabsley. The 1978 side also possessed three useful batsmen: G. Wallen, R.C. Tolchard and the captain, B.L. Matthews.

The present club was formed in 1899 and joined the Minor Counties Championship in 1901.

Dilley, Graham Roy

Born: 18 May 1959, Dartford, Kent
Career: 155 *m*; 395 wkts (av 27.63)
Tests: 26 *m*; 85 wkts (av 30.40)

Dilley made his debut for Kent in 1977. A tall, right-arm fast bowler, he bats left-handed and has made useful runs low in the order. He made his Test debut on the tour to Australia and

Philip deFreitas was England's player of the season in 1986, and one of the successes of the Ashes-winning side in Australia in 1986/87.

India in 1979/80, only Close and Compton being younger to play for England against Australia. He was in and out of the Test team for a while with injuries and run-up problems, but finally established himself as a leading strike bowler in Australia in 1986/87. He played a useful supporting innings of 56 at Headingley in 1981, when Botham's 149 not out swung the Test against Australia. They added 117 for the eighth wicket. In 1987 he left Kent to play for Worcestershire.

D'Oliveira affair

Basil d'Oliveira, the Cape Coloured cricketer, emigrated to England and qualified for Worcestershire and later by residence for England. He played in his first Test in 1966.

The MCC were scheduled to tour South Africa in the winter of 1968/69 and before the team was selected several attempts were made to obtain a clear answer from South Africa on whether d'Oliveira, if selected, would be allowed to tour.

In 1968, however, d'Oliveira had a poor season and was brought in to the England side only for the Fifth Test against, when R.M. Prideaux withdrew owing to injury. The touring party was due to be announced officially directly after the conclusion of the Test. D'Oliveira hit a brilliant 158 in the match, but his name was not among those selected to tour

South Africa. This omission caused some caustic comment from anti-apartheid groups and d'Oliveira was engaged by the *News of the World* to cover the tour as a journalist.

In September T.W. Cartwright, who had been selected, was forced to withdraw due to injury and the selectors brought in d'Oliveira in his place. The South African Prime Minister, Mr Vorster, then announced that South Africa would not accept a team chosen for political purposes and a week later MCC cancelled the tour. A special meeting of MCC was called at which one of the resolutions was that the members regretted their committee's handling of the tour. This resolution and two others were lost, but the leading supporters of the resolutions, the Rev D.S. Sheppard and J.M. Brearley, were content that the subjects had been debated.

Donkey-drop

A slow ball bowled high in the air in order to come down at an awkward angle for the batsman, but only perfected in fiction in 'Spedegue's Dropper' by Conan Doyle. C.H. Palmer, the bespectacled schoolmaster, who captained Leicestershire from 1950 to 1957, occasionally employed this delivery to some effect.

Dorset

Joining the Minor Counties Competition in 1902, having been formed as a county club in 1896, Dorset's best seasons so far have been 1922 and 1923. In the latter summer they were much inspired by their captain, the Rev W.V. Jephson, then aged 49, who hit 559 runs, averaging 50.82, as well as acting as wicketkeeper. He had previously played first-class cricket for Hampshire. The county's best post-Second World War season was 1959, when their batting was boosted by Harold Gimblett, the former England and Somerset player, and the bowling by Ray Dovey, who took 62 wickets at 11.56 each.

Double

The 'double' is a term applied usually to the feat of scoring 1,000 runs and obtaining 100 wickets in first-class cricket in an English season. In fact, statistics prove that it is much more difficult to obtain the latter than the former, a point forcibly brought home since the mid-1960s: the 1,000-run target is still achieved by most competent county batsmen, but 100 wickets is a rarity. Only Richard Hadlee of Nottinghamshire has performed the 'double' since 1969, scoring 1,179 runs and taking 117 wickets in 1984. W. Rhodes of Yorkshire achieved the feat 16 times, G.H. Hirst of Yorkshire 14 and the only other player to achieve ten 'doubles' was V.W.C. Jupp of Sussex and Northamptonshire.
(*see also* All-rounders)

Dress

A cricketing 'uniform' evolved in the 1850s and 1860s when specific teams adopted club colours, which in those days also involved a club shirt. The All-England Eleven shirt, for example, was white with pink spots. The I Zingari seem to have been the first side to wear ribbons in the club colours round their hats. This was in the 1840s, and in the following decade coloured caps began to make their appearance.

The most remarkable aspect of cricketing attire is how little

Basil d'Oliveira driving square. His selection for England and Prime Minister Vorster's reaction forced South Africa out of Test cricket.

Drive
A stroke made with the left foot (for a right-handed batsman) brought forward and the bat swinging downwards, sending the ball back towards the bowler (a straight drive), to mid-off (an off-drive) or mid-on (an on-drive), towards cover (a cover-drive) or sometimes towards point (square drive).

Duck
A batsman's score when he has failed to record a single run. Thus 'to save your duck' is to score a run. The word is short for duck's egg, being the shape of the cipher 0.

Playing for Central Districts in 1984/85, P.J. Visser managed to go to the wicket on ten successive occasions and return without scoring. In English first-class cricket B.J. Griffiths of Northamptonshire also managed this feat.

Duleep Trophy
In September 1961, the Indian Board of Control established the 'Zonal Tournament for the Duleepsinhji Trophy' to be competed for by teams representing each of the Ranji Trophy zones. The idea was to create a series of matches where the cricket was at a higher level than in the Ranji Trophy and thus improve the standard of the game in India. The West Zone, with 11 outright wins and one tie up to 1985/86, have won the title most often.

Dunedin, New Zealand
The headquarters of Otago Cricket Association is the Carisbrook Ground in Dunedin. The first first-class match on the ground was Otago v Tasmania in 1883/84, the previous venues for Otago matches being the South Dunedin Recreation Ground. The first Test Match staged on the Carisbrook Ground took place in 1954/55 when New Zealand played England. The ground is also used for football and is utilitarian rather than picturesque.

it has altered since the 1930s. Flannel trousers have given way to more lightweight material, some cricketers wear sleeveless shirts, and cricket boots with metal screwed-in spikes have given way to moulded plastic, but at first glance a county team photograph of 1986 differs little from that of 1930, except that the odd amateur with his neckerchief and striped blazer is absent.

The main change is in the amount of protective padding now used by batsmen, culminating in the helmet; to some this is a sensible precaution, to others its jars the line and grace of batsmanship.

Durham
Formed in 1882, the county tied for first place in the initial season of the Minor Counties Championship. Although they won the title twice in the inter-war period, their greatest successes have been since the mid-1970s, when the title has been won four times. The side have managed to blend in one or two overseas Test stars with a nucleus of local talent. N.A. Riddell, P.J. Kippax, S. Greensword and B.R. Lander are some of the more notable cricketers reinforced by Wasim Raja, B.L. Cairns and A.S. Patel among other internationals.

E

East Africa
East Africa joined the ICC in 1966 and in 1975 took part in the first Prudential World Cup, and during that season played one first-class match against Sri Lanka in England. A number of first-class matches involving East Africa have also taken place on home territory.

East Africa have provided a team for each of the three ICC Trophy competitions but have not been particularly successful. Kenya now play as a separate unit, so that East African teams are drawn from Uganda, Tanzania and Zambia.

Edgbaston
The Warwickshire County Cricket Club obtained the lease of the land on which the Edgbaston Ground is laid out in 1884 and the first important match there took place in 1886. Warwickshire became a first-class county in 1894 and the first Test Match to be staged on the ground took place in 1902, but not until the 1950s did Edgbaston become a regular Test Match venue. During the ten years after the Second World War the ground was virtually transformed, mainly through the enterprise of the secretary, Leslie Deakins, whose energy and inspiration brought money into the county club in numerous ways. Thus Warwickshire could afford the modernisation plans which brought it up to the standard of the other Test Match grounds. Despite the building of new stands and offices, the site still has room for ample car-parking, a facility not found on most of the other English Test grounds. The ground is situated about a mile from the centre of Birmingham, on the south side.

Edmonds, Philippe-Henri
Born: 8 March 1951, Lusaka, N. Rhodesia
Career: 365 *m*; 1,185 wkts (av 25.24)
Tests: 46 *m*; 121 wkts (av 33.42)
Edmonds made his debut for Middlesex in 1971, when he won the first of his three blues at Cambridge University. A slow left-arm bowler, he forced his way into the England side in 1975, but although appearing spasmodically ever since, he acquired the reputation of being outspoken and was not picked as often as he might.

In the mid-1980s, however, he became a regular and struck up a good Test match partnership with his Middlesex slow-bowling colleague Emburey.

Egypt
Although of little consequence today, cricket in Egypt was of some note in the first half of the 20th century, and between 1929 and 1939 a strong amateur side under H.M. Martineau toured the country each year, playing 'Test Matches' against Egypt. The Egyptian side was composed almost entirely of British servicemen stationed in the country and the only native Egyptian to make any mark was the spin bowler Abdou. During the Second World War many first-class and also Test cricketers played in matches in Egypt and in 1951 an Egyptian side made a short tour of England, the fixture list including a game against MCC at Lord's.

Emburey, John Ernest
Born: 20 August 1952, Peckham, London
Career: 296 *m*; 953 wkts (av 24.01)
Tests: 42 *m*; 115 wkts (av 31.59)
Emburey has proved the leading English spinner of the middle 1980s. He made his debut for Middlesex in 1973, and his Test debut in 1978. An off-break bowler, excellent field and useful batsman, he became a master of containing batsmen, even in one-day games. He went on the rebel SAB tour to South Africa in 1981/82, which cost him three years of Test cricket, but bowled well against Australia in 1985, and was vice-captain on the Ashes-retaining tour of 1986/87.

England
The structure of top-class cricket in England has always been fundamentally different from that in other countries. Only in England are the ordinary first-class county players fully employed throughout the season. Elsewhere the cricketer takes days off from his normal occupation in order to represent the equivalent of his county; only when a player reaches international level does cricket begin to oust his day-to-day job as his main source of income.

English cricket as a spectator sport with paid players began in the first half of the 18th century, when a number of wealthy patrons amused themselves, and found a vehicle for their gambling appetites, by promoting matches and employing some of the key cricketers. After the Napoleonic Wars the wealthy individuals created cricket clubs, based on counties usually, with the Marylebone Cricket Club as a pattern, that club having been formed in the 1780s and being a metropolitan version of the even earlier Hambledon Club in Hampshire.

In a few cases the professional players themselves created their own county club, Nottinghamshire being the prime example; this was however very much the exception.

The creation of an England team to play international matches was the brainchild of the independent professionals, and it was the Nottinghamshire professional captain, George Parr, who led the first England team overseas to North America. Thus the first *bona fide* international match involving England's leading cricketers took place in Montreal in September 1859, when the all-professional England side opposed Twenty-two of Lower Canada. With one or two exceptions, the major English overseas touring teams were organised by the leading English professionals, or 'paid' amateurs, until the first years of the 20th century, when through a series of circumstances MCC took on the role of promoting and selecting the major tours. It is only since 1977/78 that the Test and County Cricket Board (TCCB) has taken on this task and teams have been designated 'England', rather than 'MCC'.

Representative 'England' teams which opposed major touring teams in England began in 1880, when C.W. Alcock, the Surrey secretary, organised the first Test, at the Oval. Until 1899 the English teams were selected by the authorities on whose ground the Test was to be played, but a Board of Control was then set up to select such teams. The Board is now amalgamated with the TCCB.

As with the arrangements for the overseas tours, so with major domestic cricket – the control moved from the professionals themselves to county committees elected by subscribers and then to MCC and only since 1968 has control gone back to the counties. The reason for this last move is that cricket had to be governed by a representative body, rather than a private club.

The Test Match has therefore been the major feature of English cricket since 1880 and since 1928 (except 1940-45) Test Matches have been staged annually; augmented since 1971 by one-day internationals. The county has been the principal unit of important domestic cricket ever since travelling conditions allowed teams to cross the length and breadth of England with relative ease. The standard pattern of three-day inter-county games was set up in the 1860s with initially some half-dozen sides, and increased to the present 17 by 1921; since 1963 various one-day county competitions have been added to the three-day matches. Below the major counties' level comes a competition on similar lines for other county clubs. Theoretically this system covers England and Wales, but only one Welsh county competes: Glamorgan. There is a separate North Wales inter-county competition. (see also the succeeding entries, and individual entries for counties, cricketers, competitions and grounds)

England v Australia

Results: Played 262; England won 88; Australia won 97; Drawn 77

The first match between the two countries took place in Melbourne in March 1877 and resulted in an Australian victory by 45 runs, due mainly to Charles Bannerman who scored 165 retired hurt. The English team, which were an entirely professional side under the captaincy of James Lillywhite jun, had their revenge in the return match on the same ground, winning by four wickets.

The first Test in England, arranged by C.W. Alcock, was staged at the Oval in 1880. W.G. Grace became the first English cricketer to record a century in Test cricket and England won the game by five wickets. It was on the next tour, in 1882, that Australia achieved their first win on English soil and provoked the famous obituary notice regarding the demise of English cricket and thus arose the 'Ashes' (q.v.), which the following English team travelled to Australia to capture.

Test matches between the two countries were exceedingly common through the 1880s, simply because the touring sides which went in alternate years hither and thither were purely speculative ventures, and so long as the public paid to see the matches and the organisers of the touring parties made a handsome profit, the visits continued unabated. In 1887/88, however, greed killed the golden calf, when two rival English teams set out simultaneously for Australia. They combined forces for one single 'Test', but unfortunately the Australian players were also divided into two factions and both touring teams made financial losses.

Lord Sheffield, the Sussex cricket patron, was persuaded to resume tours to Australia and managed, at some great expense, to secure the services of the Grand Old Man of English cricket, W.G. Grace. The Australians won this series by two matches to one, but Grace regained the Ashes when the Australians came over to England in 1893.

Stoddart continued England's domination on the 1894/95 tour, whilst Grace led England to a third successive series victory in 1896. A.C. MacLaren, however, was not so fortunate and lost three successive series, Australia's winning captain being Joe Darling on each occasion. The teams were fairly even in the series until 1912, when, because of internal squabbles, Australia sent a second-rate side to England.

The first two series after the First World War belonged to the famous fast bowlers, Gregory and McDonald, under the command of Warwick Armstrong, and England failed to win a single match in 1920/21 or in 1921, whilst Australia picked up eight victories. England managed to beat Australia once when Gilligan's side went 'down under' in 1924/25, but Australia won the other four Tests and so it was not until 1926 that England at last won a post-war series: the first four Tests were all drawn and for the fifth match at the Oval England sacked their captain, A.W. Carr, and turned to the young A.P.F. Chapman as leader.

The decisive game was won by the large margin of 289 runs, with the great opening batsmen, Hobbs and Sutcliffe, both making hundreds. Chapman took the 1928/29 team to Australia and proved that this solitary win was no fluke by winning the series four matches to one.

Then Don Bradman came to England and the picture altered dramatically. Bradman averaged 139.14 in the series, making a triple hundred, two double hundreds and another single hundred. Australia gained the Ashes by two matches to one. This massive scoring produced Jardine's plans of leg-theory which unfolded during the 1932/33 tour to Australia. Larwood and Voce by methods which were severely criticised reduced Bradman's batting average to near normality and brought the Ashes back to England (see also Bodyline).

With Jardine, Larwood and Voce all diplomatically absent when Australia fought the Test series of 1934, the Ashes quickly changed ownership again. G.O.B. Allen captained the England side of 1936/37 and, through some brilliant bowling by the restored Voce, won the first two Tests, only to lose the remaining three.

High scoring was the feature of the 1938 series, culminating in Len Hutton's record-breaking 364 at the Oval, which brought an England victory by no less a margin than an innings and 579 runs, but this just squared the series.

After the Second World War, Bradman remained the master of the crease, whilst Australia acquired two new fast bowlers, Lindwall and Miller. The Australians won three successive series, 3-0, 4-0 and 4-1. It was almost a repeat of the immediate post-First World War pattern, and history continued to play tricks when the 1953 series arrived, producing four drawn matches and a final victory for England at the Oval under Len Hutton.

It was now England's turn to produce a fast bowler. Frank Tyson took Australia by storm in the 1954/55 series, enabling Hutton to retain the Ashes, then came the miracle of Jim Laker in 1956 and his memorable 19 wickets in the Old Trafford Test. England, now under Peter May, thereby winning a third successive series.

Richie Benaud, through his leadership and leg-breaks, soon restored Australia's fortunes, beating May's team both

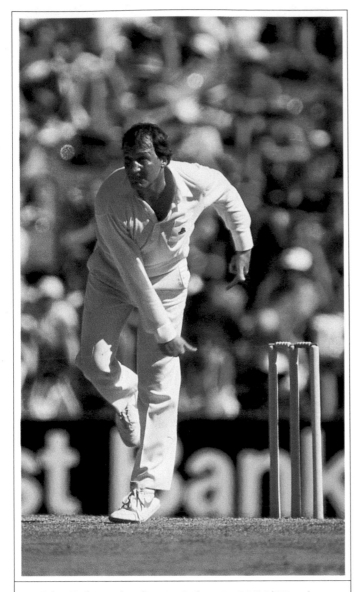

John Emburey bowling in Sydney in 1986/87, when he was the world's leading off-spinner.

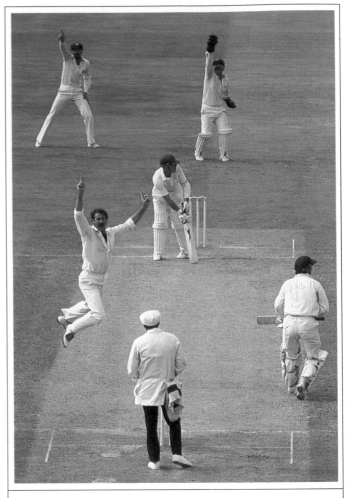

Two stalwarts of recent Ashes Test Matches in action. Geoffrey Boycott lbw to Dennis Lillee at the Oval in 1981.

home and away and then drawing a series against Ted Dexter. England tried Cowdrey and M.J.K. Smith as captain, but in vain, and it was not until the arrival of Ray Illingworth in 1970/71, after a lapse of 14 years, that the Ashes were brought back to England.

The Chappell brothers, Ian and Greg, put Australia back on top, including the famous win in the Centenary Test at Melbourne, when the home side's victory margin was identical to that of the very first Test, namely 45 runs, and as in the pioneering match there was a memorable individual hundred: 174 by an almost unknown England batsman, Derek Randall.

The next two series were pale shadows, with the politics and intrigue of the Packer WSC making any real challenge impossible. England under Brearley thus won both with ease. Greg Chappell, however, restored to the Australian side with the rest of the rebels, beat England three matches to none in 1979/80, Dennis Lillee's bowling being a deciding factor.

Brearley retired, allowing his protégé, Ian Botham, to lead

England, but after two poor matches, the former was persuaded to return, and with some outstanding all-round cricket from Botham, England won the 1981 series three matches to one.

The 1982/83 series saw the Ashes change hands yet again, but in 1985 David Gower took full advantage of the rather threadbare Australian bowling and England won the home series by three matches to one. Under another new captain, Mike Gatting, England retained the Ashes in Australia in 1986/87 by a margin of two to one.

England v India
Results: Played 75; England won 30; India won 11; Drawn 34

Although India won the 1971 series in England, their success in 1986 was a much more convincing one, and Kapil Dev and his men can be justly proud of their cricket. One of the remarkable features of the 1986 side was the depth in their batting. For too long India had relied on a few brilliant batsmen with the lower order very weak, especially under English conditions. In 1986, except for Maninder Singh, the whole team were capable of making runs in a resolute manner; the comparative failure of their veteran star, Sunil

*The Third Test at Headingley in 1981, with Ian Botham hitting
out in his famous innings which turned the match around.*

Gavaskar, was therefore nothing like as serious as it would have been not so many years back. The outstanding batsman of the 1986 series was Dilip Vengsarkar. India won the First Test by five wickets and the Second by 279 runs; the Third Test was drawn.

Prior to the Second World War there were three official Test series between the two countries, though the first of the three was in fact a single match at Lord's in 1932, which England won by 158 runs. D.R. Jardine led the 1933/34 MCC side to India and won the three-match series, two to nil.

India returned to England in 1936 under the Maharajkumar of Vizianagram. Although the side had a number of talented cricketers there was a lack of harmony and team spirit, which was dealt an almost fatal blow just before the First Test, when Lala Amarnath, one of the best all-rounders, was sent home for indiscipline. V.M. Merchant and Cotar Ramaswami were India's leading batsmen, but the English attack, led by G.O.B. Allen and Hedley Verity, enabled the home side to win by two matches to nil.

The next India side was led by the Nawab of Pataudi, who had already been awarded a Test cap by England. This series took place during the first English season following the end of the Second World War. England won the First Test due to the bowling of Alec Bedser, who was making his Test debut, and a double century by Joe Hardstaff. India were fortunate to escape with a draw in the Second Test, but in the Third Test, when their batting at last came off, they had no chance to exploit this advantage since rain washed out play.

A five-match series in India in 1951/52 was tied, one match each. The all-round cricket of Vinoo Mankad was a feature of this series. Freddie Trueman was the outstanding player when the Indians came to England in 1952. The young Yorkshire fast bowler took 29 wickets at 13.31 runs each and England won the series by three matches to nil.

Seven years later India returned to England, but Trueman was again England's principal wicket-taker, and in combination with Brian Statham won the series five matches to nil. England managed to raise only a moderate side for their 1961/62 visit to India and paid the price, being beaten in two matches with the remaining three drawn. S.A. Durani was India's main bowler in the victorious matches, whilst one of the leading batsmen was the young Nawab of Pataudi, son of the 1946 captain. With an interval of only one season, England returned for another five-match series. India, now led by the young Pataudi, drew all five games, but under Brian Close, England won all three matches of the 1967 series in England, Ray Illingworth being the home country's most effective bowler.

So far as India were concerned the next four series belonged to their spin bowlers, Chandrasekhar, Bedi, Prasanna and Venkataraghavan. They won the rubbers of 1971 and 1972/73, but lost those of 1974 and 1976/77, the last one through some brilliant bowling by Derek Underwood, the Kent medium-pace spin bowler. During these series Sunil Gavaskar remorselessly moved on his way to his record Test run aggregate, though only in 1979 did English spectators see him regularly make high scores.

There was a single Jubilee Match in Bombay in 1979/80 when Ian Botham stole all the credits by taking 6 for 58 and 7 for 48, then hitting 114, the most outstanding all-round performance yet attained in Test cricket.

India won the 1981/82 series by dint of victory in the First Test in Bombay and then batting through to a draw in the remaining four matches. England then played the same trick, when India sent their 1982 side over: England won the First Test at Lord's, and then piled up runs so high – Botham was in fine form – that India had no chance in the remaining games.

England won one of the more exciting recent series in 1984/85, when England lost the First Test but won the series by two matches to one.

Now India have won the 1986 series, it rests with England to seize the initiative.

England v New Zealand

Results: Played 63; England won 30; New Zealand won 4; Drawn 29

The series began in 1929/30, when MCC decided to run two major tours simultaneously – the other tour was to the West Indies. The modest MCC team which represented England won the First Test in Christchurch by eight wickets, but New Zealand, led by T.C. Lowry, and with Stewie Dempster as their leading batsman, held England to draws in the other three matches. In fact the home side almost certainly threw away victory in the Second Test by dropping vital catches.

Lowry again led New Zealand in 1931 when the Kiwis arrived in England for their first Test tour (they had previously toured in 1927). Only three Tests were arranged and rain at Old Trafford meant that in effect there were only two of consequence. Dempster's batting saved the tourists at Lord's, but they failed twice at the Oval, giving England victory by an innings.

Wally Hammond turned the two Tests of 1932/33 into a personal batting exhibition. Having hit 227 at Christchurch, he went to Auckland where he created a new Test record with an unbeaten 336. Both these England innings were declared closed with well over 500 on the board and no time to dismiss New Zealand, so both ended as draws.

The MCC sent a side to New Zealand in 1935/36 under E.R.T Holmes. Four matches were played against the representative New Zealand team, but the games were not accorded Test Match status, due to the unrepresentative nature of the England side. It was curious therefore that Test Match status was also denied to the next meeting in New Zealand in 1936/37, when the MCC party, having played five Tests in Australia, met a New Zealand team at Wellington. Walter Hadlee played a brilliant innings of 82 to save his side.

When New Zealand came to England in 1937, as in 1931, only three Tests were played, the feature of which was the batting of Joe Hardstaff, and for the tourists, the fast bowling of Jack Cowie, the only bowler on either side to take more than ten wickets in the series.

New Zealand in 1946/47 saw another draw, Hammond being the highest English scorer in his farewell Test appearance. New Zealand were given four Tests for their 1949 visit, but the authorities restricted each match to three days, and on the easy wickets of that season not a single Test was finished. Martin Donnelly and Bert Sutcliffe were New Zealand's star batsmen, whilst Hutton was England's best.

There were two brief series in New Zealand, in 1950/51 and 1954/55, both appendages to England tours to Australia; England won three of the four games involved and it was not until 1958 that New Zealand returned to England, for what, to date, is the only five-match series the two countries have played.

England won the series four matches to nil and indeed

England's superiority continued uninterrupted through eight more series until 1977/78. In this season, the England side spent half the winter in Pakistan and then travelled on to New Zealand for a three-match series. The First Test took place at Wellington, with Boycott leading England in place of the injured Brearley. England, batting last, required only 137 to win, but Richard Hadlee bowled irresistibly, taking 6 for 26 (making 10 for 100 in the match) and New Zealand beat England for the first time. The Second Test was won by England and the Third drawn. The following summer New Zealand came to England, but they were unable to repeat their success. Richard Hadlee was New Zealand's leading bowler, but for England Botham and Edmonds proved even more effective, and only Geoff Howarth coped adequately with them, the series being lost three to nil.

The 1983 season provided another landmark in New Zealand history, when the Kiwis won a Test in England for the first time – for once Richard Hadlee failed to take a wicket and it was Lance Cairns who took ten wickets in the match: Hadlee did, however, hit 75 in the first innings and was at the crease when victory by five wickets was obtained.

The following two series, 1983/84 and 1986, have provided further evidence of New Zealand's current strength. Both series were won by New Zealand, each by the margin of one match to nil. Richard Hadlee played a great part in these historic events, but in Jeff and Martin Crowe New Zealand had found two other notable cricketers and the runs made by the opening batsman John Wright were also invaluable. New Zealand cricket has come a long way in the 1980s.

England v Pakistan

Results: Played 39; England won 13; Pakistan won 3; Drawn 23

Although Pakistan played MCC in a series of matches in 1951/52, these games were not granted Test Match status, which was fortunate for England, as Pakistan won.

The first official Test series between the two countries was in England in 1954. England won the Second Test by an innings and were very much on top in the First and Third Tests; in the Fourth and final match, the England selectors tempted fate by a few experiments and Fazal Mahmood made them pay a heavy price. Taking 12 wickets, he dismissed England for 130 and 143, to provide Pakistan with their first Test win in England by 24 runs.

The next series did not take place until England went to Pakistan in 1961/62 under Ted Dexter. England won the First Test in Lahore, but some excellent batting by Hanif Mohammad, including two centuries in the Second Test, meant that the other two fixtures were drawn.

It was Hanif's brother, Mushtaq, who was the leading Pakistani batsman during the five-match series in 1962, but even he could not prevent England winning the rubber by four matches to nil. The combination of Statham and Trueman was too much for many of the visiting players.

After this the next three series in Pakistan proved exceedingly dull, not a single definite result being obtained due to high scoring on both sides. The Pakistani wickets came in for a great deal of criticism. Meanwhile in England the home country had things very much their own way.

It was not until 1982 that Pakistan won their second Test against England. This victory came at Lord's. Pakistan batted first and Mohsin Khan hit exactly 200 in a very patient innings lasting 491 minutes. England collapsed, initially to the pace of Sarfraz and the captain, Imran Khan, but later to the leg-breaks of Abdul Qadir. The follow-on was enforced and this time it was Mudassar Nazar who bowled out the home side, taking 6 for 32. Pakistan required 76 off 18 overs and a very confident Mohsin Kahn helped them knock off the runs in 13.1 overs, without the loss of a wicket. The Third and deciding Test of this series was staged at Headingley. Pakistan, mainly through some brilliant all-round cricket by Imran, gained a narrow first-innings lead. Botham and Willis then dismissed Pakistan for 199, leaving England wanting 219. Tavaré and Fowler put on 103 for the first wicket and England looked secure when the total was 172 for 2. Five wickets then went down for a mere 27 runs, Imran and Mudassar being the bowlers. Vic Marks and the wicketkeeper, Bob Taylor, then held firm and England won by three wickets.

The next series was held in Pakistan in 1983/84, with Zaheer Abbas leading his country. In the First Test at Karachi, England won the toss, but collapsed before the contrasting combination of Sarfraz and Qadir. Although Zaheer was dismissed by Botham without scoring, Pakistan managed a lead of 95. England disintegrated a second time, only Gower reaching 50, which meant that the home side needed just 66. Nick Cook obtained cheap wickets and the score suddenly read 26 for 3. Panic set in. Another three wickets went down with the addition of 14 runs and it required the calm sense of the young wicketkeeper, Anil Dalpat, to provide Pakistan with their first home Test victory against England after 22 years. It was sad that few spectators witnessed this event, the lack of supporters being due to student riots, or the threat of them.

Following the glut of wickets in Karachi came the superabundance of runs in Faisalabad. Botham was unable to play due to injury and Willis due to food poisoning. Gower led his weak attack well and Pakistan's leading batsmen did not take proper advantage of the situation. However, they reached 449 for 8 before declaring. Gower played a true captain's innings and the match meandered to a draw.

Pakistan ought to have won the final game, but again their batting made a mess of what should have been a formality and the game was drawn – at least Pakistan took the rubber.

England v South Africa

Results: Played 102; England won 46; South Africa won 18; Drawn 38

The whole series is dominated by two notorious matches. The Fifth Test at Durban in 1938/39 was the longest Test ever played. As there had been only one definite result in the four preceding matches, it was agreed that this last game should be played out. The match began on 3 March and continued until 14 March 1939, there being ten playing days, one of which was washed out by rain. Even after this length of time the game still ended in a draw, because England had to catch the boat home and the date of sailing could not be postponed. In all 1,981 runs were scored, which at the time was a match aggregate record. England were set 696 to win in the final innings and actually scored 654 for 5 when the game ended. No fewer than 16 individual innings exceeded 50, and there were six centuries, Bill Edrich's 219 being the highest.

At Lord's in 1960 came the incident in which the young South Africa fast bowler Geoff Griffin was continuously noballed for throwing and in order to complete his over

Mohsin Khan batting in the Second Test at Lord's in 1982, when he scored 200 and helped Pakistan to an excellent victory.

Duleep Mendis on his way to a century off only 112 balls for Sri Lanka, who gained the better of a draw against England at Lord's in 1984.

delivered his final three balls underarm. This occurred in the exhibition match arranged to entertain the crowd when the Test Match ended early, but Griffin had also been no-balled in the Test itself, the first bowler to be no-balled for throwing in a Test in England. A further curiosity was that Griffin performed a hat-trick in the game and was thus the first bowler to achieve such a feat in a Test at Lord's. England won the match by an innings and 73 runs, though South Africa won the exhibition game by three wickets!

England won every match in the first four series between the two countries, but as noted elsewhere (*see* South Africa) the early games do not really deserve their Test Match status. The South Africans caused a great sensation in 1905/06 when their side completely outplayed Pelham Warner's England team by the use of a trio of leg-break and googly bowlers: A.E.E. Vogler, G.A. Faulkner and R.O. Schwartz. South Africa won the series four matches to one.

The first series in England took place in 1907 and the home country won the only match with a definite result, but South Africa's spinners bounced back in 1909/10, taking that rubber three matches to two.

Of the next six series England won five and the other was

tied, so that not until 1930/31 did South Africa succeed in reversing the trend. Nearly all the games between the two countries during the 1930s were run riots. Of the 15 matches played South Africa won two, England one and the other 12 were drawn, including the famous match noted at the beginning of this entry.

The first series after the Second World War belonged to Edrich and Compton. The Middlesex twins took full advantage of some glorious batting wickets. Bill Edrich averaged 110.40 and Denis Compton 94.12; the best South African bowler took 15 wickets at 40.20 runs each, and England won the series by three matches to nil. England also won all three of the series played during the 1950s, as well as the first two in the 1960s, but in 1965 some fresh faces meant that South African cricket was entering a new era. The Pollock brothers, Peter and Graeme, were the leading figures, but there were also such players as Colin Bland, whose fielding was quite extraordinary, and Eddie Barlow. South Africa won the series by a single victory, with two matches drawn.

England had arranged to tour South Africa in 1968/69, but the South African authorities would not permit d'Oliveira to be a member of the English touring team and therefore the

West Indies' Joel Garner bowling to Ian Botham at Lord's in 1984.
West Indies won all five Test Matches on the tour.

MCC formally cancelled the visit (*see* D'Oliveira affair). In 1970 the South Africans were due to come to England, but after much debate the tour was cancelled. Since then the only series between England and South Africa took place in 1981/82, with England represented by an unofficial team under Graham Gooch. South Africa won the series with a single victory, the two other games being drawn. The English 'rebels' were banned from Test cricket by the TCCB for a period of three years.

England v Sri Lanka

Results: Played 2; England won 1; Drawn 1

The England team travelled to Sri Lanka after their six-match Test series against India in 1981/82 and the home team played their first Test ever in Colombo at the Saravanamuttu Oval in February 1982. Sri Lanka won the toss and batted, the most remarkable feature of their innings being the half-century by the schoolboy, Arjuna Ranatunga. England struggled to gain a first-innings lead, only David Gower batting with real assurance. Sri Lanka reached 167 for 3 in their second innings, then Emburey had a spell of 5 for 5 and the home side's hopes of victory vanished, England having little difficulty in winning by seven wickets.

It was a shell-shocked England which met Sri Lanka at Lord's in 1984: the English team had just been beaten, five matches to nil, by West Indies. Sri Lanka batted first and Ranatunga made 84, but the two Sri Lankan heroes were Sidath Wettimuny and the captain L.R.D. Mendis. The former made 190, occupying the crease for 10 hours and 42 minutes, the longest Test innings played up to that time at Lord's. In contrast Mendis hit Botham for three sixes and reached his hundred off 112 deliveries. Sri Lanka declared at 491 for 7. England then gave a lacklustre response against some rather modest bowling and found themselves with a deficit of 121. Sri Lanka's second innings was not of great importance, except to S.A.R. Silva, who hit an unbeaten 102 and Mendis, who with 94 came very close to performing the feat of two hundreds in the same match.

England v West Indies

Results: Played 90; England won 21; West Indies won 35; drawn 34

In the ten years 1976 to 1985/86 there have been five series of Test Matches between the two sides and in a total of 24 matches, England have failed to win a single game. Not even Australia at their strongest have managed such a formidable record against England, and it cannot be to England's credit that all the rest of West Indies' Test opponents during the period have managed at least one victory over the Caribbean combination.

The last two series, in 1984 and 1985/86, resulted in ten wins from ten matches, a state of affairs unparalleled in any Test Match sequence by any country. This West Indian success was primarily due to Joel Garner and Malcolm Marshall, who, in the ten matches, took 66 and 67 wickets respectively at low cost. They were more than adequately supported by the second-line bowlers and by the batting of Viv Richards, Gordon Greenidge and Desmond Haynes. Clive Lloyd captained West Indies in 1984 and Richards in 1985/86.

The two previous series, although won by West Indies, were not so decisive, in that four out of five games were drawn in 1980 and two of the four drawn in 1980/81 (the match at Georgetown being cancelled for political reasons). In 1980, Garner was again the leading bowler, but Michael Holding and Colin Croft destroyed England in 1980/81. In both these series Viv Richards was the outstanding batsman, and generally speaking the less said about the individual England players the better, though there were some defiant innings, notably by David Gower and Graham Gooch.

Prior to the advent of Garner, Andy Roberts provided the West Indies with the means to destroy England in the 1976 series, and Gary Sobers' all-round cricket brought West Indies success in 1973.

It is necessary to go back to 1967/68 to locate a series in which England came out on top. Captained by Colin Cowdrey, the team played 16 matches on the tour and were not defeated once. They won the Test series by virtue of a single victory at Port of Spain in the Fourth Test – it must be stated however that they owed their win more to the over-optimism of the West Indian captain, Gary Sobers, than to their own initiative. West Indies declared in the first innings at 526 for 7, bowled out England for 414 and then declared a second time at 92 for 2, setting England 215 to make in 165 minutes. Cowdrey hit 71 in 76 minutes and Geoff Boycott made an unbeaten 80 to see England home with seven wickets in hand. England then had a very lucky escape in the Fifth Test, Knott making a defiant unbeaten 73 and being in with the last man when time was called. Boycott and Cowdrey were the English batting successes of the series, each averaging 66. The leading West Indian bowler was the spinner Lance Gibbs, whilst John Snow took 27 wickets for England.

West Indies began their Test cricket at Lord's in 1928, but they really came to the top in 1950. Under the captaincy of John Goddard, the spinners, Sonny Ramadhin and Alf Valentine, achieved a series victory in England for the first time. West Indies had won the 1947/48 series, but England had been without several leading players, and those who went were very badly hit by illness and injury, so much so that the visit has gone down in history as the 'Cripples' Tour'.

Prior to the Second World War the two most celebrated West Indian players were the batsman, George Headley, and the all-rounder, Learie Constantine. Even these two cricketers were unable to obtain a single victory for West Indies in either the 1933 or 1939 series in England, though they proved most effective at home.

After the Cripples' Tour, England sent their full strength to West Indies in 1953/54 under Len Hutton. Hutton was at his most determined, very rarely failed, and the series was tied.

The West Indian bowling was at a low ebb in 1957 under Frank Worrell, whilst England possessed Trueman, Statham, Loader and Lock (Laker, the destroyer of Australia 12 months before, was only fifth in the England bowling table), so England were able to take the series by three matches to nil, repeating the victory in the West Indies in 1959/60 under P.B.H. May by one victory, with four games drawn. West Indies won by three matches to one in England in 1963, in which series Cowdrey came out to bat in the final over at Lord's with a broken arm – The match was drawn with England (XX) runs short of victory with their last pair together. The same margin of victory was achieved by Gary Sobers' team in 1966 in England, which point returns the saga to Cowdrey's victory of 1967/68.

English Schools Cricket Association

ESCA is the official body which looks after schools' cricket in England. It was founded in 1948 and is run by counties. In 1985 and 1986 the ESCA North XI opposed ESCA South XI at the MCC Schools Festival held in Oxford. This Festival is a new departure and also includes the HMC (Head Masters Conference) schools. From all the players involved the MCC Schools XI for Lord's is chosen.

County Competitions are staged at all levels from Under-11 to Under-19 and the principal object of ESCA is to try to raise the standard of cricket in schools throughout the country.

Essex

Without question Essex are the county of the 1980s. Some might argue that Somerset deserve that accolade, but their success is in instant cricket, whereas Essex have proved the solidity of their power beyond the froth of one-day miracles by consistently winning the first-class title as well.

The transformation of the quasi-amateur body that was Essex into the efficient professional organisation of the present day began under Brian Taylor in the mid-1960s. The county committee were at the time as ruthless as their captain. Chelmsford, little more than a backwater, became a headquarters fit for champions, and in due course – 1979 to be pedantic – the champions arrived.

The team were led by Keith Fletcher, the England batsman, whose own run-getting efforts were augmented by the not inconsiderable talents of the South African, Ken McEwan, and that native of Leytonstone, Graham Gooch. Two remarkable opening bowlers, John Lever and the West Indian, Norbert Phillip, were assisted by the spin of David Acfield and the comicalities of Ray East, together with the all-round talent of Stuart Turner. Derek Pringle and Neil Foster have added further to the reservoir of talent. In each of three seasons, 1979, 1984 and 1985, the county have carried off two titles and have dominated county cricket to an extent which was last linked with the Surrey of the 1950s.

Before this surfeit of honours, the story of Essex cricket is a grey one with just a hint of brightness now and then to lift the spirit. For a long time Essex failed to find the right centre for the county's cricket. Hornchurch boasted its talents in the days of Hambledon; Brentwood was the spot at which the county club of 1876 dropped anchor; within ten years Leyton had been adopted and that drab venue in the hinterland beyond the East End was eventually swopped for the present ground at Chelmsford, but for many years the club was peripatetic – Westcliff, Southend, Ilford, Romford, Clacton and Colchester all took in the wanderers.

Essex had joined the first-class counties in 1894 and in 1897 caused a minor stir by being third in the Championship, due to the talents of three amateurs, the express bowler, C.J. Kortright, and batsmen Percy Perrin and Charles McGahey. This remained the highwater mark until recent times, though there was a modicum of respectability in the 1930s under Tom Pearce, and again in the 1950s led by Doug Insole and Trevor Bailey. All however are overshadowed by the present.

Evans, Thomas Godfrey

Born: 18 August 1920, Finchley, Middlesex
Career: 465 *m*; 14,882 runs (av 21.22); 816 *ct*; 250 *st*
Tests: 91 *m*; 2,439 runs (av 20.49); 173 *ct*; 46 *st*
Godfrey Evans made his first appearance for Kent in 1939.

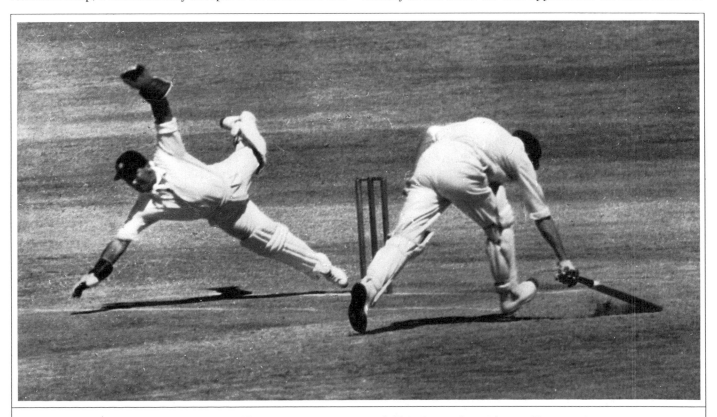

An acrobatic dive by Godfrey Evans attempting to field a shy at the wicket as Hutton tries to run out Bill Johnston at Adelaide in 1951.

After the war he took over as Kent and England keeper from L.E.G. Ames, remaining first choice for 13 years.

Evans was an extrovert cricketer, and deliberately flamboyant behind the stumps, an attitude which did not lessen his effectiveness. He was the best in the world through most of the 1940s and 1950s. He was a particular inspiration to Alec Bedser, standing up to this fast-medium bowler and even making leg-side stumpings off him. At the time of his retirement, he headed the list of Test Match career dismissals, with 219.

He might have been a better batsman had he taken batting more seriously, but he made two Test Match centuries, and on one famous occasion in 1946/47 batted for England for 95 minutes before scoring to help save a Test at Adelaide.

Extras

A general term describing runs which are not credited to batsmen, namely wides, no-balls, byes and leg-byes. The total number of extras is given in a line on a printed scoresheet directly after the last batsman.

The most extras in a single first-class innings is 74 by British Guiana v W. Shepherd's IX, Georgetown, 1909/10.

In Australia the term used for extras is 'sundries'.

F

Families

There is only one instance of four generations of the same family playing in English first-class cricket, namely Frank Townsend, C.L. Townsend, D.C.H. Townsend and J.R.A. Townsend. The first two played for Gloucestershire and the other two for Oxford University. There are 11 other instances of three generations in English first-class cricket:

G. Beet, G.H.C. Beet and G.A. Beet
E.V. Bligh, L.E. Bligh and A.S. Bligh
J.L. Carr, D.B Carr and J.D. Carr
A.G. Doggart, G.H.G. Doggart and S. Doggart
E.C. Freeman, E.J. Freeman and D.P. Freeman
C.B. Fry, S. Fry and C.A. Fry
J. Hardstaff sen, J. Hardstaff jun and J. Hardstaff
D. Hayward sen, D. Hayward jun and T.W. Hayward
G.M. Hoare, C.H. Hoare and C.T. Hoare
F.W. Lillywhite, John Lillywhite and Jas Lillywhite
J.H. Parks, J.M. Parks and R.J. Parks

Of the above the Parks family have come nearest to all representing England since the first two have done so and R.J. Parks acted as substitute wicketkeeper in one of the 1986 Tests in England.

(see also Brothers)

Fast bowlers

The first impulse of a cricketing tyro is to bowl as fast as possible, for no player captures the public imagination quite so much as the successful exponent of that difficult and transitory art. The first cartoon ever to appear in *Punch* on the subject of cricket concerned the fastest and most feared bowler of the day, John Jackson: 'He was one of the straightest, fastest and best bowlers that has ever appeared and though his speed was so great, he delivered easily to himself... By some he was called "the demon bowler".' Thus noted the historian Arthur Haygarth. Jackson's career lasted little more than ten years and he was the natural successor to George Brown, the deadliest of the underarm fast bowlers and Alfred Mynn, the early roundarm bowler from Kent. In the 1860s, George Tarrant followed Jackson, but this 'Cambridge Tearaway' lasted only half a dozen years at the top and

One of the outstanding fast bowlers of the 1970s and early 1980s, Michael Holding, bowling against England at the Oval in 1976, when he took 14 wickets.

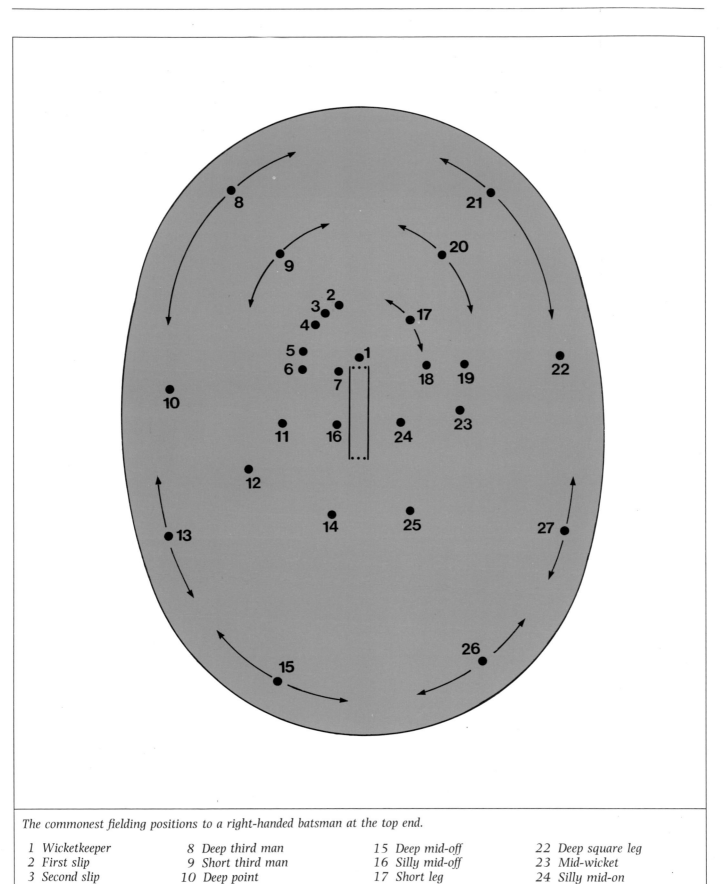

The commonest fielding positions to a right-handed batsman at the top end.

1 Wicketkeeper	8 Deep third man	15 Deep mid-off	22 Deep square leg
2 First slip	9 Short third man	16 Silly mid-off	23 Mid-wicket
3 Second slip	10 Deep point	17 Short leg	24 Silly mid-on
4 Third slip	11 Cover point	18 Short square leg	25 Mid-on
5 Gully	12 Extra cover	19 Square leg	26 Deep mid-on
6 Point	13 Deep extra cover	20 Fine leg	27 Deep mid-wicket
7 Silly point	14 Mid-off	21 Deep fine leg	

himself was succeeded by the Yorkshireman, George Freeman, whose deliveries 'whipped off the pitch like lightning.' For a brief period Yorkshire were fortunate to possess a formidable pair of fast bowlers in Freeman and Tom Emmett and they enabled their county to win the Championship for the first time in 1867 – Emmett took 48 wickets at 7.66 each and Freeman 66 at 8.36 in all first-class matches. Unlike many fast bowlers Emmett had a sense of humour. 'There's an epidemic here today,' he said, 'but it ain't bloody catching'. The circumstances can be visualised!

The next pair of fast bowlers of real class playing for the same county were Tom Richardson and Billy Lockwood for Surrey in the 1890s – in 1893 Lockwood picked up 150 wickets and Richardson 174, but oddly Yorkshire won the Championship, though Surrey won in the two preceding and two following years. In the first two Lohmann partnered Lockwood and in the other two Richardson partnered Lohmann. Around the turn of the century the Essex amateur, C.J. Kortright, was regarded as the fastest bowler in England; the first 25 years of the 20th century however did not see any really great English fast bowlers – spin and the medium-fast deliveries of S.F. Barnes and Tom Wass predominated.

Directly the First World War ended, the speed of the Australians J.M. Gregory and E.A. McDonald dominated the scene; England had no answer. The last great Australian fast bowler had been Ernest Jones whose short-pitched delivery shot once through W.G.'s beard. Before him had been the famous F.R. Spofforth, a member of the early touring sides to England, whose deadliest delivery was his disguised slower ball.

It was not until 1926 that England found their hero – Harold Larwood. By 1932, he had a fearsome partner in Bill Voce and 'bodyline' (q.v.) was born. One of the curious features of Test cricket is that when one country develops a pair of really effective fast bowlers, the other countries find their cupboards bare. After Larwood and Voce in the 1930s, came Ray Lindwall and Keith Miller for Australia in the 1940s. Lindwall and Miller were at their height in the 1946/47 and 1948 series. As they faded Australia found only medium-pace replacements and it was England's turn. Trueman and Statham with the meteoric Tyson of 1954/55 provided England with a fierce combination for a decade, whilst Australia searched desperately and became entangled in the throwing controversy of Meckiff and company.

Suddenly the fast bowling supremacy left the old countries and Wes Hall and Charlie Griffith were the names in the public eye. The West Indian reputation for fearful tearaways was beginning in earnest. There had of course been Constantine and Martindale before the Second World War, but in those days West Indies played few Test Matches.

In the 1960s England found John Snow and then, as his career was coming to a close, Bob Willis' reputation grew, but it was the Australians who found a matching pair in Dennis Lillee and the wayward Jeff Thomson. Not that West Indies faded with the retirement of Hall and Griffith; their seam of fast bowlers now appears almost too rich: Andy Roberts, Colin Croft, Michael Holding, Joel Garner, Malcolm Marshall. Players such as Van Holder and Wayne Daniel found themselves, excellent though they were, unable to command a regular Test place.

Of the other countries, only New Zealand's Richard Hadlee and Imran Khan from Pakistan come into the highest class. In 1986 both England and Australia were in search of a pair of fast bowlers and the West Indies continued to hold the stage. (see also Medium-pace bowlers, Slow bowlers and individual cricketers' entries)

Fast scoring

In recent years fast scoring has been reckoned on the number of balls received by the batsman rather than the time taken. Whilst mathematically this is obviously a much fairer measurement with which to compare the rate of scoring of batsmen, the spectator is more likely to appreciate the measurement by time. In terms of number of balls received the fastest hundred is perhaps D.W. Hookes, off 34 balls for South Australia v Victoria at Adelaide in 1982/83, but in terms of time six batsmen have hit faster hundreds and two of these have come eight minutes faster than Hookes' 43 minutes, namely P.G.H. Fender for Surrey v Northants at Northampton in 1920 and S.J. O'Shaughnessy for Lancashire v Leicestershire at Old Trafford in 1983.

O'Shaughnessy's feat, however, raises another problem. The Leicester bowlers deliberately sent down full tosses and long hops for him to hit, in order to encourage the Lancashire captain to declare and set Leicestershire a target. The same remark applies to the fastest 50, made in eight minutes by Clive Inman for Leicestershire v Notts at Trent Bridge in 1965.

The most renowned batsman for consistent fast scoring was the Gloucestershire amateur, G.L. Jessop. His fastest hundred came in 40 minutes for Gloucestershire v Yorkshire at Harrogate in 1897, and his fastest double century in 120 minutes, again for Gloucestershire, against Sussex at Hove in 1903.

E.B. Alletson hit 139 in 30 minutes for Nottinghamshire v Sussex at Hove in 1911, when he took his score from 50 to 189, and this remains the most astonishing innings of all in English first-class county championship cricket.

Fatalities

The only cricketer to be killed as a result of being hit on the head by a cricket ball whilst playing in English first-class cricket was George Summers. He was batting for Notts v MCC at Lord's in 1870 when a delivery from J.T.B.D. Platts struck him on the side of the head. Summers unwisely travelled back to Nottingham but died there four days later.

Fiction

Several well-known first-class cricketers have tried their hands at writing a novel with cricketing connections. Ted Dexter is a fairly recent example and between the wars Jack Hobbs and M.D. Lyon also put pen to paper.

In its day the most popular novel by a county cricketer was possibly 'Willow The King' by J.C. Snaith, but few would venture to read it today.

The two most famous men of literature to appear in first-class cricket are Conan Doyle and the Irish playwright, Samuel Beckett. Conan Doyle wrote only one cricketing story 'The Story of Spedegue's Dropper', and it is well worth reading. The most amusing cricket tale appears in A.G Macdonnell's 'England, Their England' and this can be found in Alan Ross's compilation 'The Cricketer's Companion', which also includes Charles Dickens' description of Dingley

Dell v All Muggleton and Thomas Hughes' account of Tom Brown's last match, among many other pieces.

Sir J.M. Barrie ran his own cricket team, the Allahak-barries, and in his 'The Greenwood Hat' describes the formation of the side, which contained mainly literary folk, but Barrie wrote very little on cricket.

Hugh de Selincourt's 'The Cricket Match' is generally regarded as the most accomplished novel on the game, and P.G. Wodehouse, himself a useful player, often brought cricket into his novels. One of the problems with cricket is that the actual events are more bizarre than an author would dare to make them in fiction.

Fielding circles
In 1981 for the English Benson & Hedges Cup, the 'fielding circle' was introduced. The 'circle' is, in fact, a semi-circle behind each wicket with a radius of 30 yards, the two semi-circles being joined by parallel lines 60 yards apart. Four fieldsmen plus the bowler and wicketkeeper must be stationed within the 'circle' when the bowler delivers the ball. This regulation now applies to all domestic limited-overs county competitions.

Fieldsman
Also referred to as 'fielder'. A player who is positioned in the field in order to stop the ball which has been hit by the batsman and return it to the wicketkeeper or bowler, thus preventing any more runs than necessary being scored off that delivery. See diagram for the commonly used fielding positions on page 63.

Fiji
Although they have played in all three ICC Trophy competitions, Fiji have not fared well, though each time they have shown an improvement on the previous competition, which indicates a slow revival in Fijian cricket.

The first recorded match in Fiji took place in 1874 and so rapid was the development of the game that in 1894/95, a Fijian team toured New Zealand and played first-class matches; similar tours took place in 1947/48 and 1953/54.

The two major figures in promoting cricket in the islands are J.S. Udal, who was Attorney-General of Fiji, and P.A. Snow, brother of the Leicestershire cricket historian, Eric Snow.

No first-class matches have been staged in Fiji and because of its location few touring teams have gone there.

Films
The three strongest connections between cricket and the cinema are the film *The Final Test* (1953), which depicted Jack Warner playing in his last Test with some of the 1953 English team as extras, the comedy actors Basil Radford and Naunton Wayne lost somewhere on the continent forever wondering what the latest Test score was in *The Lady Vanishes* (1938), and the figure of former England captain Sir C. Aubrey Smith in the role of 'a benevolent British gentleman of prominence' in many Hollywood films. The magazine *Wisden Cricket Monthly* published an article on cricket in films in December 1984, which was followed by a deluge of letters producing lists of other films with cricketing scenes, but most observers seem agreed that the screen has yet to produce a convincing film which is based on cricket.

First-class cricket
Since 1947, a first-class match has been defined as one arranged for three days minimum between two teams of 11 players each, with each team allowed two innings. Each of the two teams should be regarded as of first-class standard by the relevant body controlling cricket in the country in which the match was played.

The cricket 'averages' published in newspapers and other periodicals are usually compiled from performances in first-class matches only, unless stated otherwise. This means that players' performances in one-day internationals, the Sunday League, the NatWest Trophy and Benson & Hedges Cup are not included in the 'first-class' averages.

Prior to 1947, the press generally decided which matches qualified as 'first-class', and provided the teams were playing two innings a side and involved 'first-class' cricketers, the press included matches arranged for two days, matches involving 12 players on each side and in the second half of the 19th century some matches in which 11 players opposed 12, 13, 14 or 15 opponents.

The concept of having 'first-class' matches evolved around the middle of the 19th century and by the time overarm bowling was legalised in 1864 'first-class' cricket was established and definitive 'averages' and records could be compiled from such matches.

Floodlights
World Series Cricket, run by Kerry Packer's organisation, staged the first floodlit cricket match at the VFL Stadium in Melbourne on 14 December 1977 when an Australian XI opposed a World XI. The match began in daylight at 2.30; at 6.30 the floodlights were switched on and a white ball used against black sightscreens. The two major Australian cricket grounds, at Sydney and Melbourne, are both now equipped with floodlights, and these matches are a regular feature of Australian cricket, the players wearing coloured shirts and trousers. Some floodlit cricket matches were staged in England on football grounds in 1980 and 1981, but did not achieve much popularity.

Following-on
In a match in which teams are allowed two innings each, when the side that bats second are dismissed cheaply and have a large deficit on the first innings, they can be asked to take their second innings immediately. The team which batted first reserves the right to bat again. When a team continues their second innings directly after their first in this way, the team 'follows on'.

The first law governing this was published in 1835, when the follow-on was compulsory if a side were 100 or more runs behind.

As the Law now stands the follow-on regulation is optional and the amount of runs required as the difference between the sides depends on the number of days arranged for the match: for a five-day match it is 200 runs; three- or four-day match 150; two-day 100 and one-day 75.

Floodlit cricket at Sydney in 1979. This match, between Australia and the West Indies, was the first World Series Cricket match in which coloured gear was worn.

It is fairly unusual for a team to win after being forced to follow on and the most remarkable victory in these circumstances was by Barbados in 1926/27. Barbados made 175 in reply to Trinidad's 559, thus being 384 behind. Barbados hit 726 for 7 declared in their second innings and then dismissed Trinidad for 217, thereby winning the game. The feat has been performed twice in Test Matches, each time by England against Australia, in 1894/95 and 1981.

Forfeiting an innings

In first-class County Championship matches Brian Close became the first captain to forfeit an innings, when he did so in the match between Yorkshire and Lancashire at Old Trafford in 1966. Play was limited to 95 minutes on the first day and then rain totally washed out the second. Yorkshire declared their first innings at lunch on the third day; Lancashire batted one over and declared; Close then forfeited Yorkshire's second innings and as Yorkshire went on to bowl out Lancashire in their second innings, Close's tactics won the match – by 12 runs. In recent years it is not uncommon for both captains to forfeit an innings.

Frank Worrell Trophy

In appreciation of the famous West Indian captain, who led his country in the 1960/61 series against Australia, which included the first tied Test, the Frank Worrell Trophy was instituted in 1964 for series between West Indies and Australia.

(*see also* Australia v West Indies)

French cricket

A children's game in which there are no stumps or pitch. The batsman holds his bat vertically against his legs and his legs act as the wicket. The batsman is therefore either bowled out or caught. The fielders form a circle around the batsman and whichever fielder stops the ball then bowls the next delivery, which is underarm. The bowler tries to bowl as quickly as possible before the batsman can get his bat in place to protect his legs.

Fry, Charles Burgess

Born: 25 April 1872, West Croydon, Surrey

Died: 7 September 1956, Hampstead, London
Career: 394 *m*; 30,886 runs (av 50.32)
Tests: 26 *m*; 1,223 runs (av 32.18)

Fry was perhaps the most talented of all athletes. Apart from his cricket prowess, he played for England at soccer and was a holder of the world long jump record. He was also an excellent rugby player. He was also a scholar, published his own cricket magazine, was India's representative at the League of Nations through his friendship with Ranjitsinhji and was offered the Kingship of Albania.

Most of his cricket was for Sussex. His Test career ran from 1895/96 to 1912, when he captained England. He declined tours to Australia, which restricted his Test appearances. He was a classical batsman, always top or near the top of the averages, who in 1901 scored a record six successive centuries.

Full toss

A delivery by the bowler which reaches the batsman without hitting the ground. Not used intentionally by the bowler, except as a very occasional surprise. Also called a 'full pitch'.

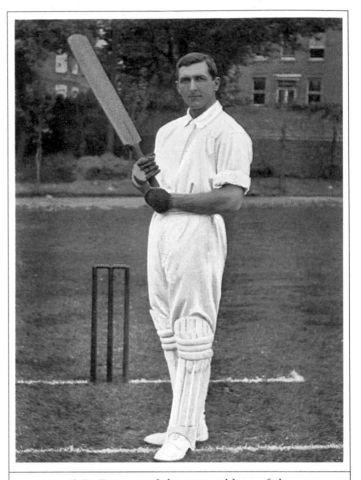

C.B. Fry, one of the great athletes of the golden age of cricket, an all-round sportsman who captained England at cricket.

G

Gambling

In the 18th century many of the great cricket matches were played for high stakes, in addition to which spectators would bet on individual batsmen making a given number of runs. Bookmakers attended matches in the same way as they attend horse racing today and the odds would move according to each fall of wicket or rise in the score. Problems arose when the players themselves became involved in the gambling, and from there it was only a step to players taking bribes to lose matches.

There are two celebrated examples of this bribery. The first in the early 19th century concerned William Lambert of Surrey, who was the best professional all-rounder of his day. He was banned from matches at Lord's after reportedly selling the England v Nottingham match of 1817. The other case occurred in Australia in the 1880s, when two of the English touring team were paid to lose a match and tried to persuade a third member of the side to join forces with them. Unfortu-nately for them he reported the matter to Alfred Shaw, who was captain of the eleven.

One of the betting swindles which some England cricketers used on the more innocent in country matches where the England team opposed a side of 22 players was that the player would receive good odds by claiming he could forecast the exact score of each individual in the 22. The player would forecast nought for all 22 and since the odds meant that he had only to forecast two or three correctly to make a profit, he usually ended with a tidy sum for a small outlay.

Garner, Joel

Born: 16 December 1952, Christchurch, Barbados
Career: 835 wkts (av 18.52)
Tests: 247 wkts (av 21.16)

The 'Big Bird' stands 6 feet 8 inches tall, bringing his fast right-arm deliveries down from a great height with the natural ability to exploit any bounce in the wicket. After only one season in first-class cricket with Barbados, he made his Test debut in 1976/77 and then came to England to play for Somerset in 1977. He had also spent one season with South Australia. He toured England with the West Indian sides of 1980 and 1984, topping the Test and first-class bowling tables on his first visit. He has also toured Australia three times and been to New Zealand and Pakistan. In 1985 he was awarded the MBE for his services to cricket. At the close of the 1986 English season his contract with Somerset was not renewed (together with that of Viv Richards) and this caused much controversy.

Gatting, Michael William

Born: 6 June 1957, Kingsbury, Middlesex
Career: 281 m; 16,920 runs (av 46.86)
Tests: 53 m; 3,118 runs (av 38.97)
Gatting is an aggressive middle-order right-hand batsman, who made his debut for Middlesex when just 18 and little more than two years later made his Test debut on the tour to Pakistan and New Zealand in 1977/78. While he was a consistently heavy scorer for Middlesex, initially his Test career was patchy and he needed all his determination to keep his place. His form turned round on the tour of India in 1984/85, when he finally made his first Test century and his highest Test score of 207. He was equally successful against Australia in 1985, when he averaged 87.83.

Gatting had become captain of Middlesex in 1983, and in 1986, when Gower was relieved of the England captaincy, he was appointed captain of his country. Although the home series against India and New Zealand were lost, he led the touring party to Australia in 1986/87 and impressively retained the Ashes.

Gavaskar, Sunil Manohar

Born: 10 July 1949, Bombay, India
Career: 333 m; 24,749 runs (av 51.24)
Tests: 115 m; 9,367 runs (av 50.63)
Sunny Gavaskar is a model for all opening batsmen: calm, secure in defence, polished in technique and possessing all the strokes. These qualities enabled the 5 feet 5 inch batsman to become the most prolific in Test Match history.

He made his first-class debut for Vazir Sultan Colts in 1966/67, and the following year joined Bombay, making the Test team in 1970/71 for the tour to the West Indies. His four-match aggregate was 774, average 154.80, and since then the West Indies have been on the receiving end of some of his best performances.

Gavaskar first captained India in 1979/80, but has not always seen eye-to-eye with the authorities, and in the 1980s he and Kapil Dev tended to swop the captaincy. Of his many great innings, the last-day 221 against England at the Oval in 1979, which helped India to 429 for 8, chasing 438 to win, will be remembered. His highest Test score was 238 not out against West Indies at Bombay in 1983/84. Earlier in the series he passed Geoff Boycott's Test aggregate record. His highest score is 340 for Bombay v Bengal, in 1981/82.

Geddes Grant/Harrison Line Trophy

The leading one-day limited-overs competition in the West Indies. This was instituted in 1975/76 under the sponsorship of Gillette, but has been sponsored by the present combination since 1977/78. The six first-class sides in the West Indies, apart from the Windward Islands, have all had their share of victories and it has been a very keenly fought series.

Gentlemen v Players

The annual match between the amateurs and professionals was staged at Lord's in most seasons between 1806 and 1962 – a total of 137 matches of which the Gentlemen won 41 and the Players 68. Matches were also played under this title at Scarborough, Kennington Oval and a few times at other venues. Such matches were not generally played in countries outside the British Isles except in pre-First World War United States.

Georgetown

The Bourda Ground at Georgetown, Guyana, has staged Test cricket since 1929/30 when West Indies played England. The ground, which is the home of Georgetown Cricket Club, has also been the setting for matches by Demerera since the first inter-colonial games were introduced (Demerera since changing to British Guiana, and now Guyana).

Ghana

The major international match against Nigeria began in 1904, and between the wars the matches were treated very seriously with Ghana (then the Gold Coast) being the stronger of the two. Cricket since independence has been at a low level, and at present Ghana forms part of West Africa, which belongs to the ICC, though they have not competed in the Trophy matches.

Gibbs, Lancelot Richard

Born: 29 September 1934, Georgetown, British Guiana
Career: 330 m; 1,024 wkts (av 27.22)
Tests: 79 m; 309 wkts (av 29.09)
Gibbs was a record-breaking off-spinner who made his debut for British Guiana in 1953/54. Late in his career he also played for Warwickshire and a few matches for South Australia.

He first played for West Indies in 1957/58, and was more or less a regular until 1975/76. Tall and slim, he bowled from a 'run' of five paces, and the effort of spinning the ball on the hard pitches he frequently encountered gave him a greatly enlarged knuckle on his right-hand index finger. He was an excellent fieldsman but the weakest of batsmen.

In his last Test, against Australia, he passed Trueman's record aggregate of Test wickets and retired.

Gibraltar

Gibraltar won only one match in the 1986 ICC Trophy, a slight improvement on 1982 when not a single victory was recorded. A team was entered for the first Trophy competition in 1979, but had to be withdrawn due to a lack of qualified players, most of the cricket on the Rock being played by servicemen stationed there. Few of the native population seem interested in the game.

Gillette Cup
see NatWest Trophy

Glamorgan

The story of county cricket in Glamorgan is one of sudden spasms of delight between long periods of mediocrity. Joining the first-class counties in 1921, Glamorgan struggled for two decades, then to the utter amazement of all carried off the Championship in 1948, only to subside again as quickly as they had arisen. Wilf Wooller was the Aladdin who rubbed the lamp on that occasion, when success was attributed largely to the magnificence of the fielding. Wooller was not far away in 1969, when the Championship was carried off a second time by the side under the able captaincy of Tony Lewis. The third example of spontaneous combustion came in 1977, when the county reached the final of the Gillette Cup, but were beaten by Middlesex. The captain at Lord's that day was Alan Jones, the long-serving opening batsman.

The Glamorgan Club was formed in 1888; it needed, however, all the energy and skill of J.H. Brain to keep the club going during the formative years. The bowling of Jack Nash and the batting of N.V.H. Riches pushed Glamorgan into first-class company, while the talents of J.C. Clay, as fast, then spin, bowler as well as captain, kept the county afloat until Wooller arrived from North Wales to assist.

It has long been the ambition of Glamorgan to field an all-Welsh team, but this has yet to be achieved, and like all but Yorkshire, the county have had the help of some talented overseas cricketers since the mid-1960s. Javed Miandad and Majid Khan, the Pakistani Test cricketers, have played some fine cricket for the county.

The headquarters of the county used to be the famous Cardiff Arms Park, which was shared by the Rugby Football Club but in 1967 the Cricket Club moved to Sophia Gardens. The St Helen's Ground at Swansea is also a regular venue, but the county's adventures to such faraway places as Colwyn Bay and Aberystwyth seem to be a thing of the past.

Glance

A batting stroke, more precisely a 'leg-glance', when a delivery on the leg side of the wicket is steered by deflection between square leg and fine leg. The glide is a similar stroke but with less attempt to steer the ball.

Gloucestershire

The county of the Graces, with the dominant figure of W.G. overshadowing all, have gone through some difficult times since the county club was formed out of the Grace family and a rather motley collection of fellow amateurs. Between 1873 and 1877 the county won the Championship four times. The crowds flocked to see W.G. and his band challenge and defeat the mighty professional counties of the north. But in his 30th summer as captain, Gloucestershire tired of their colossus and to all intents and purposes threw him out, so the greatest of cricketers ended his days in the relative solitude of the Crystal Palace.

In the Edwardian era came the hurricane hitting of Gilbert Jessop and during the inter-world war period the polished batting of Wally Hammond with such bowlers as Charlie Parker and Tom Goddard, but only in 1930 did the club look likely to regain the crown.

Since the war the county's path has been an erratic one – in 1969 for example they finished runners-up in the table, the following year they plunged to bottom place. The batting was usually adequate, though they foolishly allowed Tom Graveney to become so disgruntled that he moved to Worcestershire. Spin, with a helpful Bristol wicket, predominated: Tom Goddard in his slower style, Sam Cook, Bomber Wells, David Allen, John Mortimore, but there was a shortage of good opening bowlers too often. The two names which came to the fore when overseas cricketers arrived in batches were Mike Procter, the brilliant South African all-rounder, and Zaheer Abbas, the Pakistani batsman, and more than once Gloucestershire came back into the reckoning, only to drift away when Procter went. The mid-1980s have, however, seen another revival. Procter also changed the county's fortunes in one-day cricket, and in the 1970s, both the Gillette Cup and Benson & Hedges Cup were won.

Just as the early days of the county club were unusual in that it was run by one family – though the Walkers and Middlesex are similar in that respect – its early home venues were out of the ordinary. For nearly 20 years the county played the majority of 'home' matches on the school grounds at Clifton or Cheltenham during the summer holidays. It was not until 1889 that Gloucestershire found a proper home; this was the present ground at Ashley Down, Bristol. Beset by debts the club has had to sell the ground twice – once in 1916 to the chocolate firm of Fry's and again in 1976 to the Phoenix Assurance Co. The finances of the county club have thus been as erratic as its form on the field.

Golden Age

The 'Golden Age' of cricket is a term often used to describe the period from about 1900 to the First World War in 1914, at its peak in 1902 when England and Australia each had one of their strongest sides. It was a period of patronage, when many of the leading batsmen were dashing and stylish amateurs who drove handsomely off the front foot. Typical figures of the era were R.H. Spooner, A.C. MacLaren, Gilbert Jessop and the Hon F.S. Jackson.

Gooch, Graham Alan
Born: 23 July 1953, Leytonstone, Essex
Career: 341 *m*; 22,835 runs (av 43.00); 179 wkts (av 32.26)
Tests: 59 *m*; 3,746 runs (av 37.08); 13 wkts (av 42.00)
Gooch began his career as a middle-order right-hand batsman for Essex in 1973, and was so promising that he made his Test debut two years later against Australia. But he made a pair in his first Test and was dropped after the second. When he returned against Pakistan in 1978 he was a more mature and aggressive opening bat who made the position his own. Strangely he had to wait to his 36th Test innings to make his first century, against West Indies at Lord's in 1980. In 1981/82, he captained the rebel SAB team to South Africa, and was banned from Test cricket for three years. On his return he established himself again as one of his country's most talented batsmen, but he declined the tour to Australia in 1986/87, preferring to stay at home with his family. The previous season he took over from Fletcher as captain of Essex, and led them to the Championship.

'Big Bird' Joel Garner in mid-air, about to bowl
from a great height to an English batsman
in Trinidad.

Sumil Gavaskar, record-breaking Test cricketer
with more runs and centuries than anybody else,
a model opening batsman.

Mike Gatting took many Tests to establish himself
in the England Test side, but took over as captain
in 1986 and enjoyed a very successful tour of
Australia in 1986/87.

Graham Gooch, in one of his bearded spells,
hooking high. Converted from middle order to
opening batsmen, he became one of the most aggressive
and stylish of the day.

David Gower playing a typical shot in the Sydney Test Match of 1986/87.
He is one of the most attractive batsmen of the 1980s.

Googly

A delivery from a slow bowler which from his action seems to be going to turn in from the leg, but in fact turns the other way. The delivery was perfected by B.J.T. Bosanquet, the Oxford University and England bowler, and thus is also referred to as a 'Bosie'.

Gower, David Ivon

Born: 1 April 1957, Tunbridge Wells, Kent
Career: 290 *m*; 16,867 runs (av 40.06)
Tests: 91 *m*; 6,553 runs (av 45.50)

Gower was an excellent left-hand batsman from schoolboy days, and made his debut for Leicestershire in 1975, when 18. In 1978 he made his Test debut against Pakistan, hitting his first ball in Test cricket for four. He had a long period of success, climaxed by a lovely innings of 200 not out against India in 1979, but then began periods of uncertainty. Gower is the most attractive of modern batsmen, his off-side drives from square through mid-off and his hooks and sweeps to leg being jewels of timing, but when the timing is slightly awry he gets out in amateur style.

He took over the captaincy of England in Pakistan in 1983/84, and despite losing 5-0 to West Indies in 1984, he kept the job, won excellently in India in 1984/85 and in 1985 had his best series when regaining the Ashes, scoring 732 runs, average 81.33, in the series, including his highest career score, 215, at Edgbaston. However, all went wrong in the West Indies in 1985/86, when there was much criticism of the English discipline as West Indies won 5-0 again, and after a bad start against India in 1986, Gower's pleasant and laid-back style of captaincy was dispensed with.

He remained in the side, and played well in Australia in 1986/87, where his dignity and support for Gatting were much admired.

Grace, William Gilbert

Born: 18 July 1848, Downend, Bristol
Died: 23 October 1915, Mottingham, Kent
Career: 869 *m*; 54,211 runs (av 39.45); 2,808 wkts (av 18.15)
Tests: 22 *m*; 1,098 runs (av 32.29); 9 wkts (av 26.22)

Dr W.G. Grace, with his big black beard, is both the most recognisable and the most famous cricketer of all time. For over 30 years he dominated cricket. He and his brothers, E.M. and G.F., established Gloucestershire as a leading county, whose four championships in the 1870s have not been added to since. All three Graces played in the first Test played in England, and W.G., with 152, scored England's first-ever Test century.

W.G. first played for Gloucestershire in 1870 and England in 1880. His only tours were to North America and Australia (twice), but only the last was first class. From 1888 to 1899 he captained England when he played.

Grace was in theory an amateur, but in reality made more from cricket than any professional of his day. He was something of a law unto himself – a famous story about him claims he refused to leave the wicket when out early, telling the bowler that 'people have paid to see me bat, not you bowl'.

He created most of the cricket records, which have since, one by one, been beaten. He was the first to score 1,000 runs in May, the first to score 100 centuries, the first to perform the

W.G. Grace as a young player. He dominated cricket from 1870 to the end of the century, and 100 years later remains, to Englishmen at least, the most recognisable of all sportsmen.

'double' (as well as being a commanding batsman, he was a more than useful roundarm bowler). His career aggregate stood for many years. Nobody has yet passed the 28 times he made 1,000 runs in a season, although Woolley equalled it. His last first-class match was for Gentleman of England in 1908, when he was 60.

Greenidge, Cuthbert Gordon

Born: 1 May 1951, Black Bess, Barbados
Career: 435 *m*; 31,074 runs (av 45.76)
Tests: 71 *m*; 5,033 runs (av 48.39)

Although born in the West Indies, Greenidge came to England as a boy and made his first-class debut with Hampshire in 1970. He quickly established himself in the county side and was asked if he was available to play for England, but he preferred to represent West Indies and made his Test debut in 1974/75. He has toured England with the West Indies in: 1976, 1980 and 1984 and has been a most dependable right-hand opening batsman for both county and country. In addition he has made his mark in one-day cricket, at one time holding the Hampshire batting records for all three English competitions. His highest first-class score is 273 not out for D.H. Robins' XI v Pakistanis at Eastbourne in 1974 and in Tests 223 against England at Old Trafford in 1984.

Grimmett, Clarence Victor
Born: 25 December 1891, Dunedin, New Zealand
Died: 2 May 1980, Adelaide, Australia
Career: 248 *m*; 1,424 wkts (av 22.28)
Tests: 37 *m*; 216 wkts (av 24.21)
Grimmett began his first-class career in New Zealand with Wellington in 1911/12, played five matches in five years for Victoria after the First World War, then switched to South Australia, where he finally established himself, aged 33, and forced himself into the Test team.

He took so long to reach the top because he was short, balding, and would trundle to the wicket and bowl leg-breaks with a low arm action – it was not pretty and did not look menacing. However, in his first Test, he took 11 England wickets for 82 and continued from there.

He toured England three times, claiming his best innings

analysis with 10 for 37 against Yorkshire at Bramall Lane in 1930. In South Africa in 1935/36 he first passed Barnes' record aggregate of Test wickets (189), in the next Test achieved his best Test analysis of 7 for 40 and became the first to pass 200 Test wickets, and in the next Test, his last, he took 13 wickets.

Guard
At the start of his innings, the batsman 'takes guard' by holding his bat vertically in front of the wicket and on the line of the popping crease, whilst the umpire at the bowler's end advises him as to the position of the bat in a direct line between the two sets of wickets, until the bat covers either the middle stump, leg stump, off stump or midway between middle and leg, or middle and off, according to which guard the batsman requests. The batsman marks on the turf which position he desires for the purpose of guarding his wicket.

Gully
A fielding position between point and slips, which according to some observers was created by the England and Nottinghamshire captain, A.O. Jones, before the First World War.

H

Hadlee, Richard John
Born: 3 July 1951, Christchurch, New Zealand
Career: 287 *m*; 9,806 runs (av 30.26); 1,221 wkts (av 18.48)
Tests: 66 *m*; 2,397 runs (av 25.77); 334 wkts (av 22.51)
New Zealand's best-ever bowler, Hadlee was one of the great all-rounders who distinguished cricket in the 1970s and 1980s. The son of a former New Zealand captain, Hadlee made his debut for Canterbury in 1971/72, and in 1978 began a successful English career with Nottinghamshire. He made his first Test appearance in 1972/73.

Hadlee is a genuine fast bowler. Wiry rather than muscular, he achieves zip and life from a comparatively short run. He bowls right-handed, but bats left-handed in an aggressive but scientific manner at about No. 7. He scored a Test century against West Indies in 1979/80.

Hadlee has been instrumental in New Zealand's rise to true Test standard. He took ten wickets in their first-ever defeat of England in 1977/78; his century helped in their first home series win; he was at the crease when England were beaten by New Zealand for the first time in England; he took 33 wickets in three Tests when Australia were beaten for the first time in a series in 1985/86, and took ten wickets in the defeat of England at Trent Bridge in 1986 which won New Zealand's first series in England.

To emphasise Hadlee's all-round qualities, in 1983 he became the only player to perform the 'double' since the Championship season was reduced in 1969.

Half-volley
A ball delivered by the bowler, which pitches just in front of the batsman and thus can be hit with relative ease just as it comes off the ground.

Hambledon
This small Hampshire village was the headquarters of the leading cricketers in England for about 30 years immediately prior to the rise of the MCC. The team raised by the Hambledon Club challenged and beat the Rest of England and in 1833 Charles Cowden Clarke compiled, from the recollection of John Nyren, 'The Cricketers of My Time', which remains one of cricket's greatest books and which describes many of the players who played at Hambledon. The matches were staged on Broadhalfpenny Down and latterly on Windmill Down. The captain of the Hambledon side was Richard Nyren, who had learnt his cricket from Richard Newland of Slindon, one of the greatest cricketers of the 1740s. Richard Nyren was landlord of the Bat and Ball Inn, Hambledon and then the George Inn in the same village. C.C. Clarke noted: 'When Richard Nyren left Hambledon the club broke up and never resumed from that day.'

Hammond, Walter Reginald
Born: 19 June 1903, Dover, Kent
Died: 1 July 1965, Durban, South Africa

Career: 634 *m*; 50,551 runs (av 56.10); 732 wkts (av 30.58)

Tests: 85 *m*; 7,249 runs (av 58.45); 83 wkts (av 37.80)

Hammond was the outstanding English batsman of the 1930s, being the leading Englishman in the batting averages for eight consecutive seasons. He made his debut for Gloucestershire in 1920, but difficulties over his registration and severe illness in 1926 hindered his progress. He first appeared for England on the tour of South Africa in 1927/28. The following winter he scored 905 runs in a series against Australia, average 113.12.

Hammond was a burly figure at the wicket whose driving was of great power – his off-drive was one of cricket's classic shots. In 1932/33 he made the then record score in a Test Match, 336 not out in New Zealand – he scored 563 in his two Test innings, which was his series average.

Hammond was a more than useful fast-medium bowler, and one of the greatest of specialist slip fielders, taking a record ten catches in a match against Surrey in 1928, in which he incidentally scored a century in each innings.

Hammond became an amateur in 1938 and led England in three series before the war and three afterwards. He made a marvellous 240 against Australia at Lord's in 1938, but was not in good health after the war, and he retired in 1951.

*Wally Hammond walking out to bat for England.
He was England's outstanding player of the 1930s, who
turned amateur to captain his country after the war.*

Hampshire

The 1970s saw the county win three titles – two John Player and a County Championship – and is therefore the most successful decade for Hampshire in modern times. West Indian cricketers Roy Marshall, Andy Roberts and Gordon Greenidge have been three outstanding postwar stars, with Malcolm Marshall as a brilliant more recent addition from the Caribbean. The South African Barry Richards also contributed to the trophy-gathering until he tired of county cricket. Most notable of the postwar English players are the bowlers Derek Shackleton and Peter Sainsbury, who dominated the attack through the 1950s and 1960s, as the county gradually awoke under the leadership of Desmond Eagar and Colin Ingleby-Mackenzie from their long slumber.

The mythical splendour of the Hambledon Club and the Hampshire team that it generated still survives in cricket's folklore. Richard Nyren, the chosen General of all the matches, Tom Walker, John Wells, William Beldham, David Harris, John Small, father and son, were just some of the names connected with the Hambledon Club, which produced a Hampshire team capable of taking on the Rest of England. Through the 19th century journalists would hail each attempt at reviving Hampshire cricket by proclaiming the resurrection of Hambledon's glory, only to find within a few years the county had collapsed again.

Officially Hampshire regained first-class status in 1895, but in the 20 summers prior to the outbreak of the First World War, it made precious little impact on the destiny of the Championship crown.

Lord Tennyson's flamboyant grandson led the county during most of the inter-war period, but never raised Hampshire above sixth place. The stalwart Phil Mead ground out 2,000 runs a season with the precision of a batting machine and Alec Kennedy took his 100 wickets with the same regularity, but they made little impression on the hardened pros of the north.

Thus it was that Hampshire supporters had to wait 200 years for a revival of fortune. The cricketers had descended from Broadhalfpenny Down into Southampton, with annual forays east and west to Portsmouth and Bournemouth and the occasional match at Basingstoke.

Handled the ball

A batsman can be given out if he picks up or deliberately

Tavare caught Smith bowled Hadlee at Christchurch in 1983/84, and New Zealand are well on their way to the victory which brought their first series win over England.

The pavilion at Headingley, the Test ground in Leeds which has seen some famous innings, notably from Bradman and local batsman Boycott.

touches the ball with his hand whilst it is in play. His dismissal is then recorded in the scorebook as 'Handled Ball', but his wicket is not credited to the bowler. This mode of dismissal is given in the earliest Laws of 1744.

The most recent example in English first-class cricket is A. Rees of Glamorgan v Middlesex at Lord's in 1965, and in Test cricket Desmond Haynes was given out for handling the ball in a match against India at Bombay in 1983/84.

Hanif Mohammad
Born: 21 December 1934, Junagadh, India
Career: 238 *m*; 17,059 runs (av 52.32)
Tests: 55 *m*; 3,915 runs (av 43.98)

Hanif came from a cricketing family, his brothers Wazir, Mushtaq and Sadiq and son Shoaib all playing for Pakistan, and various others of his family playing first-class cricket. He was a great batsman from an early age, making his Test debut when only 17. He kept wicket in this match, but was only an occasional keeper and bowler.

He was mainly a very solid opening batsman, who has the distinction of making the highest score in first-class cricket, 499 for Karachi against Bahawalpur in 1958/59 – he was run out attempting his 500th. He also played the longest Test innings, 16 hours and 10 minutes for 337 against West Indies in 1957/58. He captained his country in 11 Tests.

Harvey, Robert Neil
Born: 8 October 1928, Fitzroy, Victoria, Australia
Career: 306 *m*; 21,699 runs (av 50.93)
Tests: 79 *m*; 6,149 runs (av 48.41)

Neil Harvey was one of the best of Australia's post-Second World War batsmen. He made his debut for Victoria in 1946/47, and 12 years later switched to New South Wales. A brilliant, attractive left-hand batsman, he made his Test debut aged only 18, toured England with Bradman's all-conquering 1948 Australians, and scored a century in his first Test there. By the time he retired from Tests, he had appeared more often than any other Australian until then, and scored more runs than all except Bradman.

Harvey's highest Test score was 205 against South Africa, his highest career score 231 not out for New South Wales against South Australia. He had no interest in statistics, however, preferring to get on with the game. He is a small man, who used dazzling footwork to attack the bowlers. His nimbleness also made him a brilliant fieldsman, usually at cover-point.

Hat-tricks
The first recorded instance of a player being given a hat, when achieving the feat of taking three wickets in three consecutive balls, occurred in 1858. D.V.P. Wright of Kent, with seven instances has performed the hat-trick, as the feat came to be known, most often in first-class matches and six bowlers have performed the feat twice in the same match in first-class cricket.

Haynes, Desmond Leo
Born: 15 February 1956, Holders Hill, Barbados
Career: 141 *m*; 9,162 runs (av 43.42)

Tests: 59 *m*; 3,703 runs (av 42.56)

An excellent right-hand opening batsman, he made his first-class debut for Barbados in 1976/77 and his Test debut the following season against Australia, when he was an immediate success. His Test career was interrupted by a season with Packer's World Series Cricket, but since then he has been a regular member of the West Indies team and came to England with both the 1980 and 1984 sides, being particularly successful on the first tour, when he averaged over 50 in the Test series and was second only to Richards.

Headingley
The first first-class match played on the Headingley Ground, Leeds, took place in September 1890 when the North of England played the Australians. In the following season Yorkshire played on the ground for the first time. The ground is actually owned by the Leeds Cricket, Football and Athletic Club, and one half of the ground is used for Rugby League matches, including internationals. The first Test Match was staged there in 1899, but only since 1921 has it been a regular venue for such matches. The largest attendance at a three-day county match was 78,792 for the Roses game of 1904, but the five-day Test of 1948 saw 158,000 people present to watch England play Australia. It is believed that this is the largest recorded attendance for a match in England.

The ground is the headquarters of Yorkshire County Cricket Club.

Headley, George Alphonso
Born: 30 May 1909, Colon, Panama
Died: 30 November 1983, Kingston, Jamaica
Career: 103 *m*; 9,921 runs (av 69.86)
Tests: 22 *m*; 2,190 runs (av 60.83)

Headley was called the 'Black Bradman' in the 1930s – he was the greatest West Indian batsman before the Second World War, and indeed there have been few batsmen his equal anywhere in the world.

He went to school in the West Indies (he was born in Panama where West Indians largely built the Canal) and learned cricket, becoming a brilliant natural batsman, especially strong on the on-side. He played for Jamaica for 26 years from 1927/28, making his Test debut in 1929/30. His Test career lasted 24 years, but he was not the same player in his three post-Second World War Tests. Before the war, he succeeded in every series he played.

His highest Test score was 270 not out against England at Kingston in 1934/35, his highest career score 344 not out for Jamaica, against Lord Tennyson's tourists in 1931/32. On both his tours to England he hit two double centuries. Considering that he batted at No. 3 with his side's fortunes usually resting entirely on him, his career and Test averages are remarkably high.

Helmets
On 4 August 1978, the TCCB at its Summer Meeting ruled that a batsman could not be caught off a ball which rebounded off a protective helmet worn by a fielder and thus 'helmets' entered into the regulations of the game for the first time. This was then enshrined in the 1980 Code of the Laws.

It was during the 1978 English season that helmets came

The great West Indian batsman George Headley, who averaged 66 and 72 on his two tours of England. He was among the world's best batsmen of the 1930s.

Dennis Amiss with his new design of helmet, during the Warwickshire v New Zealand match at Edgbaston in 1978.

to be introduced in force in first-class county cricket. Dennis Amiss, the Warwickshire batsman, organised the manufacture of helmets and some 100 were sold to county players at £29 each. Prior to this Mike Brearley had improvised his own which was worn under his cap, but for batting only. There was a loud cry from the aesthetes, but within a season or two bareheaded batsmen became a rarity in top-class cricket.

Hertfordshire

Formed in 1876, the county club were founder members of the Minor Counties Championship and have appeared every season. Under the captaincy of their wicketkeeper, F.E. Collyer, the county last captured the title in 1983. Collyer had also led the county in 1975 when they claimed the title by a convincing margin. D.G. Ottley, A.R. Garofall and B.G. Collins were all leading figures in both summers.

The only other season of success was in 1936, when the slow left-arm professional, Ted Roberts, carried all before him, taking 97 wickets at 9.81 runs each, and the county won eight of their 12 fixtures. Roberts was well supported by C.B. Fordham's off-breaks and the latter also did well as a batsman.

Historians

The first textbook of the game which contained its history and

made a lasting impression on several generations of cricketers was 'The Cricket Field' by the Rev James Pycroft. His book first appeared in 1851 and then re-appeared at intervals for over 30 years. Whilst therefore Pycroft might be described as

Mike Brearley, batting for England against Australia in 1977 with the protective headgear he wore before the modern conventional helmet became fashionable.

cricket's popular historian, Arthur Haygarth, the dry researcher, spent his life gathering together his monumental 'Scores and Biographies'.

Two historians devoted their time to the task of checking through pre-Victorian newspapers and collecting cricket notices. H.T. Waghorn published 'Cricket Scores, Notes Etc' in 1899 and then 'The Dawn of Cricket' in 1906. Later on the scene came G.B. Buckley, who also issued two similar books of cricket notices in 1935 and 1937.

Another researcher into the distant past was P.F. Thomas, who issued a series of booklets in the 1920s, which not only contain some hitherto unknown facts but make important deductions from the various gleanings.

Much more prolific than Thomas was F.S. Ashley-Cooper, who dealt in both history and statistics. His published works range from a definitive history of Nottinghamshire cricket and 'The Hambledon Cricket Chronicle' to numerous pamphlets, all of which contain items of interest and are highly valued by collectors.

Since the Second World War, a number of researchers have continued to delve into unexplored archives and have increased our knowledge of the game's history. The most notable of these present-day historians are Irving Rosenwater, John Arlott, Peter Wynne-Thomas and, on a more limited scale, John Goulstone and David Rayvern Allen. (*see also* Reference books)

Hit ball twice

The batsman can be given out if he hits the ball twice, unless he does so to prevent the ball hitting his wicket. This mode of dismissal is recorded in the earliest Laws of 1744, but only very rarely have batsmen been so dismissed. The bowler is not credited with the wicket.

It has not occurred in English first-class cricket since 1906 when J.H. King of Leicestershire v Surrey at the Oval was the guilty party.

Hit wicket

If in the course of making a stroke, the batsman dislodges a bail, either with his bat or his person, he can be given out. The bowler is credited with the wicket. This mode of dismissal appears in the earliest Laws of 1744.

Hobbs, John Berry

Born: 16 December 1882, Cambridge
Died: 21 December 1963, Hove, Sussex
Career: 834 *m*; 61,760 runs (av 50.66); 108 wkts (av 25.04)
Tests: 61 *m*; 5,410 runs (av 56.94)
Jack Hobbs was called 'The Master'. Some claim he was the best batsman of all. His figures were surpassed by Bradman,

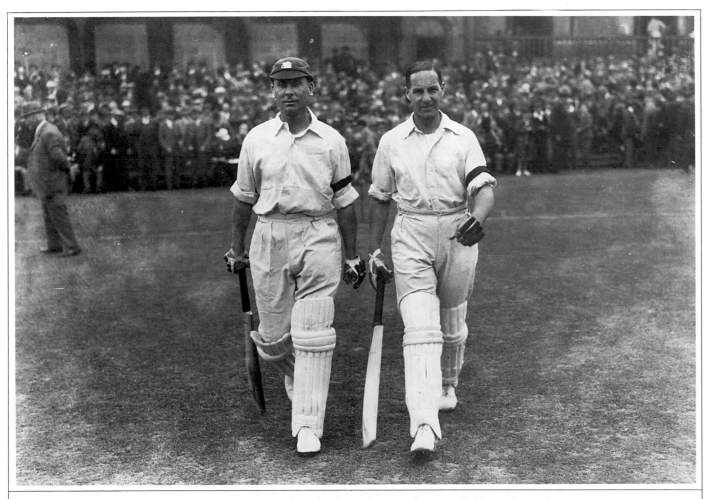

Jack Hobbs (left) and Herbert Sutcliffe, the most famous of all opening pairs, going out to bat for England at Trent Bridge in 1930.

but the grace and elegance of his batting, his genius on difficult wickets and his lack of interest in big scores for their own sake give the figures alone a false value. Nevertheless his own were impressive. Nobody has ever scored more first-class runs or centuries.

Hobbs played for Surrey for 29 years from 1905. His Test career began in 1907/08 and lasted until 1930. Probably no English batsman was more highly regarded in Australia, where he was a great success on five consecutive tours.

Hobbs was an opening batsman who found two outstanding partners for Surrey: Hayward and Sandham. But his most famous partnership was with Sutcliffe for England. In 26 Tests in which they opened, they made a century partnership in 15, 11 of them against Australia.

In all, Hobbs took part in 166 century opening partnerships. His highest Test score was 211 against South Africa at Lord's, his highest career score 316 not out for Surrey against Middlesex. This was his only score over 300, and the highest ever made at Lord's.

Hobbs was an occasional medium-pace bowler and outstanding cover-point, who on the 1911/12 tour of Australia ran out 15 batsmen. He was a true sportsman, modest and kind, and was knighted in 1953.

Holland

Dutch cricket is very much on the rise, and having reached the final of the 1986 ICC Trophy, their team made a very creditable showing against Zimbabwe, losing by only 25 runs. This result is a vast improvement on their performances in the previous ICC Competitions of 1979 and 1982, but it is misleading to suggest that cricket is a relatively recent import to the Netherlands. The first match took place there in 1845 and the Dutch Cricket League was founded in 1891.

Prior to their success in 1986, the most famous Dutch match was in 1964, when the Australians, who were touring England, paid a brief visit and were beaten in a one-day match. Before the First World War, Holland had one famous cricketer, C.J. Posthuma, who came to England in 1903 and appeared in several first-class matches. He is regarded as the W.G. Grace of Dutch cricket, being a splendid all-rounder.

Hook

A batsman's stroke which is used to deal with a short pitched delivery when the ball is rising. The batsman moves back towards his wicket and strikes the ball, with a horizontal bat, in the direction of square leg. The invention of this stroke is credited to E.M. Grace, brother of W.G.

Hong Kong

The Hong Kong Cricket Club was formed in 1851 and from 1866 for many years the principal fixture was against Shanghai. It was returning from Shanghai in 1882 that Hong Kong lost their entire team, when the steamer in which they were travelling sank during a typhoon.

Apart from Shanghai, Hong Kong played against Ceylon and the Straits Settlements. Since the Second World War many teams have played in Hong Kong, but the first English tour made by the colony did not take place until 1976. Hong Kong won two matches in the 1982 ICC Trophy and three in 1986.

Horse cricket

Sir Horace Mann, the great patron of Kent cricket, arranged a match on horseback, with the bats being specially constructed with long handles. The game took place about 1800 at Harrietsham.

Hove

The present ground at Eaton Road, Hove, was opened in May 1872 as the new headquarters of Sussex County Cricket Club. The county had had three previous grounds in the Brighton and Hove area, namely Ireland's Gardens, 1791 to 1847; Lillywhite's Ground, 1834 to 1844; and Brunswick Ground, 1848 to 1871.

The ground falls about 20 feet from north to south, which can be a little disconcerting to players unaccustomed to the venue.

Hutton, Leonard
Born: 23 June 1916, Pudsey, Yorkshire

The young Len Hutton, who was to become England's outstanding post-war batsman, and the first professional to be regularly appointed captain of England.

Career: 513 *m*; 40,140 runs (av 55.51); 173 wkts (av 29.51)

Tests: 79 *m*; 6,971 runs (av 56.67)

Len Hutton was the first professional to be regularly appointed as England's captain, a reward for being the outstanding opening batsman of his era. He first appeared for Yorkshire in 1934, aged 18, and for England in 1937, when he made 0 and 1, but a century in the next Test. He entered the record books in 1938, when, just over 22, he broke the Test innings record with 364 against Australia at the Oval.

An accident during the Second World War led to his left arm being slightly shorter than his right, but he overcame this handicap: 1949 was his best season with 3,429 runs. He is the only player to carry his bat for England twice – he made 202 not out from 344 against West Indies in 1950 and 156 not out for 272 against Australia in 1950/51. Both matches were lost, and Hutton was often burdened with attempting to save his side.

When made captain in 1953, he won back the Ashes, and retained them in 1954/55, but he soon retired, finding being captain and best batsman a strain. He was knighted in 1956.

His style and technique were of the highest class, and whether attacking, as he preferred, or being forced by circumstances to defend, he was an attractive batsman.

I

ICC Trophy

This competition has been staged three times, each time being in England. The teams which take part are from the associate membership countries of the International Cricket Conference (q.v.). All associate members are eligible, but not every one has competed in the competitions. The matches are all of limited overs, with one innings per side.

The results of the finals were:

1979 Sri Lanka 324-8 beat Canada 264-5 by 60 runs
1982 Zimbabwe 232-5 beat Bermuda 231-8 by 5 wkts
1986 Zimbabwe 243-9 beat Holland 218 by 25 runs

Ice matches

In the 19th century cricket on ice was relatively common. One of the first matches of which the full score is preserved took place on 15 February 1870 on the Mere Fen at Swavesey, Cambridge. The Cambridgeshire county eleven scored 230 for 9 against 16 of Cambridge who made 125 all out. In the 1890s, Lord Sheffield organised several ice matches at Sheffield Park with a number of well-known cricketers taking part.

Imran Khan

Born: 25 November 1952, Lahore, Pakistan

Career: 328 *m*; 15,349 runs (av 36.03); 1,145 wkts (av 21.84)

Tests: 57 *m*; 2,140 runs (av 30.14); 264 wkts (av 22.18)

Imran has been one of the great all-rounders of the 1980s – one of the six cricketers who can claim 2,000 Test runs and 200 Test wickets. Eight of his cousins played first-class cricket; two, Majid Khan and Javed Burki, captained Pakistan and Imran joined them.

He made his debut for Lahore aged 16½. Later he played for PIA, and also Worcestershire and Sussex in England. He made his Test debut in 1971 in England, but was not a regular member of the side until 1976/77, after he had studied at Oxford University.

Imran gradually developed into an outstanding fast bowler and attacking middle-order batsman. He became his coun-try's leading Test wicket-taker, and one of the world's most formidable cricketers.

India

Calcutta Cricket Club, once regarded as the MCC of India, was established as long ago as 1792, but for the best part of 100 years cricket remained a game played in India almost solely by Europeans.

The first Indians to adopt the game were the Parsis of Bombay. In 1886 they sent the first Indian team to England, but found themselves very much outplayed. Not discouraged by defeat, the Parsis redoubled their efforts and in 1889/90 were the only side to defeat Vernon's English team on their pioneering visit to the sub-continent. Three years later the Parsis were able to challenge the Europeans in India and this was the start of first-class domestic matches – the Presidency Matches, which developed into the Bombay Pentagular series as the Hindus, Muslims and 'The Rest' also entered teams.

The first Indian side to be granted first-class status when touring England came in 1911 under the captaincy of the Maharajah of Patiala and he was just one of many of the Indian rulers who actively encouraged the playing of cricket, not only by participating themselves, but by raising their own teams and employing professional coaches from England.

The MCC took a strong side to India in 1926/27, playing 34 matches in a programme which extended to both Burma and Ceylon. A second MCC tour was arranged for 1930/31, but had to be cancelled due to political unrest, which also caused the Bombay Tournament to be temporarily suspended. India was granted Test Match status when their team toured England in 1932 and after the MCC tour of 1933/34, the Indian Board of Control established the Ranji Trophy (q.v.) as India's equivalent to England's County Championship. The Ranji Trophy soon superseded the Bombay Tournament as India's major first-class competition, but the leading native Indian rulers also had their own competition, the Moin-ud-Dowlah Gold Cup Tournament (q.v.), which ranked as first class from 1930/31 to 1937/38 and then 1962/63 to 1973/74, being run latterly by Hyderabad CA.

Nationally, India's strength in the 1940s and 1950s lay in

batting and huge scores were made in home Test and domestic first-class games, both by teams and individuals, but India were rarely seen to much advantage overseas until the emergence of some formidable spin bowlers in the 1960s and 1970s. India's greatest success so far came in 1983 when the side, under the leadership of Kapil Dev, won the Prudential World Cup final at Lord's, defeating the West Indies, who were regarded as the favourites. The victory was the cause of great celebrations in India – and rightly so.

(see also the succeeding entries, Australia v India, England v India, West Indies v India, New Zealand v India and individual entries for cricketers, competitions and grounds)

India v Pakistan

Results: Played 35; India won 4; Pakistan won 6; Drawn 25

With only ten definite results out of 35 games, the meetings between the two countries have too often been dominated by a combination of batting wickets and the desire to avoid defeat.

The first series heralded Pakistan's introduction into Test cricket in 1952/53. The First Test was staged at New Delhi and proved to be Mankad's match; he took 13 wickets, as India gained an innings victory. India then foolishly omitted their leading players for the Second Test and were themselves in consequence defeated by an innings at Lucknow, Fazal Mahmood taking 12 wickets and Nazar Mohammad carrying out his bat for 124, made in 517 minutes: he was on the field throughout the entire game. India brought back their missing men for the Third Test and Mankad took the opportunity to complete the 'double' of 1,000 runs and 100 wickets in Tests, but it was Amarnath who broke the Pakistan batting in the first innings. With Hazare and Adhikari both making hundreds, India won by ten wickets. Torrential rain prevented even a first-innings result in the Fourth Test and the Fifth was drawn, the most notable feature being 110 by the left-handed Shodan, coming in at No.8 in his first Test.

The next two series consisted of ten drawn matches, after which, for political reasons, there was a break of 18 years in the contests, which eventually resumed in 1978/79, when Bedi's side went to Pakistan. The First Test in this revival was a run-glutted draw with hundreds from Zaheer, Javed Miandad and Asif Iqbal for the Pakistanis and 145 from Viswanath for the visitors. The dreadful succession of draws came to a halt at Lahore in the Second Test, when Mushtaq won the toss and put India in, Imran and Sarfraz bowling them out for 199. Zaheer then hit an undefeated 235 in Pakistan's 539 for 6 declared and though India managed 465 in their second innings they still lost by eight wickets. The bowling of Imran and Sarfraz also enabled Pakistan to win the Third Test and therefore the series by two matches to nil.

In more recent times the draw has returned with a vengeance, no definite result having been recorded in two series in the mid-1980s. The last time victory was gained was in January 1983 when Pakistan won by an innings, Mudassar Nazar and Javed Miandad both making double hundreds and Imran and Sarfraz, with eight and seven wickets respectively, dismissing India for 189 and 273. Since then there have been seven successive draws.

One interesting record was achieved at Lahore in 1982/83 when Mudassar Nazar carried his bat through the completed

Imran Khan, one of the outstanding all-rounders of the 1980s. His main strength is as a fast bowler, but he is also a good batsman, fielder and captain.

Pakistani innings, thus emulating his father, Nazar Mohammad, who performed the feat noted earlier in this entry.

India v Sri Lanka

Results: Played 4; Sir Lanka won 1; Drawn 3

The inaugural series consisted of a single match between the two sides at Madras in 1982/83. L.R.D. Mendis celebrated the occasion by scoring a century in each innings, but as Gavaskar and S.M. Patil scored hundreds for the opposition, the game was left drawn, with India failing to score 175 in less than two hours in the final innings.

India visited Sri Lanka to play Test cricket for the first time in 1985/86, and Sri Lanka by winning the Second Test and drawing the remaining two won this series. Their success was mainly due to the bowling of Ratnayake who took nine

The Second Test between Pakistan and India at Lahore in 1978/79.
Asif Iqbal is bowled by Chandrasekhar, but Pakistan won after 13 draws.

wickets, thus dismissing India for 244 and 198. India's ill fortune was to an extent self-imposed, there being a conflict between the captain, Kapil Dev, and his predecessor, Gavaskar, who for some reason batted at no. 5 or no. 6 instead of opening the innings.

Indoor cricket

The NCA national six-a-side indoor cricket competition was first staged in 1975/76, when the final was won by Durham City who beat Enville at the Michael Sobell Centre in Islington, over 500 clubs having competed in the competition. In the following year the number of competing clubs had doubled. Since the opening of the Indoor Centre at Lord's, the finals have been staged there.

In the winter of 1983/84 came the rival Australian eight-a-side indoor game, when Derek Randall's Cricket Centre was opened in Nottingham. There are now three commercial eight-a-side varieties of the game in England with over a dozen centres competing for trade.

The NCA six-a-side version is also flourishing, over 2,000 clubs entering the 1985/86 national competition.

The first organised indoor competition in England seems to have taken place in 1970/71 in Shropshire, being devised by E.J. Rowe, M.D. Vockins and P. Sellars. This first league was a six-a-side competition.

Innings

A term used to describe the time occupied, or the number of runs scored, by a batsman between his arrival on the field of play and his dismissal. It is used of the whole team in the same way.

If a team wins by an 'innings' this means that their opponents failed in two complete innings to equal the score made by the other side in a single innings.

In-swinger

A delivery which the bowler makes swerve in the air from the off to the leg. One of most effective of the earlier exponents of this delivery was J.B. King, the Philadelphian cricketer, at the turn of the century.

International Cricket Conference

Founded in 1909 as the Imperial Cricket Conference by England, Australia and South Africa at the instigation of Sir Abe Bailey, its membership increased to six countries in 1926 with the admission of India, New Zealand and West Indies. Pakistan were admitted in 1952, and when South Africa left the Commonwealth in 1961, their membership of the ICC ceased. At this time its rules included 'Membership shall be restricted to recognised Governing Bodies of countries of the British Commonwealth of which the representative teams are accepted as qualified to play official Test Matches.'

In 1965 the body was renamed the 'International Cricket Conference' and new rules were adopted allowing for the admission of all cricketing countries – those which did not play Test Matches being eligible as Associate Members. In the same year, Ceylon, Fiji and the United States became the first Associate Members. Since then the following other countries have joined: 1966 Bermuda, Denmark, East Africa and the Netherlands; 1967 Malaysia, 1968 Canada, 1969 Hong Kong and Gibraltar, 1973 Papua-New Guinea, 1974 Argentina, Israel and Singapore; 1976 West Africa; 1977 Bangladesh, 1981 Zimbabwe and Kenya. Ceylon, now Sri Lanka, became a full member in 1981.

Thus the Conference has developed into an important international cricket organization.
(*see also* Administration, ICC Trophy)

Ireland

The Irish Cricket Union was originally founded in 1884/85, but the present organisation, which is the governing body of cricket in Ireland, came into being in 1923. Dublin University was for long the stronghold of Irish cricket and the majority of international matches were, until 1963, staged on its ground.

The first-class status, or otherwise, of matches played by Ireland has been a complex problem for 100 years and at present is not satisfactorily resolved. The 'Guide to First-class Matches in the British Isles' by the Association of Cricket Statisticians explains the problem in detail. Certain Irish matches are regarded as first-class commencing 1902, but matches from 1895 to 1926 by Dublin University have in some cases been granted first-class status.

Irish Interprovincial Tournament

Founded in 1966 and sponsored until 1985 by Guinness, the tournament is the nearest equivalent to the English County Championship. The six competing teams in 1986 were North West, South Leinster, North Leinster, Munster, Ulster Country and Ulster Town, the first named becoming the holders of the title, when they won four out of five matches. The Ulster teams, which for so long dominated the competition, are now not so strong.

Israel

The first cricket league in Israel was established in 1966 and the country joined the ICC in 1974. A team have been entered for each of the three ICC Trophy competitions, but in all three, only one victory has been recorded.

J

Javed Miandad Khan
Born: 12 June 1957, Karachi, Pakistan
Career: 324 *m*; 23,133 runs (av 53.30)
Tests: 74 *m*; 5,413 runs (av 55.23)
An attacking right-hand middle-order batsman, Javed made his first-class debut at the age of 16 and was playing for Sussex and for Pakistan in Tests at the age of 19. His highest Test innings was 280 not out for Pakistan v India at Hyderabad in 1982/83, but at the age of 17 he created something of a sensation by hitting 311 in a domestic first-class match in Pakistan. In 1980 he left Sussex to join Glamorgan and was most successful in 1981, hitting 2,083 runs with eight hundreds for the county – a Glamorgan record. His record in Test cricket is just as impressive and he hit 163 against New Zealand on his Test debut. He toured England in 1978 and 1982. Although expected to play for Glamorgan in 1986, he failed to report at the start of the season and his contract with the county was ended after several weeks of speculation and discussion.

Johannesburg
The present Wanderers Ground in Johannesburg was opened on 16 November 1956, when Transvaal played Natal, and the first Test Match was staged there between England and South Africa later in the same season. The ground replaced the old Wanderers ground which was near the centre of the city and is now part of the present railway terminal. For some years between the closure of the old ground and the opening of the new, the major cricket matches were played at Ellis Park, the home of Transvaal rugby.

The attendance record for a day's play at the new ground is 36,057 on 26 December 1957, when South Africa played Australia.

Journalists
Until the First World War, the journalists who reported on cricket for the national and provincial press were largely anonymous. A series of splendid articles by J.D. Coldham published in *The Journal of the Cricket Society*, Vols 10 and 11, removes much of this anonymity, but it was the writing of Neville Cardus in the *Manchester Guardian* which changed cricket reporting and gave it an individuality which the public could readily identify. A second writer who quickly made a name for himself in the inter-war period was the Somerset amateur, R.C. Robertson-Glasgow, first in the *Morning Post* and then *The Observer*.

After the Second World War, E.W. Swanton transferred from the London *Evening Standard* to the *Daily Telegraph* and established himself as an authoritative voice. John Arlott, though better known to the general public as a cricket broadcaster, wrote pieces in a distinctive style for the *Manchester Guardian* and Alan Ross provided his own flavour to the columns of *The Observer* for nearly 20 years. John Woodcock has been the correspondent for *The Times* for many years and is the senior member of the current press corps in cricketing circles. Matthew Engel has in the last few summers established his own style in *The Guardian*.

One of the most prolific of Australian correspondents was Ray Robinson, whose career in journalism took off in 1930 when he was appointed chief cricket writer of the *Melbourne Star*. Later he moved to Sydney and in his last years worked for the *Sun-Herald*. Robinson died in 1982. Another well-known Australian journalist who died in the 1980s was the Test batsman, Jack Fingleton, whose writing appeared in England and South Africa as well as his native Australia.

Most of the above journalists have had selections of their writings collected in books.
(*see also* Broadcasting, Magazines).

K

Kanpur
The Oxford Authentics played a match here against Northern India in 1902/03, the city being known as Cawnpore until the 1940s, but neither of the inter-war MCC sides staged matches in Cawnpore and it was not until 1945/46 that United Provinces played their first Ranji Trophy match there.

The Test Match, India v England, in 1951/52 would appear to be only the third first-class match ever played on the Green Park Ground at Kanpur. Although it has regularly staged Test Matches since the 1950s, the number of Ranji Trophy games played on the ground by the home side, Uttar Pradesh, have been exceedingly few.

Originally matches were played on jute matting, but since the 1960s grass pitches have been prepared in such a way as to favour the batsmen to a ridiculous extent, with one or two exceptions.

Kapil Dev
Born: 6 January 1959, Chandigarh, India
Career: 192 *m*; 7,888 runs (av 31.80); 619 wkts (av 26.52)
Tests: 77 *m*; 3,132 runs (av 29.82); 291 wkts (av 28.72)
Kapil Dev, with Botham, Imran and Hadlee, has been one of

*Javed Miandad, Pakistan's mercurial batsman,
who is one of the few to average over 50
in Test matches.*

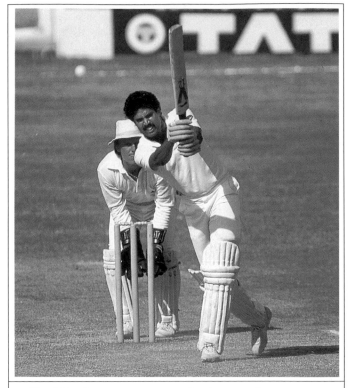

*Kapil Dev batting against England at Bombay in 1984.
One of India's best-ever fast bowlers, he is also
one of the world's most exciting
fast scorers with the bat.*

*Part of the crowd at the National Stadium, Karachi, during the Third Test with England
in 1977/78. The match was the eleventh successive draw between the countries.*

The famous landmarks at the Oval, the gasholders. The first Test Match in England was played here. This is England playing Pakistan in 1978.

the four great all-rounders of the 1980s who has registered 2,000 runs and 200 wickets in Test cricket. Early in the 1986/87 season he became the second man to 3,000 and 300.

Kapil made his debut for Haryana in 1975/76 near his 17th birthday, and for India when not quite 20. A fast-medium opening bowler and hard-hitting middle-order batsman, his career has similarities with Botham's. In 1 year and 105 days he had 100 Test wickets, being the youngest to reach this target, and the quickest. Two days later he became the youngest player to score 1,000 Test runs. He slowed down a little after this, but remained India's main strike bowler and a dashing scorer.

He became captain of India in 1982/83 and led his country to the World Cup, playing an outrageous innings against Zimbabwe, taking the score from 17 for 5 to 266 for 8, smashing 175 not out, a World Cup record. His highest career score is 193, and in Tests 126 not out against the West Indies in 1978/79. He also achieved his best analysis against West Indies, 9 for 83 in 1983/84.

Karachi

The National Stadium in Karachi has been the venue of Test Matches since 1954/55 when Pakistan played India there. At that time cricket was played on matting wickets, but in the 1960s grass wickets were introduced.

The Sind Tournament, which was founded in 1919/20, was staged in Karachi, but the first first-class match was not staged in the city until 1926/27 when the MCC side opened its tour with four matches there. Karachi was the headquarters of the Sind Cricket Association which played in the Ranji Trophy prior to Partition; the major matches were then played on the Gymkhana Ground, which was still being used for first-class matches in 1985/86.

Kennington Oval

The home of Surrey County Cricket Club, Kennington Oval was originally a market garden. In 1844, when the Montpelier Cricket Club of Walworth were in search of a new ground, it was vacant and Mr Houghton, the President of the Montpelier Club, with money from the Club funds, took over the land and laid out a cricket ground, which was ready for use in 1845. The ground at that time covered some four acres, but at present is some ten acres in extent.

During 1845 a meeting of cricket enthusiasts revived Surrey County Cricket Club and arranged that their county matches should be played at the Oval.

In 1854, the proprietor, in order to increase the revenue from the ground, organised poultry shows and other entertainments and the Duchy of Cornwall, which owned the freehold, refused to continue Mr Houghton's lease. As a result three trustees on behalf of Surrey CCC took up the lease and the ground has been under the control of the county club ever since.

A large new pavilion was erected on the ground in 1858. The present pavilion was erected in 1897/98 at a cost of £38,000, the architect being the same as that for the Old Trafford pavilion and the design being somewhat similar.

The first Test Match ever staged in England took place at the Oval in 1880. Between 1873 and 1889 England also played soccer internationals on the ground and from 1871/72 to 1891/92 the FA Cup Final took place there. In 1895 the members of the Surrey Club voted by two to one to stop the playing of soccer on the ground.

Two men who were responsible for the organising of events at the Oval in the last 30 years of the 19th century were William Burnup and C.W. Alcock, and English sports followers owe a great deal to their enterprise.

Over 80,000 spectators watched the Surrey v Yorkshire County Championship match at the Oval in 1906: the largest recorded attendance for an inter-county game. It was on this ground in 1938 that England made 903 for 7 declared against Australia, the highest team total ever in England.

Kent

To the casual follower Kent are the county of wicketkeepers: the England Test team are slightly askew when the wicketkeeper is not from Kent. Ames, Evans and Knott dominated the position from the late 1920s to the middle 1980s. Knott is arguably the greatest of all wicketkeepers; Ames scarcely equalled as a wicketkeeper-batsman; the flamboyant Evans was the man who cheered the drab post Second World War era.

Kent, however, to the historian, are much more than a succession of stumpers. The present Kent officials seem to mark their county from the year 1871, almost as if they are ashamed of their murky past. Why this should be is a baffling mystery. Kent reorganised their county club in 1870/71, but that had little effect on the calibre of the cricketers.

The match between Kent and England played in 1744, which the county won by one wicket, must remain, historically, one of the, if not *the*, most important games ever staged. For the next 100 years Kent were either pre-eminent or, at worst, the equal of the two or three other leading counties – the 1830s and 1840s were the heady days of Alfred Mynn and Fuller Pilch. By the 1860s, however, a slow decline had set in and even the machinations of Lord Harris did not bring relief until Edward VII had been on the throne for some years. The left-arm slows of Blythe then augmented the fast bowling of Fielder, and in 1906 the Championship was won. It was a significant year indeed, for it was the one in which Frank Woolley first made his mark. The batting depended on one or two sound professionals – Seymour and Humphreys initially – and an array of gifted amateurs, who came and went, then came again. C.J. Burnup, K.L. Hutchings, E.W. Dillon and J.R. Mason were the most distinguished at this time. The county won the championship again in 1909, 1910 and 1913.

Between the wars, the batting remained strong – Hardinge, Woolley and Ashdown maintained the professional side, with A.P.F. Chapman and B.H. Valentine being two of several notable amateurs. The bowling, however, relied too much on 'Tich' Freeman, with Ames breaking records as a wicketkeeper as a result.

After two good seasons in 1946 and 1947, the county had some 15 undistinguished years, when the bowling was weak – Doug Wright's fast leg-break alternated between unplayable and expensive.

Colin Cowdrey, Derek Underwood and the West Indian John Shepherd brought back a title in 1967 – the Gillette Cup – and the county demonstrated their all-round ability by coming second in the Championship. In 1970 the Championship was won, a success repeated in 1977 and 1978 – through all these years Underwood remained the outstanding bowler, with Knott behind the stumps, but the batting was in the hands of Asif Iqbal, Chris Tavaré and Bob Woolmer. Also in the 1970s, both Benson & Hedges and Player League titles were each won three times. No such success was to come as the 1980s progressed.

Kenya

From 1910 to 1964 the principal match of the season was Officials v Settlers. In the 1930s, however, the Asian population of Kenya developed an interest in the game and an annual match Europeans v Asians was inaugurated. A number of Kenyan-born Asians have made their mark in English county cricket since the mid-1960s, the first notable figure being Basharat Hassan. The first international match series was played against Uganda and founded in 1914.

Kenya played in the 1979 ICC Trophy as part of East Africa, but in 1982 and 1986 played as a separate unit, and in the latter season won three of their six matches.

Kingston

The first English team to visit Jamaica played their principal match against the colony at the Sabina Park Ground in April 1895. The ground remains the headquarters of cricket in Jamaica and the first Test Match was staged there in 1929/30 when West Indies played England. It was on this ground in 1957/58 that Gary Sobers created a new Test record by scoring 365 not out against Pakistan. The boundaries on the ground are shorter than on most major Test centres and this brings the often explosive spectators much more into the actual cricket.

First-class matches in Kingston have also been played at Melbourne Park, but no Tests have taken place there.

Knighthoods

The first person to be knighted for services to cricket was the retiring MCC Secretary, F.E. Lacey, in 1926; he was followed by Fred Toone, who was Secretary of Yorkshire from 1903 until 1930 and was knighted in 1929.

In 1936 the Rajkumar of Vizianagram was knighted during the Indian tour of England, he being the captain of the touring side, his award being similar to that of Fred Toone, whose citation read 'in recognition of his great work in helping to promote the best relations between Commonwealth and Mother Country.'

The following year a knighthood was bestowed on Pelham Warner, but it was not until 1949 that a cricketer was knighted strictly for his efforts on the cricket field itself, this honour going to Sir Don Bradman. Jack Hobbs and H.D.G. Leveson-Gower received knighthoods in 1953, Len Hutton in 1956, Frank Worrell in 1964 and Gary Sobers in 1975. (The awards of OBE, MBE and CBE have been fairly frequently bestowed on cricketers since the Second World War, but Freddie Brown is, it is believed, the only player to receive the MBE and then the CBE.)

Knott, Alan Philip Eric

Born: 9 April 1946, Belvedere, Kent
Career: 478 *m*; 17,431 runs (av 30.47); 1,129 *ct*; 131 *st*
Tests: 95 *m*; 4,389 runs (av 32.75); 250 *ct*; 19 *st*
Knott was one of the great Kent wicketkeepers. In the county side at 18, and the England side at 21, he was an automatic choice for his country for 10 years. A health and fitness fanatic, who ate the right foods, he did his calisthenics at the wicket, forever bending and stretching between deliveries, whether keeping or batting. It kept his short frame in condition for the darting and diving way in which he kept wicket.

He was no mean batsman, scoring runs in the same impish and perky manner, often when they were most required. An ideal No. 7 for England, he hit five Test centuries, his highest score, 135, coming against Australia in 1977 – with England 82 for 5 he put on 215 with Boycott.

World Series Cricket interrupted his Test career, the rebel South African tour and an unwillingness to spend every winter abroad practically ended it in 1981.

L

Lahore

The Lahore Tournament, which was played between 1922/23 and 1938/39, was staged on the Gymkhana Ground, Lawrence Gardens, and Northern India used the ground for Ranji Trophy matches until Partition. The ground was first used for Test cricket in 1954/55 when Pakistan played India and, now known as the Bagh-e-Jinnah Ground, it is still used for first-class matches, though Lahore Test Matches have been held since 1959/60 at the Gaddafi Stadium, which can accommodate over 50,000 spectators.

Laker, James Charles

Born: 9 February 1922, Bradford, Yorkshire
Died: 23 April 1986, London
Career: 450 *m*; 1,944 wkts (av 18.41)
Tests: 46 *m*; 193 wkts (av 21.24)
Laker will always be remembered for the most astonishing Test Match record of all: 19 wickets in one match, a feat he achieved against Australia at Old Trafford in 1956.

He did not make his first-class debut until after the Second World War, for Surrey. In the 1950s he was one of the main

Alan Knott, the leading wicketkeeper of modern times, who combined agility with reliability.

Jim Laker bowling against South Africa at the Oval in 1951.
Five years later he set the most astonishing Test Match record of all against Australia.

reasons the county won seven successive Championships, a record. After two seasons he made his Test debut on the 1947/48 tour to the West Indies, where he was England's most successful bowler. Unfortunately the selectors frequently under-rated his off-spin, and he toured Australia only once, a fact which rankled. He was probably the greatest of all off-spinners, with a mastery of all aspects of the craft, and should have had more Test wickets.

He twice took ten wickets in an innings, each time against Australia, in the same season – once for Surrey. On retirement he became an excellent television commentator.

Lamb, Allan Joseph

Born: 20 June 1954, Cape Province, South Africa
Career: 272 m; 18,199 runs (av 47.64)
Tests: 51 m; 2,644 runs (av 32.64)
Lamb first played for Western Province in 1972/73, and joined Northants in 1978, qualifying by residence for England, for whom he made his debut soon after becoming eligible, in 1982. A middle-order right-hand batsman, who possesses all the shots and plays forcefully all round the wicket, he was at the time the most consistent batsman qualified for England. Despite having one or two less impressive patches, his Test place has rarely seriously been in doubt.

Lancashire

Although Lancashire are bracketed with Yorkshire and Notts as one of the great northern counties which dominated professional cricket until the Second World War, probably the most triumphant period in the Red Rose county's history was the early 1970s, and perhaps their two outstanding matches, the semi-finals of the Gillette Cup in 1971 and 1972. The latter, staged at Old Trafford, was the famous game which continued until 8.50 pm and made David Hughes the hero of the hour when in the semi-darkness he hit John Mortimore for 24 off one over to clinch the game. Jackie Bond went on to lead Lancashire to the title in both years as well as in 1970; he also won the Player League in 1969 and 1970. The side had some excellent batsmen in Clive Lloyd, Barry Wood, David Lloyd, Harry Pilling and Farokh Engineer and in Jack Simmons and David Hughes two ideal all-rounders for one-day cricket, and Bond got the most out of his players.

In the County Championship Lancashire's great days are now a distant memory. The late 1920s saw them win six Championships in ten years. They were immortalised in prose by Neville Cardus in the *Manchester Guardian*: the Tyldesleys, Makepeace, who 'never forces admiration out of you; he woos it', Iddon, Watson, Hallows and the Australian fast bowler, Ted McDonald. Those were the days when the Lancashire v Yorkshire matches could decide the Championship: 78,000 turned up to watch the 1926 game at Old Trafford, which at the end of three full days' cricket just reached a decision on first innings. The report nicely describes this war of attrition: 'Makepeace and Ernest Tyldesley withstood the Yorkshire attack for three hours and a quarter' – and that was the middle of the first day.

The county were perhaps unfortunate not to win more honours in the immediate post-Second World War period. In Statham, Tattersall and Hilton they possessed three of the most talented bowlers in England, whilst in Washbrook and

Place they had a very sound pair of opening batsmen, but the best this side could muster was one tied Championship title in 1950.

In the 19th century the county bred some brilliant amateur batsmen – Archie MacLaren still retains the record score in England of 424, made against Somerset in 1895, but for some inexplicable reason the county found bowlers impossible to find, and the fact that they imported their three most successful men – McIntyre, Crossland and Briggs – from Notts, led to some cross-fire between the two counties at a time when the title was fought out between the two.

Lancashire's history is thus one of very contrasting images. The sparkle of MacLaren, the steadiness of Makepeace and the merry band of one-day specialists under Bond, all flourished despite Old Trafford's reputation for inclement weather.

Lancashire League

Formed in 1890 as the North-East Lancashire Cricket League, the league changed to its present title in 1892. In the days before overseas Test players could qualify immediately for a first-class county, many notable world-class players were Lancashire League professionals, including Learie Constantine (Nelson), Everton Weekes (Bacup), Bobby Simpson (Accrington), Charlie Griffith (Burnley), Ted McDonald (Nelson) and many others. In 1986 there were still some well-known Test players, Mudassar Nazar (Burnley), Winston Davis (Rishton) and John Maguire (Church) being three. The 1986 league title was won by Nelson after a play-off, when they finished level on points with Todmorden – the latter are the only Yorkshire team in the league. The league is sponsored by Matthew Brown.

Larwood, Harold

Born: 14 November 1904, Nuncargate, Notts
Career: 361 m; 1,427 wkts (av 17.51)
Tests: 21 m; 78 wkts (av 28.35)
Larwood is not a tall man, but his bowling action was considered about perfect for a fast bowler, and some contemporaries claim that there never was a faster bowler.

He played exactly 300 first-class games for Notts from 1924 to 1938, but it is with the 1932/33 Test Match series in Australia that his name will be forever linked. In an era of batting mastery on easy wickets, when Bradman was almost a run-machine, Larwood was the very fast, very accurate bowler ideal for Jardine's 'bodyline' tactics (q.v.) which won the series. Larwood took 33 wickets in the five Tests, but such was the ill-feeling caused by the matches that he was not picked for England again.

Larwood was no mean batsman, and scored 98 against Australia in the 'bodyline' Tests. In 1949 he emigrated to Australia, where he remains a popular figure.

Lawrence Trophy

Instituted in 1934 by Sir Walter Lawrence as an award to the scorer of the fastest hundred in English county cricket in a season. In 1939 with the outbreak of the Second World War, the Trophy was in abeyance. Sir Walter Lawrence died in the same year.

In 1966 the directors of Sir Walter Lawrence's building firm re-established the award, but for Test cricket in a calendar year. In 1971 however it was changed back to the original concept of the fastest hundred in county cricket.

Laws of cricket

The history of the Laws has been told in a well researched book *The Laws of Cricket* by the former secretary of the MCC, Col R.S. Rait Kerr, published by Longmans in 1950.

The earliest known set of Laws which appear in a book, magazine or periodical, were printed in *The New Universal Magazine* of November 1752 and were entitled 'The Game at Cricket, as settled by the Cricket-Club, in 1744, and play'd at the Artillery-Ground, London.' There are however, linen handkerchiefs of the 1740s with a version of the Laws printed around the border of an adaptation of Francis Hayman's painting of cricket in Marylebone Fields. It seems agreed that there must have been earlier versions and that the 1744 edition was a revision, but as yet no one has located any definite evidence on this point. The Laws were first issued as a booklet in 1755 and the first code which was produced by the MCC was written in 1788, since which year the MCC has remained the body in charge of the Laws.

Although the present Laws now involve a 28-page booklet, they contain the basic elements of the earliest known version. The distance between the wickets has remained at 22 yards, two umpires have controlled the game and the system of innings and overs remains unchanged as well as the principal ways of dismissing a batsman.

Leg

The cricket field is divided into two halves by an imaginary line running parallel to and through the centre of the pitch. The side of the stumps at which the batsman stands when preparing to receive a delivery from the bowler is referred to as the 'leg side'; all the fielders on that half of the field are described as leg-side fielders and if the batsman hits the ball to that side it is described as a leg hit (*see* Glance, Hook, Drive etc). The other side of the field is referred to as the 'off-side'.

A left-handed batsman stands on the other side of the stumps, when receiving the ball, in comparison with a right-handed batsman, thus when a left and a right-handed batsman are in at the same time, the fielders change positions each time the two batsmen change ends and the terms leg-side and off-side alternate accordingly, much to the confusion of the casual observer. The leg side is also called the on side.

Leg before wicket

Normally abbreviated to 'l.b.w.' or 'lbw', this mode of dismissal occurs when any part of the batsman's person, apart from his hand and forearm, is situated between the two sets of stumps and in the opinion of the umpire prevents a ball, which either hit him on the full, or pitched on a line between the two wickets, from hitting the stumps. The Law was introduced in the 1774 revision for the first time and is now more complex than in the description above, since the batsman can be given out 'lbw' if the ball pitches on the off-side of the stumps and would have hit the wicket, but for the batsman preventing it by means of his person, UNLESS he did so whilst attempting to play a stroke.

As can be imagined the lbw law causes more argument than any other form of dismissal.

Leg-break

A delivery from a bowler which deviates when it hits the ground by moving from the leg side to the off. A leg-break bowler is one who employs this delivery. It is more difficult to bowl than the off-break (q.v.) and therefore leg-break bowlers tend to be less accurate. This type of bowler, once relatively common, is now rarely seen in English county cricket.

Leg-bye

A run scored is thus termed when the ball is deflected by the batsman's person. Until the 1850s, leg-byes were not scored separately but simply given as 'byes'. The present Laws state that the batting team can be credited with a leg-bye only if either the batsman attempts a stroke, or makes a deliberate attempt to avoid the ball.

Leicestershire

Leicestershire cricket has been 'first-class' since 1894, but for 60 years it was frequently a struggle to maintain that status. The image of the county as a title-winning combination is entirely modern. C.H. Palmer, the Worcester schoolmaster, began to change the county's image during the 1950s. He retired as captain in 1959 when F.M. Turner was appointed as secretary/manager and the Yorkshire batsman, Willie Watson, captain. Tony Lock continued the up-grading in the later 1960s, so that the arrival of Ray Illingworth found a team ready for glory.

The Benson & Hedges Cup was won in 1972, the Player League in 1974 and the County Championship in 1975, with the B&H for a second time in the same year. The team were one with four notable all-rounders, an unusual circumstance in county cricket. Illingworth, John Steele, J.C. Balderstone and J. Birkenshaw were a remarkable quartet. Balderstone even went off in the middle of the final vital Championship game of 1975 to play League football for Doncaster Rovers in an evening match – he was 51 not out prior to his evening of football, and returned the following morning to reach 116. He then picked up 3 for 28, as Derbyshire were dismissed cheaply on the final afternoon, giving Leicestershire victory by 135 runs and the Championship.

The county won the Benson & Hedges Cup for the third time in 1985, under the leadership of David Gower – having one of England's best batsmen as captain and match-winning run-getter is not without its disadvantages and makes winning the County Championship exceedingly difficult.

Even before their success of the 1970s, the county seemed to be dominated by all-rounders. Astill and Geary were the two major figures of the inter-war period, Astill being among the elite who have 20,000 runs and 2,000 wickets to their names. Jackson and Walsh were two Australians imported in the late 1930s who toiled long and hard for their adopted county in careers which spanned almost 20 years.

At the beginning of the 19th century Leicester vied with Nottingham and Sheffield as the principal centres of cricket away from the south east, but partially due to their small population, Leicester soon fell behind their two rivals and in the important formative years in the middle of the century lacked the catalyst, whom both Sheffield and Nottingham possessed, to create a viable county eleven. It was not until 1878/79 that county cricket in Leicester put its house in order, and though they gained some kudos in 1880 by arranging a

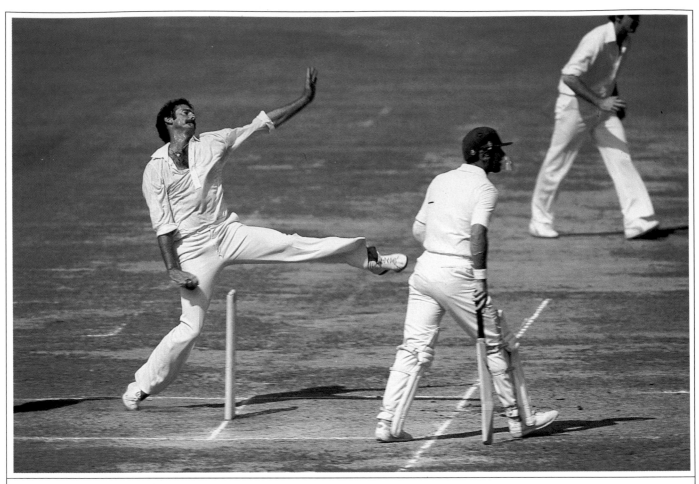

Dennis Lillee, the outstanding fast bowler of the 1970s, overcame back injuries to claim 355 Test victims, at the time a world record.

The pavilion at Lord's, the 'headquarters' of cricket. The current ground is on the third site chosen by Thomas Lord for his sacred turf.

The most successful of Test Match captains, Clive Lloyd, batting for the
West Indies at Lord's in 1984, when his side beat England 5-0 in the Test series.

fixture with the Australians when most of the other counties cold-shouldered the visitors, Leicestershire remained among the also-rans until the 1970s.

Length

The distance between the stumps and the place where the ball lands when bowled by the bowler. A 'good length' is an essential attribute of a successful bowler; the distance varies according to the speed at which the ball is delivered. (*see also* Blind spot).

Lillee, Dennis Keith

Born: 18 July 1949, Subiaco, Western Australia
Career: 184 *m*; 845 wkts (av 22.86)
Tests: 70 *m*; 355 wkts (av 23.92)

Lillee was the best fast bowler of his generation – he had an excellent action and an aggressive nature, which earned a record number of Test wickets, since exceeded by Botham. He first appeared for Western Australia when 20, and made his Test debut in 1970/71. His name will be linked with two other cricketers: Jeff Thomson, a fellow fast bowler, with whom he destroyed England in 1974/75 (the pair were sometimes known as 'Lilian Thomson'), and Rod Marsh, his Western Australian colleague and wicketkeeper, with whom he shared 95 Test wickets.

Lillee was a cricketer who courted trouble – trying to play with an aluminium bat and kicking Javed Miandad being two regrettable incidents. Another form of trouble, a back injury, he overcame splendidly. He helped make Australia the most powerful side of the mid-1970s, prior to World Series Cricket.

Lincolnshire

The present county club was formed in 1906 and joined the Minor Counties Competition the following year. The title was won for the only time in 1966 under the inspiring captaincy of R.N. Beeson, who also kept wicket exceptionally well. The side had a well-balanced attack with Norman McVicker, J.B. Evans and the old Somerset pro, Johnny Lawrence, all in good form. Martin Maslin topped the batting table.

Perhaps their other best season was back in 1909, when the competition was in four groups and Lincolnshire won the Eastern section with seven wins in ten games. The Rev C.G. Ward topped the batting and Riley took 40 wickets at 9.67 each to head the bowlers.

Lincolnshire have possessed many talented players, but in their early days lacked a strong county club, the one which began in 1906 was the fifth Lincolnshire County Cricket Club, and even that struggled in the years directly following the First World War, not returning to the Championship until 1924.

Lindwall, Raymond Russell

Born: 3 October, 1921, Mascot, NSW, Australia
Career: 228 *m*; 5,042 runs (av 21.82); 794 wkts (av 21.35)
Tests: 61 *m*; 1,502 runs (av 21.15); 228 wkts (av 23.03)

Lindwall was the outstanding fast bowler of the days following the Second World War. Like Larwood, he was not a tall man, and he achieved his mastery by virtue of a perfect sideways-on action.

He was 20 when he made his debut for New South Wales, and began his Test career when international cricket resumed after the Second World War. He was immediately successful, and in 1948 took 27 Test wickets in England, including 6 for 20 when England were dismissed for 52 at the Oval. He was equally successful in a losing side in England in 1953. Strangely, for such a great bowler, he never took more than seven wickets in an innings.

Lindwall, who captained Australia once, was a good lower-order batsman, with a highest score of 134 not out, and two Test Match centuries.

Lloyd, Clive Hubert

Born: 31 August, 1944, Georgetown, British Guiana
Career: 490 *m*; 31,232 runs (av 49.26)
Tests: 110 *m*; 7,515 runs (av 46.67)

Lloyd was the captain of West Indies who shaped a collection of talented individuals into the most powerful cricket team of recent times.

His debut was for British Guiana (which became Guyana) in 1963/64, and his first Test came three years later. His tall, bespectacled figure became known on cricket grounds all over the world. He was a very aggressive, hard-hitting, left-handed middle-order batsman who could destroy a bowler with his long reach and powerful shots. At first he was a good right-arm change bowler, but bowled less as his career progressed. He was always a good fielder, but in his early days, before knee injuries, he was outstanding, prowling in the covers and throwing with speed and accuracy.

In 1968 he began playing regularly for Lancashire, whom he captained, and in 1974/75 he took over the West Indies captaincy. In all he captained West Indies 74 times in Tests, a record, and won 36 of them. His captaincy was sometimes criticised for using the intimidatory nature of his fast bowling battery to excess, but he obtained results.

He played many spectacular innings, particularly in one-day games (his century in the first World Cup final was outstanding). He made 19 Test centuries, the highest (and his career highest) being 242 not out against India in 1974/75.

Lob

A type of delivery used by a slow underarm bowler. This mode of delivery has vanished from first-class cricket. The last exponent of the art in the English Test team was G.H.T. Simpson-Hayward, who also played for Cambridge University and Worcestershire, his best season being 1908.

Long field

The area of the cricket field which is nearer to the boundary than to the pitch itself. Fielders are therefore described as 'long-off' i.e. near the boundary behind the bowler but on the off side, similarly 'long-on'. 'Long-leg' is near the boundary on the leg side behind the wicketkeeper, and 'long-stop', now not much used, is directly behind the wicketkeeper.

Lord's

Considered as the world headquarters of cricket, the ground is named after its founder, Thomas Lord. A Yorkshireman, he moved to London in the 1770s, and during the following decade was general factotum to the White Conduit Cricket Club, which played in the Islington area of London. In 1786 the Earl of Winchelsea and Charles Lennox (later 4th Duke of Richmond), who were members of the club, suggested that Lord should lay out a new ground for their use and in the following year the first matches were played on Lord's ground on the Portman Estate (now Dorset Square). This ground remained in use until 1810, when it was taken for building, Lord having secured the lease of some land on the St John's Wood Estate. Lord moved the turf to this new ground but in 1812 Parliament decreed that the Regent's Canal should be routed through this site and Lord was forced to move a second time. This was to the present site, the first match being played there in 1814.

In 1825, Lord determined to build houses on part of the ground, but William Ward, a noted cricketer and member of the Marylebone Cricket Club, who used the ground as their headquarters, bought out Lord, thus saving the venue.

The original pavilion on the ground, which was erected by Lord, was burnt down in 1825. A new pavilion was erected for the following year and was extended in 1865, and the foundation stone of the present pavilion was laid in 1889.

Until 1877, the ground was used only by the MCC, but in that year Middlesex CCC moved there and from that season, Lord's has been home to both clubs.

The first Test Match was staged on the ground in 1884, against Australia, since when one Test in every series played in England has been played there, a unique distinction.

Lord's was the headquarters of the Board of Control which was set up in 1899 and has remained the centre for the various bodies which have been formed to administer cricket in the United Kingdom since then.

The finals of the NatWest Trophy and the Benson & Hedges Cup are played there annually and the present ground capacity is about 25,000.

Lunch intervals

In the 18th century intervals for 'dinner' were usually between 2.00 and 3.00. Before the 19th century was out 'dinner' had become 'luncheon', but it is only in recent years in England that the interval has been standardised to begin at 1.15 for most matches, and 1.00 for Tests.

(Tea intervals were not introduced as common practice until about 1910. Prior to this it was not uncommon for tea to be taken on to the field, in the same way now adopted for 'drinks'. However in the 19th century intervals between innings were very variable and could stretch to half-an-hour, rather than the standard 10 minutes now so carefully measured.)

M

McCabe, Stanley Joseph

Born: 16 July 1910, Grenfell, NSW, Australia
Died: 25 August 1968, Mosman, NSW, Australia
Career: 182 *m*; 11,951 runs (av 49.38); 159 wkts (av 33.72)
Tests: 39 *m*; 2,748 runs (av 48.21); 36 wkts (av 42.86)
McCabe was a brilliant middle-order batsman, and a useful medium-pace bowler. Perfectly balanced, he could play all the attacking strokes, and was at ease against all bowling, but was particularly good against the fastest. Of medium height and very strong, he could drive and hook equally impressively.

McCabe is particularly remembered for two of the greatest Test innings of all time. He made 187 not out against England in 1932/33, the highest score against the 'bodyline' tourists, and at Trent Bridge in 1938 against England he made 232 out of 411, including 72 out of 77 added for the last wicket. It was said that Bradman told his team they would never see such a fine innings again.

McDonald's Cup

Australia's major limited-overs competition is a knock-out competition between the six first-class states. Innings are limited to 50 overs per side. The competition has had three previous sponsors, namely V&G in 1969/70 and 1970/71, Coca-Cola in 1971/72 and 1972/73, and Gillette from 1973/

74 to 1978/79, since when it has been sponsored by McDonald's. The winners have been as follows:

1969/70	New Zealand	1978/79	Tasmania
1970/71	Western Australia	1979/80	Victoria
1971/72	Victoria	1980/81	Queensland
1972/73	New Zealand	1981/82	Queensland
1973/74	Western Australia	1982/83	Western Australia
1974/75	New Zealand	1983/84	South Australia
1975/76	Queensland	1984/85	New South Wales
1976/77	Western Australia	1985/86	Western Australia
1977/78	Western Australia		

New Zealand's national side took part in the competition until 1974/75.

Madras

The first first-class match was staged on the Chepauk ground in 1915/16 and this ground was the home of Madras Cricket Club from 1861. One of the best appointed grounds in India it has been the headquarters of Tamil Nadu since the 1960s and is now known as the Chidambaram Stadium. The first Test Match was played there in 1933/34 when India played England. In 1955/56 Test Matches began to be played on the Corporation Ground, Madras, but this change of venue for international matches was of only brief duration and Tests soon returned to the Chepauk ground.

Stan McCabe (right) walking out to bat in a Test Match with Don Bradman.
McCabe played some innings that even Bradman could not have bettered.

Part of the stand at the Chepauk ground, Madras, during the Third Test between India and England in 1976/77.

A magnificent catch by Rod Marsh. Tony Greig is caught off Gary Gilmour's bowling in a 1975 Prudential World Cup match.

Magazines

Three monthly cricket magazines command wide circulation in England in the 1980s. The oldest is *The Cricketer*, founded in 1921 by Pelham Warner and originally issued weekly during the season. The present chairman and managing director is B.G. Brocklehurst, the former Somerset amateur, and the editor is Christopher Martin-Jenkins, the cricket commentator. *Wisden Cricket Monthly*, founded by David Frith in 1979, is edited by its founder. The magazine concentrates very largely on Test and first-class cricket, whereas *The Cricketer* also gives space to club, league and school cricket in England. The third monthly is *The Club Cricketer*, founded by A. Symondson and M. Blumberg in 1983 and edited by them. This magazine gives wide coverage to league and club cricket in the British Isles.

The first magazine devoted entirely to cricket was simply entitled *Cricket* and founded by the secretary of Surrey, C.W. Alcock. It came out weekly during the season and monthly in the winter, from 1882 to 1914, though latterly under new management and a change of title.

Australia, South Africa, New Zealand and Pakistan also issue cricket magazines which appear usually monthly during the season.

Maiden

An over from which no runs have been hit off the bowler. In 1985 an additional stipulation was added that the over was not regarded as a 'maiden' if any wides or no-balls were conceded by the bowler. The most maidens bowled in succession in a single innings of a first-class match are 23 by Alfred Shaw for North v South at Trent Bridge in 1876. At this time four-ball overs were used.

Malaysia

Having failed to win a match in the ICC Trophy competition in either 1979 or 1982, Malaysia won three out of six games in 1986, so there would appear to be some improvement in the country's cricket over recent years.

The first inter-state match, Perak v Penang, was played in 1884, but for many years the major fixture was the three-day game, Malay States v Crown Colony. The country was particularly rich in talent in the 1930s, with several first-class county cricketers in residence. The Malaysian Cricket Association was formed in 1963, though Singapore formed a separate Association in 1965. Fairly regular tours have taken place, mainly from the Indian sub-continent, in recent years.

Marsh, Rodney William

Born: 11 November 1947, Armadale, Western Australia
Career: 258 *m*; 11,067 runs (av 31.35); 802 *ct*; 66 *st*
Tests: 96 *m*; 3,633 runs (av 26.51); 343 *ct*; 12 *st*
Marsh made his debut for Western Australia in 1968/69 as a batsman. He became a wicketkeeper, but his choice for Australia in 1970/71 was not universally approved. However, he went on to play a record 96 Tests for Australia, and his 355 Test victims is a world record.

Marsh was nicknamed 'Iron Gloves' at first because he kept dropping the ball; later he made some astonishing catches, particularly off his team-mate Lillee. Marsh played in all but one of Lillee's Tests, and caught 95 of Lillee's 355 Test wickets.

Marsh's left-handed middle-order batting declined as his keeping improved. He was the first Australian wicketkeeper to score a century against England – in the 1977 Centenary Test – but did little afterwards.

Marshall, Malcolm Denzil

Born: 18 April 1958, Pine, Barbados
Career: 229 *m*; 5,542 runs (av 21.73); 1,017 wkts (av 17.87)
Tests: 45 *m*; 953 runs (av 19.44); 215 wkts (av 21.57)
The equal of any of the recent West Indian fast bowlers, his career began with Barbados in 1977/78 and he gained his Test cap the following season, before joining Hampshire in 1979. His best season in county cricket was 1982 when he took 134 wickets (average 15.73), the most wickets taken in first-class cricket since 1968. He toured England with the West Indian sides of 1980 and 1984, topping the Test bowling averages in the latter year with 24 wickets (average 18.21). He has also made three tours to Australia, as well as visits to all the other Test-playing countries.

Marylebone Cricket Club

The Marylebone Cricket Club a private cricket club, which own and have their headquarters at Lord's Cricket Ground in St John's Wood, London. The membership of the Club is about 18,000, but there are some 10,000 candidates on the waiting list.

The exact year of the foundation of MCC is not known. Lord's ground (q.v.) was first opened in 1787 and the players who had been known as the 'White Conduit Club' moved to the ground, and being in Marylebone the club seems to have merely adopted a change of name to Marylebone Cricket Club. Unfortunately few details of either the White Conduit Club, or the Marylebone Club, exist for the period 1770 to 1800. The fire which destroyed the Lord's pavilion in 1825 is presumed to have also burnt all the relevant documents.

The MCC began to revise the Laws in 1788 (see under Laws) and remain the authority on this subject. During the late 19th and early 20th century the club gradually became involved in the running of cricket in England at a national and county level and this administrative function continued until the formation of the Cricket Council in the 1960s.

The club until the First World War used to employ a large staff of professional cricketers and play matches against many of the first-class counties as well as the minor counties and numerous club games; between the wars the club played annually about 12 first-class games and over 150 other matches, but since the Second World War the number of first-class games has slowly dropped to two or three per season, although the number of club games remains high. The number of professionals employed has also dropped. From 1903 to the 1970s the club also organised the major English overseas tours, but this old tradition has now changed, though MCC still run pioneering tours to non-Test playing countries, which are in themselves extremely valuable.
(*see also* Administration)

May, Peter Barker Howard

Born: 31 December 1929, Reading, Berkshire
Career: 388 *m*; 27,592 runs (av 51.00)
Tests: 66 *m*; 4,537 runs (av 46.77)

Peter May, England's first great batsman to emerge after the Second World War, showing typical easy mastery against Middlesex. J.T. Murray is the wicketkeeper.

May was the most talented English batsman to emerge after the Second World War. A brilliant schoolboy, he made 146 for Public Schools at Lord's when 17, played for Surrey and Cambridge University in 1950, and made his debut for England in 1951, scoring 138 in his first Test innings. He captained Surrey at the end of their record-breaking run of seven Championships in the 1950s, and captained England 41 times.

May was a fine stroke-maker all round the wicket, particularly strong with his on-side driving. His highest score was 285 not out for England against West Indies at Edgbaston in 1957, when he and Cowdrey put on 411, England's highest partnership, and finally conquered Ramadhin.

Business and ill-health cut short May's career (he was

forced to return from the tour to the West Indies in 1958/59), but he became chairman of selectors and a leading administrator.

MCC
see Marylebone Cricket Club

Medium-pace bowlers
These workhorses of the game are an essential part of any team, the bowlers who hold the batsmen whilst the fast men build another head of steam on the days when there is nothing in the wicket for the spinners.

William Lillywhite, who played for Sussex, is reputed to be

Malcolm Marshall, who came to the fore in the mid-1980s as the latest in West Indies' line of magnificent fast bowlers.

Huge crowds watch cricket at the Melbourne Cricket Ground.
This match is during the series for the World Championship of Cricket in 1984/85.

the pioneer of medium-pace 'length bowling', though by the time his career ended in the 1850s – Lillywhite was then over 60 – he was essentially a slow bowler. His nephew, James Lillywhite junior, assumed the title of England's medium-pacer in the 1860s and like his uncle he had a very long career. Just as Jim Lillywhite's career was drawing to a close, Dick Attewell took his place and proceeded to bore out batsmen for two decades. His teasing command of length, pegging away just on or outside the off stump, irritated even the most patient of men. His contemporaries, Johnny Briggs and George Lohmann, though also coming into the broad category of medium pace, put more work on the ball. Lohmann of Surrey tragically died at the age of 36 after being ill for a number of years, but from about 1885 to 1895 he was considered one of the most difficult bowlers in England. Whilst he possessed the 'length' of Attewell he also moved the ball in the air as well as on the ground. 'Boy' Briggs, the Lancashire left-hander, also died young. Somewhat slower than Lohmann, he was forever experimenting.

Australia possessed Charley Turner, who was faster than medium pace, but despite his title as the 'Terror' was not regarded as a fast bowler. His forte was the ability to make the ball nip off the wicket, and with Spofforth he gave the early Australian sides of the 1870s and 1880s a pair of very effective bowlers, backed up by George Palmer, whose pace was more akin to Briggs'.

Hugh Trumble, who succeeded these Australians, was in the Attewell mould and from 1893 to 1902 in successive visits to England picked up over 100 wickets on each trip. By the turn of the century however England had found a bowler of unique stature in S.F. Barnes. Somewhat over medium pace he had the ability to combine swing with movement off the wicket and of course possessed the nagging length.

Unlike many players, Maurice Tate, who was England's and Sussex's most reliable bowler in the 1920s, began as a spinner and then not being over-successful switched to brisk medium and soon found himself among the wickets. He was an ideal man to take advantage of any morning atmosphere with his ability to move the ball late. His successor in this was Alec Bedser, who carried the England attack in the first post-Second World War years. In between the two however came Bill Bowes, who was faster in his early years but latterly of medium pace. Many would rank Bowes as the equal of Barnes, but the Yorkshireman was not given as much opportunity as was his due in Test cricket and lost a vital six years during the Second World War. Australia's answer to Bedser was Alan Davidson, though the latter was left-arm and somewhat quicker, but not of the pace of the genuine fast bowlers of the Lindwall and Miller variety. In English county cricket, the medium-pacer was much in evidence: Cliff Gladwin of Derbyshire and Derek Shackleton of Hampshire were two who gained occasional England caps, whilst bowling thousands of overs in the first-class game.

The advent of one-day cricket has been a boon to the miserly medium-pace merchant, with runs being more important than wickets. Mike Hendrick of Derbyshire, and briefly of Notts, was the great master of the art of runlessness and there are several present-day bowlers not much behind him.

Two medium-pace bowlers who are 'loners' but whose names stand out are Tom Wass, the exponent of fast leg breaks using a natural action which was unique and baffled most Edwardian cricketers, and the left-arm medium pace spinner of the present day, Derek Underwood. His methods are as individual as those Wass employed and he continues to capture wickets at a cheap rate, and would no doubt hold many Test records but for his three years with the Packer World Series Cricket.

(*see also* Fast bowlers, Slow bowlers and individual cricketers' entries)

Melbourne

The Melbourne Cricket Ground, generally referred to as the MCG, was the scene of the first ever Test Match in March 1877. The Melbourne Cricket Club moved to this ground in 1853. Victoria have played most of their home matches on the ground since first meeting New South Wales in 1855/56, and twice the Victorians have scored in excess of 1,000 runs in a single innings on the ground, the record being 1,107 against New South Wales in 1926/27.

The ground has a capacity of 130,000 and was used as a venue for many of the events in the 1956 Olympics. The finals of the main Australian Rules Football competition are also staged on the ground. A total of 350,534 people attended the Third Test between England and Australia in 1936/37, this being a record for Australia, as is the single day's attendance figure of 90,800 set during the second day of the Fifth Test between Australia and West Indies in 1960/61.

Floodlights, reputed to cost £3 million, were installed on the ground in 1985 for the World Championship of Cricket, a series of one-day internationals arranged to celebrate the founding of Victoria 150 years earlier.

Middlesex

The modern county club was conceived in the back garden of the Walker family at Arnos Grove some 120 or so years ago, and for a dozen seasons they wandered around the outskirts of London with a troupe of talented amateur batsmen, who rarely all came together in a single eleven, and a pair of professional bowlers. In 1861, 1862 and 1863 the county was homeless; in 1864 they played at the Cattle Market in the Caledonian Road; in 1869 they were homeless once more; in 1871 they moved to Lillie Bridge, West Brompton; the following year found the county off Sloane Street and in 1877 Middlesex were given a niche at Lord's, where they have resided ever since.

The results Middlesex achieved in the Championship until the Second World War reflected the transient nature of their amateur talent. From the beginning until 1936 the Hearne family provided a good portion of the professional element, reinforced by two notable Australians, Jim Phillips and Albert Trott – he who struck the ball over the pavilion at Lord's. After the Walkers retired, the county were led by A.J. Webbe,

Gregor MacGregor, the Scottish rugby international and 'Plum' Warner, later the Grand Old Man of Lord's. MacGregor won the County Championship in 1903 and Warner in his last season of 1920.

By the end of the 1930s, Middlesex had acquired two bright young men, the Middlesex 'twins', Edrich and Compton, and in 1947 they piled one batting record upon another as Middlesex finally broke the stranglehold which the northern professionals had had on the Championship for 26 years.

They tied for the title in 1949, but after that came a long barren stretch. It was not to be broken until Mike Brearley used his mind-bending powers on the obviously gifted players, welding them into a match-winning unit. In 1975 Middlesex were beaten finalists in both Gillette and Benson & Hedges competitions; the following summer they captured the Championship. Phil Edmonds and Fred Titmus made the most of the dusty wickets which were the feature of that dry summer; Barlow, Featherstone, Mike Smith and Radley with Brearley provided the runs. That was only the beginning. As Gatting and Emburey matured, the team grew stronger. Brearley was able to retire in September 1982, his OBE well deserved. In the 1980s the team had obtained seven titles by 1986 and vied with Essex as the most proficient county of the decade. They are fortunate in that they have happened upon, as their main overseas player, a West Indian bowler whose considerable talent has been largely ignored by his country – Wayne Daniel. But Middlesex also possess some second-line players capable of filling the gaps created by the Test selectors. The 1980s are the finest years in Middlesex history.

Midnight cricket

The Orient liner *Lusitania* took a cruise party to Spitzbergen in August 1894 and on 12 August at midnight, by the light of the midnight sun, a cricket pitch was set up on deck. Alfred Shaw, the England bowler, bowled out about all the male passengers and ship's officers, some 40 in all, in the space of about three quarters of an hour.

Mid-off/mid-on

Mid-off is a fielding position on the off side between cover and the bowler; similarly mid-on is placed in the same position but on the leg side. Variations for both these positions are silly mid-on and deep mid-on, the former being closer to the batsman than mid-on and the latter further away.

Mid-wicket

A fielding position on the leg side between square leg and mid-on, but until the inter-world war period mid-wicket was used as a shortened form of mid-wicket on (i.e. mid-on).

Miller, Keith Ross

Born: 28 November 1919, Sunshine, Victoria, Australia
Career: 226 m; 14,183 runs (av 48.90); 497 wkts (av 22.30)
Tests: 55 m; 2,958 runs (av 36.97); 170 wkts (av 22.97)
Miller was not only a brilliant all-rounder, he was a tall man who played his cricket in a extrovert manner. He made his debut for Victoria in 1937/38, but soon after the war switched to New South Wales. After playing for the

Keith Miller cuts a ball past Evans and Edrich during the Third Test at Sydney in 1951.

Australian Services XI in England after the war, he made his Test debut in 1945/46.

At first, Miller's powerful middle-order batting was his main strength, but Bradman used him for Australia as a fast bowler. Although he had an excellent action, he would bowl off long or short runs according to how he felt, and with a liberal use of bouncers. He sometimes slipped in a leg-break or off-break. He was a brilliant fielder, with the knack of making things happen.

Miller made seven Test centuries, the highest 147 against West Indies in 1953/55. His best Test bowling, 7 for 60, was against England at Brisbane in 1946/47. After retiring, he became a journalist.

Minor Counties Championship

The Minor Counties Cricket Association was founded in 1895 and a Championship started that year. All non-first-class counties were eligible plus all second elevens of the first-class counties. Prior to this, from 1888 to 1893, there had been a competition for second-class counties, but this ended when the main competing counties were granted first-class status in 1894.

The early years of the Minor Counties Championship were dominated by Worcestershire (until granted first-class status in 1899) and Northants, who were elevated in 1905. Between 1930 and 1970 the first-class counties' second elevens more often than not were the leading teams, notably Yorkshire, Lancashire and Surrey, but the creation of the Second Eleven Championship has caused the first-class counties to withdraw one by one, until in 1986 only Somerset remained. Of recent years Durham have been the strongest county, but in 1986 the tables were turned when Cumberland, so often one of the also-rans, were proclaimed champions.

(*see also* entries for individual counties)

Moin-Ud-Dowlah Gold Cup

This knock-out tournament was held in various forms between 1927/28 and 1978/79. It is however regarded as a first-class competition only from 1930/31 to 1937/38 and 1962/63 to 1973/74.

An invitation competition, the principal matches in the 1930s were staged between teams raised by various Indian rulers. In the 1960s and 1970s a number of the teams were sponsored by commercial undertakings. The matches were originally played at Secunderabad, but latterly in neighbouring Hyderabad, when they were organised by the Hyderabad Cricket Association.

N

National Cricket Association

The National Cricket Association (NCA) was set up in 1968 as an organisation to represent cricket clubs and cricketers at all but first-class level in English cricket, and consists of representatives from 51 county cricket associations and another 17 national cricketing organisations. J.D. Robson is the chairman, B.J. Aspital the secretary and the former Northants and England wicketkeeper, K.V. Andrew, is director of coaching.

(*see also* Administration)

NatWest Bank Trophy

The first major limited-overs competition involving the English first-class counties, this tournament of 60 overs per side was sponsored by Gillette Industries from its start in 1963 to 1980, during which time it was called the Gillette Cup. Since then it has been sponsored by the NatWest Bank under the current name. The competition is between 32 teams, namely the 17 first-class counties, Scotland, Ireland and the 13 leading minor counties. The winners have been:

1963 Sussex	1968 Warwickshire	1973 Gloucestershire
1964 Sussex	1969 Yorkshire	1974 Kent
1965 Yorkshire	1970 Lancashire	1975 Lancashire
1966 Warwickshire	1971 Lancashire	1976 Northamptonshire
1967 Kent	1972 Lancashire	1977 Middlesex

1978 Sussex	1981 Derbyshire	1984 Middlesex
1979 Somerset	1982 Surrey	1985 Essex
1980 Middlesex	1983 Somerset	1986 Sussex

The most exciting final occurred in 1981. Derbyshire required seven to win at the start of the final over. G. Miller hit two off the first ball and a single off the second. No runs came off the third, but Tunnicliffe scored one off the fourth, Miller hit one off the fifth, thus two were needed off the final ball to overtake the Northants total of 235. Tunnicliffe could only hit a single and the scores being tied, the destination of the Trophy had to be decided on fewest wickets lost. Derbyshire having only lost six to Northants' nine, were thus declared the winners.

Nets

In 1845 'Felix on the Bat' advocated: 'The way to secure much practice off either a professional bowler or a catapult is to procure a large net about twenty yards long and six feet in height.' In 1850, R. Richardson of New Road, London, was advertising 'cricket nets' for sale. Within a few years the idea of having side nets as well as a back net was introduced, and also the logical extension, a series of 'nets' side by side. 'Practice nets' at Eton were in use as early as 1840.

The use of large barns for practice during the winter months was also in vogue by the middle of the 19th century, and by the end of the century 'indoor nets', as they are known today, had been in use for some years.

New South Wales
Having won the Sheffield Shield 37 times, New South Wales can boast a supremacy over the other Australian states. The title was won six times in succession, commencing 1901/02, but this record was beaten with a run of nine titles starting in 1953/54.

The Edwardian team was perhaps the strongest ever assembled. The renowned Victor Trumper was aided by M.A. Noble, R.A. Duff, C.G. Macartney, Warren Bardsley and Syd Gregory. Between the wars came Bill O'Reilly and Arthur Mailey. The great team of the 1950s included Richie Benaud, Alan Davidson, Norman O'Neill and Bobby Simpson.

New South Wales played their first first-class match against Victoria in March 1856; there is some confusion over the date on which the New South Wales Cricket Association was established, either 1857 or 1859 being suggested, but either way it was a much better organised body than that in Victoria. The great dynasty of the early years was the Gregorys – five Gregory brothers represented the colony, as well as other members of the clan, the second generation producing the famous fast bowler, J.M. Gregory, among others.

Don Bradman played his early cricket for New South Wales and Keith Miller left Victoria to join New South Wales in 1947/48.

New Zealand
For long under the shadow of Australia, New Zealand have emerged in the 1980s as a major force on the scene of international cricket; this transformation has been due to the brilliant all-round cricket of Richard Hadlee, but credit must also go to several other players who gained valuable experience in English county cricket, notably Glenn Turner, John Wright and Geoff Howarth.

Although first-class matches began in New Zealand with the match between Otago and Canterbury in 1863/64, it was not until 1902/03 that an English touring team opposed any New Zealand side on even terms and the first New Zealand tour to England did not take place until 1927. There were, however, fairly frequent visits by Australian sides to New Zealand, Tasmania in 1883/84 being the first such to play first-class matches.

The Plunket Shield (q.v.) – a challenge competition between the major New Zealand cricket associations – began in 1906/07. It was literally a challenge trophy until 1921/22, when the cricket associations were formed into a league. The Plunket Shield (named after Lord Plunket, a Governor-General of New Zealand) ended in 1974/75, when this main domestic competition was altered to the Shell Series (being sponsored by the Shell Oil Company).

New Zealand was elevated to Test Match status in 1929/30 when four matches were played between a representative New Zealand eleven and the MCC touring side; the only other Test team to oppose New Zealand before the Second World War were South Africa. Australia, apart from a single match in 1945/46, did not play New Zealand at Test level until 1973/74.

The present first-class sides in New Zealand are Auckland, Canterbury, Central Districts, Northern Districts, Otago and Wellington and apart from their first-class competition, they also compete in the limited-overs Shell Cup, which under various sponsors has been running since 1971/72.

Of all their great achievements in the 1980s, the proudest must be the winning of the 1986 series of Test Matches in England, but immediately prior to this New Zealand beat Australia in two successive series, at home and away, and have also made their mark in one-day internationals.
(see also the succeeding entries, and Australia v New Zealand, England v New Zealand, South Africa v New Zealand, West Indies v New Zealand, and individual entries for cricketers, competitions and grounds)

New Zealand v India
Results: Played 25; New Zealand won 4; India won 10; Drawn 11
There have been seven series between the two countries of which only the last saw New Zealand successful. This was in New Zealand in 1980/81, when India toured under Gavaskar. The series consisted of three matches and was played following India's tied series against Australia. The First Test took place at Wellington, and due to a century from Geoff Howarth, the home captain, and then 5 for 33 by Cairns, New Zealand gained a substantial first-innings lead. In the second innings, however, New Zealand's main batting collapsed before the seam bowling of Kapil Dev and then Shastri wiped out the tail. India required 253 for victory, but some excellent bowling by Richard Hadlee, who had been out of sorts in the first innings, took New Zealand to a 62-run win. Rain prevented even a first-innings completion in the Second Test at Christchurch, though New Zealand had the advantage in what play did occur. The Kiwis also held the upper hand in the Third Test; gaining a first-innings lead of 128, they required 157 in the last innings in 243 minutes. Rain, however, caused a delay and though Hadlee was promoted in the order to get some quick runs, he failed and the score was a modest 95 for 5 when bad light ended the match.

The first series was played in India in 1955/56 as was the second nine years later. New Zealand failed to win a match in either, their first victory coming on India's initial tour in 1967/68. It was a tour of contrasts in that India looked frail against the New Zealand seam attack headed by Motz, whereas New Zealand struggled against the spinners, notably Prasanna and Bedi. The First Test was won by India, but in the Second, Dowling hit 239, enabling his side to reach 502 and India were forced to follow on, when Motz took 6 for 63, New Zealand eventually winning by six wickets. The New Zealand batting failed in four successive innings – none exceeded 200 – and India thus won the Third and Fourth Tests and the series three to one.

Two years later under the same captains, the Nawab of Pataudi and Dowling, the teams met in India, New Zealand going there on their way home from the 1969 tour of England. Prasanna and Bedi again bowled New Zealand out cheaply in the First Test at Bombay, but in the Second at Nagpur, Hedley Howarth returned the compliment, taking 9 for 100, and New Zealand won by 167 runs. New Zealand deserved to win the Third Test. India were dismissed for 89 by Dayle Hadlee and Cunis, but a cyclone washed out one complete day and a riot also interrupted play. Then on the final day rain caused a stoppage and the umpires seemed very

Edmonds and Emburey batting in the dusk near the end of the NatWest

final at Lord's in 1984, in which Middlesex beat Kent by four wickets.

reluctant to resume the match. The spectators threatened another riot and the army arrived with tear gas equipment. No further play took place.

The other two series, one in each country, found Glenn Turner opposed to Bishan Bedi. The 1975/76 series in New Zealand was tied, one match each. Prasanna once more proved New Zealand's undoing, taking 11 wickets in the First Test and giving India victory by eight wickets. After a drawn game at Christchurch, Richard Hadlee, also with 11 wickets, provided New Zealand with their victory.

The following season in India, Bedi and Chandrasekhar were too much for the New Zealand batsmen, and two of the three matches provided India with easy wins, while the other game was drawn, time alone saving New Zealand.

New Zealand v Pakistan

Results: Played 27; New Zealand won 3; Pakistan won 10; drawn 14

New Zealand achieved the first of only two successful series in 1969/70 in Pakistan: this was in fact the first time New Zealand had won a Test series against any country. In the first two Tests, Pakistan ruined any chances they had by scoring at a very slow pace. Mushtaq managed 59 runs in six hours spread over his four innings and after a draw at Karachi, New Zealand deservedly won the Second Test at Lahore by five wickets, by what was very much a team effort – no 'five wickets in an innings' and no individual hundreds.

The Pakistani batsmen scored with more rapidity in the Third Test, but Glenn Turner spent over seven hours collecting 110 runs and Burgess hit a bright hundred in New Zealand's second innings, so Pakistan needed 184 to win in 150 minutes. They had given up the chase when play ended early due to a combination of crowd trouble and rain.

New Zealand's other series success was in 1984/85, when they beat Pakistan at Eden Park, Auckland by an innings – John Reid made 158 not out, whilst Richard Hadlee, Cairns and Chatfield shared the wickets – and clinched the series at Dunedin with a two-wicket win, due to a final unbroken ninth wicket stand of 50 by Coney and Chatfield. The remaining Test was drawn.

The New Zealand victory in this series came as a surprise, since Pakistan had beaten New Zealand earlier in the same season, in Pakistan, by two matches to nil. Richard Hadlee was absent from this series, but Pakistan's great batsman, Zaheer Abbas, failed completely, so balanced out Hadlee's absence to an extent. The best batting of the series came from Javed Miandad, who scored a century in both innings at Hyderabad in the Second Test. After losing the first and second games, New Zealand derived some comfort from gaining first-innings lead in the drawn Third Test. The Pakistani umpiring came in for some criticism.

Two curiosities in the matches between the two countries: in 1969/70 three of the Mohammad brothers appeared in the same Test – Hanif, Mushtaq and Sadiq, and in the 1976/77 Test at Hyderabad Mushtaq and Sadiq both hit hundreds in the same innings, a feat by brothers in Tests only previously achieved by the Australian Chappells.

New Zealand v Sri Lanka

Results: Played 5; New Zealand won 4; Drawn 1
One series has been played in each country. D.S. de Silva led

Sri Lanka to New Zealand in 1982/83, when the visitors' batting failed in all four innings and they lost both Tests, the first by an innings and the second by six wickets.

Richard Hadlee dominated the 1983/84 series in Sri Lanka, taking 23 wickets at ten runs each in the three-match series. New Zealand won the First and Third Tests with the Second being drawn due to some slow play by Sri Lanka (both batting and bowling) and poor fielding by New Zealand.

Nightwatchman

A term used to describe a player who normally comes in to bat near the end of an innings, but is sent in just prior to the end of the day's play in order to save a better player for the morning.

There are several examples of nightwatchmen, even in Test cricket, staying the following day to hit a large score, one of the most remarkable being A.L. Mann of Australia, who hit 105 against India at Perth in 1977/78.

Nissan Shield

The major limited-overs competition in South Africa is played between the leading sides on a knock-out system with 55 overs. Nissan have been the sponsors since the 1983/84 season; prior to this the competition was sponsored by Gillette from 1969/70 to 1976/77 and Datsun from 1977/78 to 1982/83. The winners have been:

1969/70 Western Province	1978/79 Transvaal
1970/71 Western Province	1979/80 Transvaal
1971/72 Eastern Province	1980/81 Transvaal
1972/73 Western Province	1981/82 Western Province
1973/74 Transvaal	1982/83 Transvaal
1974/75 Natal	1983/84 Transvaal
1975/76 Eastern Province	1984/85 Transvaal
1976/77 Natal	1985/86 Transvaal
1977/78 Rhodesia	

No-ball

A delivery by the bowler which is declared illegal by the umpire, who is instructed to shout 'No-ball' immediately in order to allow the batsman to hit out at it, since the bowler cannot dismiss a batsman with such a delivery save by a run out, by 'hit ball twice', by 'handled ball', or 'obstructing field'.

The umpire can call 'no-ball' for the following reasons:
1 The bowler changes his mode of delivery without notice.
2 The bowler throws, rather than bowls the ball.
3 The bowler's foot or feet are beyond specified positions related to the creases.
4 If the bowler throws the ball at the wicket in an attempt to run out the striking batsman.
5 If the wicketkeeper or any of the fieldsmen are breaking the Laws relating to their position in the field.

If the striker hits a no-ball, then any runs made are credited to him; if no runs are made, the one no-ball is credited to the 'extras' (q.v.). The no-ball does not count in the bowler's over and he is obliged to deliver an additional ball to make up the required number.

Until recently a no-ball which was not hit for runs was not debited to the bowler in his analysis, but nowadays it is.

'No-ball' – the umpire at Port of Spain, Trinidad, signals a no-ball as Colin Croft fires a bouncer at Brian Rose in the First Test, West Indies v England, 1980/81.

Norfolk

The first county club was founded in 1827, and by the early 1830s, Norfolk were strong enough to play Yorkshire on even terms and were regarded as one of the best cricketing counties in England. At that time they possessed in Fuller Pilch England's most promising young batsman. By 1848 however the county club had collapsed, and Pilch had long since vanished to Kent. The present club was not formed until 1876. Founder members of the Minor Counties Championship, they tied for first place in 1895 and were one of the leading clubs in the first years of the present century. One of their best years was 1910 when they carried off the title, due to the all-round cricket of the Rev G.B. Raikes, who hit 679 runs, averaging 61.72, and took 57 wickets at 10.66 runs each. The title was won again in 1913. They have not won the title since, but ought to have been champions in 1933, when they headed the table and owing to an extraordinary mix-up with the calculation of points were then challenged by the wrong county! The great strength of the team at this time were the Rought-Rought brothers, and of course, Michael Falcon, who had captained the side since 1912. Mention must be made of the Edrich clan, young Billy appearing in 1933, but of course their years of greatness lay with more exalted company.

Northamptonshire

A record of failing to win a match for four years in the Championship – May 1935 to May 1939 – is not one easily erased. Northamptonshire gained status as a first-class county in 1905 and after some years of modest endeavour took the cricket buffs by surprise in 1912 by coming second in the Championship. The season was quite without parallel since the enlarging of the Championship in 1895 in that Northants used 12, and only 12, players throughout the year. Nine appeared in every match, Vials missed two, whilst 'Fanny' Walden and Claude Woolley, brother of the more famous Frank, shared the last place. The credit for the success belonged to Northants' main bowlers, the left-arm spinner, S.G. Smith, and the fast bowler, G.J. Thompson.

Between the wars Northants were in the bottom half of the Championship every season; in 1946, 1947 and 1948 they continued their unfortunate sequence, being 16th, 17th and 17th. In 1949 the semi-retired Surrey amateur, F.R. Brown, was persuaded to accept the Northants captaincy and changed the team overnight. Brown himself completed the 'double' and Northants moved up from bottom to sixth place. With the aid of several overseas players, notably Tribe, Livingston and Manning, the 1950s were good years and in 1957 the team were second in the Championship. They have succeeded in taking second place on two more occasions since then, but Northants first trophy at last came in the Gillette Cup of 1976. They owed a great deal at this time to Mushtaq Mohammad, the captain, Bedi and Sarfraz, the odd feature of the 1976 side being that only one of 17 who appeared in Championship games was actually born in the county.

Northants repeated their one-day success in 1980 by winning the Benson & Hedges Cup under Jim Watts. In this latter success English players took a greater part, notably Wayne Larkins, Tim Lamb and Jim Griffiths, but the South African Allan Lamb topped the batting table. Any review of Northants cricket must point out that the traditional system of players' qualifications is heavily weighted against the county, because their population is smaller than any of the other 16 first-class counties': Lancashire and Yorkshire are over ten times as large.

Northern League

Formed only in 1952 by clubs which broke away from the Ribblesdale League, the Northern League's outstanding club is possibly Blackpool, who have had as professionals Rohan Kanhai and Bill Alley. In 1986 Blackpool had Tim Shaw, the South African left-arm slow bowler, who topped the bowling table, but only put Blackpool in second place in the League, behind Lancaster. The League spreads up into Cumberland with both Kendal and Netherfield coming from that county.

Northumberland

The well-appointed Jesmond ground is the home of the Northumberland Club, which organises annual matches bringing many first-class cricketers to that venue, and there is a desire for the ground to become the headquarters of the 18th first-class county.

The county's two greatest years were 1924 and 1925, in both of which they topped the Minor Counties table, but lost the Championship by being beaten in the challenge match. In these two seasons their principal bowlers were W. Hetherton, who took 91 wickets, average 9.25, in 1925, and G.T. Milne; the leading batsmen were the amateurs J.B. Bruce and C.F. Stanger-Leathes.

The present club was founded in 1895 and joined the Minor Counties in 1896.

Nottinghamshire

Through almost all the second half of the 19th century Nottinghamshire supplied English cricket with famous and not-so-famous professional talent. It is estimated that some 300 cricketers left their Nottinghamshire homes each season to be employed by counties, clubs and schools throughout the British Isles. The county club themselves reached the height of their powers in the 1880s, when they were champion county in seven out of ten years, and but for the famous strike of their seven best players in 1881, would have gained eight out of ten. In Shrewsbury and Shaw they possessed the best professional batsman and bowler of the decade, in Barnes and Flowers the best professional all-rounders. There came a period of adjustment round the turn of the century, but the county rose again and particularly in the 1920s and early 1930s were much respected, though only actually capturing the title in 1929. It was the era of Larwood and Voce, of George Gunn and A.W. Carr. The controversial 'bodyline' crisis caused problems between England and Australia, which are well-documented, but it also split Nottinghamshire in two.

The county's bowling strength fragmented within three or four years and remained weak in the immediate post-Second World War period. Relief came in the form of Bruce Dooland's leg-breaks, but these and the subsequent signing of Gary Sobers in the following decade brought no more than a temporary upsurge in the county's record. It was not until the triumvirate of Rice, Hadlee and cricket manager K.A. Taylor emerged in the late 1970s that Notts made any real impact on the four domestic competitions. Rice and Hadlee proved to be the equal of any all-rounder in English cricket. These two overseas players were joined by three local Notts-born cricketers, the mercurial Randall, Tim Robinson and Bruce French, plus the off-spinner from Warwickshire, Eddie Hemmings, and the Championship was won in 1981. The following year the Benson & Hedges final was reached and in 1985 the NatWest final.

Until 1951, the county had a self-imposed rule that only Notts-born men could appear in the eleven. After this was abandoned the pendulum swung completely the other way, but with little better results, despite the mass import of players. The 1970s saw a fresh attempt to train local cricketers to county standard and this has most certainly paid off, in spite of the same handicap as Northants – a relatively small population.

Nourse, Arthur Dudley

Born: 12 November 1910, Durban, South Africa
Died: 14 August 1981, Durban, South Africa
Career: 175 *m*; 12,472 runs (av 51.33)
Tests: 34 *m*; 2,960 runs (av 53.81)

Dudley Nourse was the son of South Africa's first great batsman, and he became a fine middle-order batsman himself. He was also a first-class fieldsman, and captained his country in three series.

Nourse was frequently the backbone of his country's batting, and developed a stubborn, fighting quality, never better shown than when he scored 208 against England at Trent Bridge in 1951, batting in pain with a fractured thumb. It was South Africa's first double century against England and led to their first win for 28 Tests. His highest Test score was 231 against Australia in 1935/36.

O

Obstructing the field

If a batsman wilfully obstructs a fielder by word or action he can be given out. The bowler is not credited with the wicket.

This dismissal is very rare and last occurred in England in first-class cricket when Khalid Ibadulla of Warwickshire was so given out against Hampshire at Coventry in 1963.

Oddities

Cricket has such a vast literature and has attracted such eccentrics that every aspect of the game has seen its odd happenings. Here are a few of them:

Odd average W.A. 'Bill' Johnston, the Australian fast-medium left-arm Test bowler, was such a rabbit with the bat that he was a regular number 11. However, on the tour of England in 1953, by virtue of being only once dismissed in 17 innings, he became one of the handful of batsmen ever to average over 100 in an English season: 102.00

Odd bat In the Test Match against England at Perth in 1979/80, Dennis Lillee, the Australian fast bowler, began his innings with an aluminium bat. England captain Brearley objected, he was ordered to change it by the umpire, refused, and caused a long stoppage before his captain, Greg Chappell, intervened and persuaded him of the error of his ways. The score card entry of Lillee's second innings was a minor oddity in itself: Lillee c Willey b Dilley.

Odd batting order When England played a Test against the West Indies at Bridgetown, Barbados, in 1934/35, the pitch was such a 'sticky' one that England declared at 81 for 7, 21 behind West Indies' 102. West Indies then declared at 51 for 6, setting England 73 to win. To use up time, hoping the pitch might dry out, England opened the batting with their fast bowlers, C.I.J. Smith and Ken Farnes. The great batsman Wally Hammond came in at number six, and the captain and opening batsman, R.E.S. Wyatt, came in at number eight. It worked. From 48 for 6 the two added 27 and saw England home by four wickets.

Odd burial When Harry Bagshaw, a Derbyshire all-rounder who became an umpire, died in 1927 he was buried wearing his umpire's coat, and with a cricket ball in his hand. His gravestone showed an umpire's raised finger, signifying 'out'.

Odd clothing George Brown, who played for Hampshire and Sussex in the early nineteenth century, bowled under-arm, but was so fast that nearly all his fielders were behind the wicket, and his wicketkeeper, Dench, would wear a sack stuffed with straw tied to his chest to prevent injury when stopping the ball.

Odd dismissal Laurie Fishlock, the Surrey opening batsman, playing against Kent at the Oval in 1938, jumped out to drive a no-ball, made contact, but his bat broke and the ball continued to the wicketkeeper, who caught it and broke the wicket. A batsman cannot be out caught or stumped from a no-ball, but Fishlock had to go – run out.

Odd eighter In 1986, playing for Notts against Essex, Clive Rice hit the ball nearly to the boundary and ran three, but dropped his bat in the process. The Essex bowler John Lever picked it up, and when the ball was returned from the boundary stopped it with Rice's bat. For fielding the ball with anything other than 'the person' the penalty is five runs, and Rice was therefore credited with an 'eight'.

Odd entry Abdul Aziz, playing in the final of the Qaid-I-Azam Trophy in Karachi in 1958/59 was injured in the first innings, the score card reading:

Abdul Aziz retired hurt . . . 0

He died, and his second innings entry reads:

Abdul Aziz did not bat, dead . . . 0

Odd obituary A black cat called Peter made Lord's his home for 12 years and could often be seen walking round the boundary at matches. When he died in 1964 his obituary appeared in *Wisden Cricketers' Almanack*.

Odd over Playing for Barbados against British Guiana in 1946, Everton Weekes was lbw to D.F. Hill from the fourteenth ball of an over in which there were no wides or no-balls. The eight-ball over was in force, and the extra six deliveries were due to the umpire miscounting.

Odd stoppage Opening for England in the Test against South Africa at Durban in 1922/23, soon after a large sheet covering the wicket had been removed, Andy Sandham was baffled by the strange squelchy pitch of the ball. Investigation revealed hundreds of tiny frogs on the wicket. Play was held up while staff removed them in buckets.

Odd tourist Edward Pooley, the Surrey wicketkeeper of the England touring party to Australia and New Zealand in 1876/77, won a large sum in New Zealand by betting a local he could forecast the score of each of the opposition's 22 batsmen (see entry under Gambling). The 'mug' would not pay, there was a scuffle and Pooley was arrested. When the first-ever Test Match was played in Australia, the England wicketkeeper was still in jail in New Zealand. Pooley was eventually acquitted and given a gold watch and £50 by embarrassed New Zealand cricket-lovers.

Off

The off side of the field as opposed to the leg side (*see* Leg for full explanation).

Off break

A delivery from the bowler which deviates on hitting the ground by moving from the off to the leg, hence 'off-break bowler'. This type of bowling in recent years has also been referred to as 'off spin'.

The pavilion at Old Trafford, the headquarters of the county club of Lancashire for over 120 years.

Old Trafford

The first provincial England ground to stage a Test Match (in 1884), Old Trafford is the headquarters of Lancashire County Cricket Club. The present ground was opened by the Manchester Gentleman's Cricket Club in 1857 and replaced one which was required for the 'Art Treasures Exhibition' and was also situated at Old Trafford. The Manchester Club established Lancashire County Cricket Club in 1864, and in 1880 the two clubs were merged forming the Lancashire County and Manchester Cricket Club. This title, officially, survived until 1957.

The present pavilion was erected in 1894. The largest attendance at a three-day county match is 78,617 at the Lancashire v Yorkshire game of 1926. The present seating capacity is about 20,000.

During the Second World War the ground was requisitioned and used for various purposes; it was also badly damaged by enemy action. The pavilion was substantially renovated when peace returned and there have been many additional improvements in recent years.

Oldest cricketers

The oldest player to take part in a first-class match was Raja Maharaj Singh who was believed to be 72 when he played for Bombay Governor's XI v Commonwealth in Bombay on 25, 26 and 27 November 1950. B. Aislabie was 67 years and 5 months when he turned out for the MCC v Cambridge University at Lord's on 1 and 2 July 1841; in the 20th century, Lord Harris was 60 years and 5 months when he appeared for Kent v India at Catford in 1911.

J. Marshall is believed to be the oldest Australian first-class cricketer, being 58 when he appeared for Tasmania v Victoria in 1853/54.

Oldfield, William Albert Stanley

Born: 9 September 1894, Alexandria, NSW, Australia
Died: 10 August 1976, Killara, NSW, Australia
Career: 245 *m*; 6,135 runs (av 23.77); 399 *ct*; 262 *st*
Tests: 54 *m*; 1,427 runs (av 22.65); 78 *ct*; 52 *st*
Bert Oldfield was regarded as the best wicketkeeper of his generation. After touring with the AIF (services) team after the First World War, he made his debut for New South Wales in 1919/20, and began his Test career the following year. Of his many tours, four were to England, and in 1926, 1930 and 1934 he was outstanding. He played in a period of great Australian spinners (Mailey, Grimmett, O'Reilly), hence the remarkable number of stumpings in his record. In 1924/25, he stumped England's Hobbs, Woolley, Chapman and Whysall, a record for a Test innings.

Oldfield was a good lower-order batsman. It was his being struck on the head by Larwood in 1932/33 that finally sparked off the 'bodyline' crisis (q.v.).

Olympic Games

The only time cricket was played in the Olympic Games was in 1900, when Great Britain, in the form of Devon County Wanderers, beat the only other entrants, France, by 262 runs to 104, on 20 August 1900 in Paris. The gold medallists were C.B.K. Beachcroft, John Symes, Frederick Cuming, Montague Toller, Alfred Bowerman, Alfred Powlesland, William Donne, Frederick Christian, George Buckley, Francis Burchall, and Harry Corner.

Toller and Bowerman played a few games for Somerset.

On

The 'on side' is another term for 'leg side' (see Leg for full explanation).

One-day internationals

When MCC toured Australia in 1970/71, the Third Test at Melbourne was abandoned without a ball being bowled, and on what would have been the fifth day of the match, a limited-overs match was played between England and Australia, or more strictly speaking MCC v Australia. This game is regarded as the first one-day international.

In England the one-day internationals between the touring teams and England began in 1972 when they were sponsored by Prudential. The matches are limited to 55 overs and consist of two matches in a series when two teams tour in one season and otherwise three matches. Since 1984 Texaco have taken over the sponsorship.

In Australia the Benson & Hedges World Cup Series has been staged each season since 1979/80 with two invited countries plus Australia taking part in a qualifying series of 15 matches, with a best-of-three final.

(see also Prudential World Cup and World Championship Cricket)

O'Reilly, William Joseph

Born: 20 December 1905, White Cliffs, NSW, Australia
Career: 135 *m*; 744 wkts (av 16.60)
Tests: 27 *m*; 144 wkts (av 22.59)

O'Reilly was perhaps the greatest of leg-break bowlers – although because his style was so individual, it is probably unreasonable to compare him with anybody else. He was tall, bowled quite quickly from flailing arms and extracted a lot of life from the pitch. His demeanour towards batsmen was as aggressive as that usually associated with fast bowlers, and he earned the nickname 'Tiger'.

He appeared first for New South Wales in 1927/28 and for Australia four years later. On his two tours to England in 1934 and 1938 he headed the Australian averages in both first-class and Test Matches. He played in one match after the Second World War, versus New Zealand, which was later classified as a Test Match, but the war came at the wrong time for his Test career. He became a journalist whose cricket writings are as respected as his bowling was.

Origins

In the absence of any documentary evidence stating where, when and by whom cricket was conceived, historians have wrung early references to the game from every possible

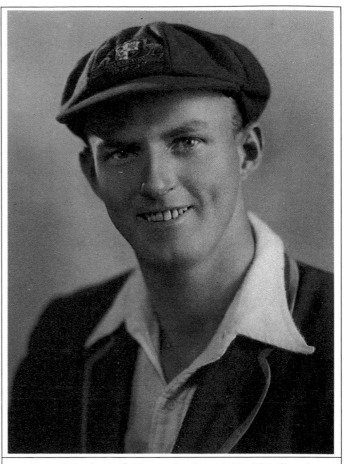

One of the best of all spin bowlers, W.J. O'Reilly of New South Wales and Australia. He headed the averages on both his tours to England in the 1930s.

written notation and many strange illustrations.

A number of 11th- and 12th-century pictures showing a person with some form of club standing adjacent to another holding a spherical object have been seriously presented as early cricket pictures. The reference to the mysterious 'creag' in the wardrobe accounts of Edward I in 1299-1300 has been claimed as the earliest mention of cricket, based, so far as one can judge, on the fact that the word begins with 'cr'. The historian, Rowland Bowen, was certain that he had found the first reference in a French document of 1478.

The first plausible reference comes from Guildford in 1598 in a dispute of some land which ended in a court case. One witness, John Derrick, stated that he used to play 'there at Creckett and other plaies' when he was a schoolboy. This would have been about 1550.

In 1611 at Sidlesham in Sussex two young men played cricket instead of attending church on Easter Sunday and were fined 12d (5p) and in the same year Randle Cotgrave's French-English Dictionary defines 'Crosse' as 'a cricket staff, or the crooked staff wherewith boyes play at cricket' and 'Crosser' as 'to play at cricket'.

In Horsted Green in Sussex, an inquest heard that Jasper Vinall was killed when he was struck by a 'small staff called a cricket batt, worth $\frac{1}{2}d$' the batsman, Edward Tye, trying to prevent Vinall from catching the ball.

These and other references, mainly in church records,

prove that cricket was common in Sussex and its adjoining counties in the first half of the 17th century.

Except that it involved hitting a ball with a bat we have no evidence on which to base the actual way the game was played at this time. Whether it was single wicket or double wicket, the numbers involved, how a batsman could be out and what constituted the wicket are not known.

There is the odd reference to cricket being banned in Ireland in 1656. Odd because it does not fit into the pattern produced by all the other references to that date, i.e. that cricket, on any scale, was only played in the south east of England. Why should Cromwell ban a game which as far as one can tell was not to be played in Ireland until 100 years after his death?

It is a rational deduction to assume that the aristocracy whom Cromwell sent to their country estates brought the game of cricket to London after the Restoration. In 1697 comes the first mention of the number of players in a team. The precise notice is typical of the many which appear in the press during the next 50 years: 'The middle of last week a great match at Cricket was played in Sussex; they were eleven a side, and they played for fifty guineas a piece.' (*Foreign Post*, 7 July 1697).

Not that it can be deduced from this, that all matches were 11 a side. The next notice three years later mentions a match of ten on each side.

In 1709 comes the first reference to inter-county cricket: Kent v Surrey at Dartford. In a pamphlet of 1712 the writer at last throws a little light on the nature of cricket using the following comments in a description of a two-a-side match: 'Sir, I can play ten times better than t'other boy, and if you'll make my crown ten shillings, I'll catch them both out in three or four stroaks . . . the boy won . . . but not so easily as imagin'd, for the Duke gave 'em several master stroaks before he was outed.' Also 'Twelvepence to a third boy to knotch the Game down exact.'

By 1718 the first cricket club is noted, 'the Rochester Punch Club Society'. In 1721 came the first mention of an event which is still too familiar: 'Will went to Stenning with the rest of our parish to play a cricket match, but the weather was so bad, they could not.'

It is in the 1720s that the first notable patrons of cricket come to light, namely the Duke of Richmond, Edward Stead, and Sir William Gage. The first-named arranged two matches with Mr A. Brodrick of Peperharrow in 1727 and by some lucky chance the 'articles of agreement' for these matches are preserved in the Library of Goodwood House. It would seem that these articles were supplementary to the Laws themselves, merely clarifying points on which a dispute might arise, but the earliest known copy of the Laws date only from 1744. In the same year occurred the most famous of 18th-century matches, Kent v All England on the Artillery Ground, and the detailed score of this match is still extant. By the middle of the 18th century the game had spread over most of England, though actual written references are not extant for many counties until the end of the century.

One of cricket's myths which still lingers is that the Hampshire village of Hambledon was the 'cradle of cricket'. The famous Hambledon Club (see under that heading for details) did not come into existence until the 1750s, by which time, as can be realised from the above brief survey, the game was thoroughly established more or less in the form known today.

Out
To be dismissed when batting. The 1744 Laws state, for example: 'If ye wicket is bowled down its out.'

Out-swinger
A delivery from a bowler which moves in the air from leg to off.

Oval
see Kennington Oval

Over
A given number of deliveries which a bowler can send down consecutively from one end. In English first-class cricket the number of balls per over was four until 1888; from 1889 to 1899 the number was five and since 1900 it has been six, except for the 1939 season when eight were tried.

In overseas first-class cricket the number has also varied. A detailed article appears in *The Cricket Statistician* No. 7 (October 1974).

In recent years a great deal of importance has been attached to the 'over-rate', which is the number of overs bowled per hour. A system of fines has been introduced into County Championship cricket for teams which fail to bowl at a minimum over-rate during the season, and in some limited-overs cricket for teams which fail to bowl the required number of overs by the time stipulated for the end of the innings.

Overarm
A style of bowling in which the hand delivers the ball above shoulder height. First legalised in 1864 and now employed almost universally at all but very junior level.
(*see also* Underarm and Roundarm)

Overthrow
One or more runs which the batsmen acquire when the fielding side make an error when throwing the ball to the wicket.

Owzat?
A corruption of 'How is that,' the expression being used by members of the fielding side in asking an umpire whether a batsman has been caught, stumped, run out, lbw, etc.

Oxford
The first first-class match was played on the Parks Ground at Oxford in May 1881 when the University opposed MCC. Since that date the ground has staged most of the University matches, but on the occasions when it has been necessary to make an admission charge, the University has used the Christ Church Ground. In the first half of the 19th century, the University also played important matches on the Magdalen Ground, Bullingdon Green and Cowley Marsh.

Oxford University
The first serious cricket involving the University was played by the Bullingdon Club, which staged matches against MCC in the last years of the 18th century, but Oxford University Cricket Club developed out of the Magdalen Club in the early part of the 19th century. The first game against Cambridge was played in 1827 and the University Match at Lord's was for many years one of the major fixtures of the season. As at Cambridge, the strength of Oxford cricket is now at a low ebb, though still officially ranked as 'first-class'.

Oxfordshire
The county possesses an intriguing riddle (maybe someone reading this book and living in the county will be inquisitive enough to burrow in the county's archives and solve it!).

There is an engraving of a youth in cricket costume with lettering in an oval border. The inscription reads: 'Oxfordshire Cricket Club 1787'. If this refers to a county cricket club it is the earliest known record of any county in England. We cannot find another reference to the existence of Oxfordshire County Cricket Club until 1844. Oxfordshire had a terrible time with their county clubs. The 1844 one died in 1848, another started in 1856, another in 1863, another in 1882, yet another in 1891. This last joined the Minor Counties Championship, but left and collapsed in 1906. So the present county club did not start until 1921! They won the Championship in 1929 and of more recent years have flourished, winning in 1974 and 1982. In 1986 they lost in the final play-off match to Cumberland. They owed much of their success to Mike Nurton, who had been their leading batsman for many seasons.

P

Pads
The leg-guards worn by batsmen and wicketkeepers. Pads came into general use in the middle of the 19th century and were first referred to as 'pads' in 1844.

'Pad-play', or stopping the ball deliberately with the pads, especially deliveries which pitched on the off side and might turn in to the wicket, became increasingly common in the 1880s and 1890s, with, in the end, a change in the leg-before-wicket law.

Pair
Abbreviated description of a 'pair of spectacles' meaning the failure of a batsman to score any runs in either of his innings in a two-innings match. First written mention is in 1862. A 'king pair' is being dismissed first ball in each innings.

Pakistan
Created in 1947 on the partition of India, Pakistan did not have to wait long to gain Test Match status, their first such game being against India in 1952/53. The young Test country then created something of a sensation by beating England on their first Test tour there in 1954, and the other major cricketing sides soon found that the 'new boy' was growing up fast. As the 1950s progressed they were fortunate to possess Hanif Mohammad and his brothers, notably Mushtaq and Sadiq, who formed the backbone of their national side.

Domestic first-class cricket in Pakistan is based principally on the Qaid-I-Azam Trophy (q.v.), which was established in 1953/54, but unlike most major domestic competitions it is not based on geographical units, but on a variety of cricket associations. In addition to this trophy several others have been granted first-class status, there being two such in the mid-1980s, the PACO Pentangular and the BCCP Patron Trophy. The major domestic limited-overs competition is the Wills Cup, which began in 1980/81.

As in India the batsmen tended to dominate the game, and many very high scoring games have been recorded – Hanif Mohammad holds the first-class score record with his innings of 499. In more recent years, Pakistan have produced some effective fast bowlers, Sarfraz Nawaz and Imran Khan being the most famous examples. In both 1979 and 1983, Pakistan reached the semi-finals of the World Cup and were unfortunate enough to be drawn against the West Indies on each occasion. They beat England, however, in the Test series of 1983/84, and Australia in both 1979/80 and 1982/83. (*see also* the succeeding entry, also Australia v Pakistan, England v Pakistan, India v Pakistan, New Zealand v Pakistan, West Indies v Pakistan and individual entries for cricketers, competitions and grounds)

Pakistan v Sri Lanka
Results: Played 9; Pakistan won 5; Sri Lanka won 1; Drawn 3
Three series have so far been played between the two countries, Pakistan having won two and the other being tied.

Sri Lanka went to Pakistan for their first series in 1981/82. In the First Test which took place in Karachi, the tourists almost matched Pakistan in the first innings (396 to 344), but they failed when set the very tall order of 354 in about five hours, trying to attack the bowling even when the position was hopeless and thus losing by 204 runs. Sri Lanka's fortunes improved in the Second Test when a century from Wettimuny and some good bowling enabled them to gain a first-innings lead of 184, but they were incapable of pressing home this advantage in the latter half of the match.

Imran's bowling routed Sri Lanka in the last Test, the Pakistani fast bowler taking 14 wickets and Pakistan won by an innings.

There were two series of three matches each between the two countries in 1985/86. The first of these, in Pakistan, was won by the home side by two matches to nil, after the First Test had been one of high scores: Qasim Omar and Javed Miandad both hit double centuries and added 197 for Pakistan's third wicket on a Faisalabad pitch which was totally dead.

At Sialkot and Karachi however the bowlers received more than a modicum of assistance from the groundsmen and the highest individual score in the two games was P.A. de Silva's 105. Imran's bowling was very much in evidence as Pakistan won by 8 and 10 wickets respectively.

The series in Sri Lanka a few months later was filled with unpleasant incidents – Miandad at one stage threatened to attack the spectators; Arjuna Ranatunga staged a walk out; Pakistan threatened to call off the series due to poor umpiring.

After each country had won one match, Pakistan simply threw away victory in the Third and deciding Test by some terrible fielding. It is to be hoped that a calmer approach is made by the players who participate in future series between the two teams.

Papua-New Guinea

Papua-New Guinea joined the ICC in 1973 and in the 1986 ICC Trophy hit the highest team total, making 455 for 9 in 60 overs against Gibraltar. The team achieved four wins in eight matches. They were most successful in the 1982 competition when they reached the semi-finals, before being beaten by Bermuda.

Cricket came to Papua at the turn of the century, introduced by various missionaries, and the first domestic competition was organised at Port Moresby in 1937. New Guinea was a German colony until the First World War; cricket was therefore not played there until the 1920s. Several Australian first-class cricketers have acted as advisers and coaches since the Second World War and the standard of cricket has risen steadily.

Perth

It was not until 1970/71 that a Test Match was staged on the Western Australian Cricket Association Ground at Perth. The first first-class match was played in Perth in 1898/99, when Western Australia opposed South Australia, but owing to Perth's geographical position, Western Australia did not join the Sheffield Shield Competition until 1947/48, so it was not until that season that first-class matches began to be played on the ground with any regularity. The pitches at Perth are regarded as the equal of any in Australia and give good opportunities to both batsmen and bowlers.

Pitch

1 The piece of turf or ground on which the two sets of stumps are set up. This area is also referred to as the 'wicket'.
2 To pitch the ball is to make it land on the ground between the two sets of stumps when bowling.
3 To pitch the stumps (or wickets) is to set up the stumps in readiness for a match.

Pitched out

After two overs had been bowled in the County Cham-pionship game between Derbyshire and Yorkshire at Queen's Park, Chesterfield, on 29 June 1946, Len Hutton, fielding at slip, queried the length of the pitch. A check discovered that it was 24 yards long. The match was then re-started on a pitch of the correct length.

Played on

The action of a batsman who hits a delivery from the bowler, but in doing so directs the ball on to his own wicket. If this action dislodges a bail, the batsman is out, in the manner described as 'played on', but in the scorebook he is shown as 'bowled' not as 'played on'.

Player League

The John Player Special League was played on Sundays between the 17 English first-class counties, each county playing its 16 competitors once. The matches were restricted to one innings each of 40 overs. The League was instituted in 1969 and the title winners are as follows:

1969 Lancashire	1978 Hampshire
1970 Lancashire	1979 Somerset
1971 Worcestershire	1980 Warwickshire
1972 Kent	1981 Essex
1973 Kent	1982 Sussex
1974 Leicestershire	1983 Yorkshire
1975 Hampshire	1984 Essex
1976 Kent	1985 Essex
1977 Leicestershire	1986 Hampshire

The most exciting season was in 1976 when no fewer than five counties finished level on points at the top: Kent, Essex, Leicestershire, Somerset and Sussex. Somerset seemed certain to win prior to the final set of matches, but lost their game by one run against Glamorgan at Cardiff, when the last man was run out. The title was awarded to Kent on the slender margin of 0.42 of a run, the teams being positioned by run rate.

Refuge Assurance took over the sponsorship of the competition for the 1987 season.

Plunket Shield

Lord Plunket, the Governor-General of New Zealand, presented a Challenge Shield for competition in 1906/07 between the major New Zealand cricket associations, namely Auckland, Wellington, Canterbury, Otago and Hawke's Bay. The New Zealand Cricket Council awarded the Shield to Canterbury, which team they judged to have been the best in that season. From that time until 1921 the major associations had to challenge the holders for the Shield.

The competition was reorganised on a league system for the 1921/22 season and continued as such until 1974/75. Hawke's Bay had dropped out of the Shield whilst it was a Challenge competition, but Central Districts joined the remaining four Associations in 1950/51 and then Northern Districts in 1956/57.

After 1974/75, the Plunket Shield was allocated to the winners of the matches between North Island and South Island. The major associations now compete for the Shell Trophy (q.v.).

Pocketed

In the match between Dartford and Camberwell in 1827, Charles Hodsell, one of the Dartford team, was batting when the ball glanced off the handle of his bat into his pocket. The wicketkeeper immediately stepped forward to try to obtain the ball and thus claim a catch. Hodsell did not dare pull the ball out of his pocket for fear of being given out 'handled ball' and so ran off across the field trying to dislodge the ball as he did so, with the wicketkeeper in hot pursuit. Hodsell managed to remove the ball and get back to his crease before it was returned.

Point

A position in the field which is on the off side in a line with the popping crease and five or six yards from the batsman. Similarly 'backward point' is slightly behind the wicket on the off side; 'deep point' is in the line with the popping crease but farther from the batsman; 'silly point' is in the same line but closer to the batsman.

Pollock, Robert Graeme

Born: 27 February 1944, Durban, South Africa
Career: 226 *m*; 18,352 runs (av 55.61)
Tests: 23 *m*; 2,256 runs (av 60.97)
The ostracism of South Africa from Test cricket from 1970 deprived the world of enjoying the skills of Graeme Pollock, who was on the brink of proving himself one of the greatest batsmen ever.

Pollock made his debut for Eastern Province in 1961/62. Before he was 17 he was the youngest to make a Currie Cup century, and two seasons later was the youngest South African double-century maker. He made his Test debut at 19 in Australia, and before he was 20 became the youngest Test century-maker for South Africa. In the following Test he and Barlow added 341 for the third wicket (Pollock 175) – this is South Africa's highest-ever Test stand.

Pollock is a tall, powerful, left-handed middle-order batsman, who used a heavy bat, which caused the ball to speed to the boundary, although he played all his shots in an unhurried classical manner.

His highest score was 274 for South Africa against Australia in 1969/70, his last Test series, the highest Test score by a South African.

Port of Spain

The Queen's Park Ground in Port of Spain, Trinidad, first staged a Test Match in 1929/30, when West Indies played England. The ground has been used for first-class matches by Trinidad since the 1880s, the very early games having been played on the St Clair Ground. The ground is the home of the Queen's Park Club and until 1934 the wickets were coconut

The Queen's Park Oval, Port of Spain, Trinidad, the most pleasant ground in the West Indies. This is the First Test against Australia in 1977/78.

Graeme Pollock, an outstanding post-war batsman, whose Test career was cut short
as it was about to blossom by South Africa's exclusion from Tests.

matting which favoured bowlers. In 1935 a switch was made to jute matting, and this substantially increased the runs. In the 1950s turf was introduced.

The ground is the best appointed in the West Indies and is most pleasantly sited.

Postal cricket

In 1753, Lord March made a bet that he could convey a letter a certain number of miles within a given time. His proposition was declared impossible, but he enclosed the letter in a cricket ball and then got 20 cricketers, who were good catchers, to form a large circle and throw the ball from one to another. By this means he won his wager.

Postcards

Considering that there are estimated to be over 5,000 cricketing postcards, the number of collectors dealing in 'deltiology' seems to be remarkably small, and thus the cost of collecting is not as grim as with most cricketana. Picture postcards were legalised in Great Britain in 1894 and the internationally recognised size adopted in 1899.

The main collecting vogue was prior to the First World War, when numerous cricketing postcards of players and teams were issued, chiefly through the photographers Hawkins and Foster. Since the Second World War several firms have from time to time published cricketing postcards.

Prudential World Cup

Three Prudential World Cup competitions had taken place by 1986, all held in England. The first such competition was held in 1975 with the then six Test-playing countries plus Sri Lanka and East Africa. There were two groups of four teams each and the top two in each group then played in knock-out semi-finals.

The second competition under the same system was held in 1979 with the same teams, except with Canada in place of East Africa.

In the third competition in 1983, with Zimbabwe now taking Canada's place, the initial group matches were increased from three per side to six, but otherwise the competition was unaltered.

The finals were as follows:
1975 West Indies 291-8 (60 overs) beat Australia 274 (58.4 overs) by 17 runs
1979 West Indies 286-9 (60 overs) beat England 194 (51 overs) by 92 runs
1983 India 183 (54.4 overs) beat West Indies 140 (52 overs) by 43 runs

Public houses

From the earliest date of organised cricket teams, the public house has been a centre for cricketers to meet. Many of the principal cricket grounds have public houses attached to them and in some famous cases, notably Trent Bridge, the pub begat the ground.

The cricketing connections with the licensed trade have been strengthened by the number of professional cricketers who have become landlords in their later years.

Few towns in England can have passed through the last 200 years without at some time having 'The Cricketers' or some similarly named hostelry in their boundaries.

A directory of cricketing pubs appeared in *Wisden Cricket Monthly* for August 1985, and subsequent issues.

Public schools

It is not perhaps generally realised that the major reason for cricket becoming such an integral part of the English way of life was its adoption by the public schools. For a century or more it was the major game in the vast majority of public schools, both in the British Isles and across the British Empire. If instead of cricket, the schools had taken up, for example, rounders, then the history of cricket would have taken an entirely different path.

Cricket was being played informally in some schools in the 18th century. Eton opposed Westminster in 1796, in defiance of the Eton headmaster, who flogged the whole team on their return. The two most famous matches before 1850, however, are the first Eton v Harrow game of 1805, when Lord Byron played for the latter, and the Rugby v MCC match which is described in 'Tom Brown's Schooldays'.

In the 1870s the Eton v Harrow match at Lord's attracted crowds which were about as large as those attending any of the other major matches of the season with maybe 10,000 spectators on a single day. The importance of public school cricket can be gauged by the space that the various cricket annuals allotted to it, and until the 1930s Ayres Cricket Companion, which came out annually, was almost entirely devoted to public schools' cricket.

Two schools' grounds, Cheltenham and Clifton, have been regularly used for first-class county matches and some minor counties play games on school premises. For many years the two major school fixtures were Southern Schools v The Rest and Public Schools v Combined Services and even in the 1950s, when the Services were a first-class team, the Public Schools side could hold its own. The days are now gone when boys spent almost as much time on the cricket field as they did in the classroom during the summer term, and the number of first-class cricketers hailing from the major public schools has dropped considerably in recent years.

Pull

A batting stroke in which the ball is 'pulled' round from the off side to the leg.

A montage of cricket postcards from the turn of the century to the Second World War, showing the Australian tourists of 1905, a Middlesex XI of about the same time, three Kent players of the early 1900s, Bill Ponsford and Len Hutton.

Mohinder Amarnath, the Man of the Match, and Kapil Dev, the Indian captain,
after India's victory in the World Cup of 1983.

The Prudential World Cup final at Lord's in 1983. The Indian opener Srikkanth
drives West Indies' Roberts early in the match.

Q

Qaid-I-Azam Trophy

Pakistan's principal first-class competition, which was instituted in 1953/54. Until 1979/80 the trophy was decided by a knock-out final, but since 1980/81 it has been run on a league system. In the early years the various Karachi teams dominated the tournament, but more recently the struggle for supremacy has been between the National and United Banks teams.

Queensland

The Queensland Cricket Association was formed in 1876, but their first first-class match was not until April 1893, when New South Wales were the opponents, and not until 1926/ 27 did the side enter the Sheffield Shield. It is unfortunate that Queensland play the majority of their matches in January and February, which are possibly the worst months for the weather in Brisbane.

Although finishing in second position several times, including three successive seasons from 1973/74 onward, Queensland have yet to take the Shield. This run of near misses was due to Greg Chappell, who moved from South Australia to join his new state as captain.

Don Tallon, the wicketkeeper in Don Bradman's last Tests, was Queensland's first really distinguished player, since when the stonewaller, Ken Mackay, has hit the headlines and later, Peter Burge. The weather is Queensland's real obstacle to success, with rain affecting too many of their matches.

R

Ranji Trophy

India's major cricket competition was officially founded at a meeting of the Board of Control for Cricket in India held at Simla in 1934 as 'The Cricket Championship of India'. The trophy for the tournament was donated by the Maharaja of Patiala to commemorate the memory of His late Highness Sir Ranjitsinhji Vibhaji of Nawanagar (the Test cricketer, K.S. Ranjitsinhji).

The Board arranged fixtures for the competition for 1934/ 35 between all the Cricket Associations then affiliated to the Board. Bengal and Rajputana however withdrew and Maharashtra was allowed to enter later. The trophy was organised by dividing India into four zones: North, South, East and West. Each zonal competition was by knock-out with the zonal winners then meeting in two semi-finals and a final. In 1948/49 the zones were abolished and the whole competition run as one knock-out cup, but this scheme lasted just one year. In 1952/53, a fifth, Central, zone was added and since 1957/58 the zones have been run on a league system. Forty-nine differently styled teams have competed in the competition and it is outside the scope of this entry to detail the complicated changes of teams.

Bombay have been the outstanding team over the years and had won the title 30 times to 1985/86.

Ranjitsinhji, Kumar Shri

Born: 10 September 1872, Sarodar, India
Died: 2 April 1933, Jamnagar, India
Career: 307 *m*; 24,692 runs (av 56.37); 133 wkts (av 34.59)
Tests: 15 *m*; 989 runs (av 44.95)

Prince Ranjitsinhji, later the Maharaja Jam Sahib of Nawanager, usually called Ranji, was the first great Indian player. He made his first-class debut for Cambridge University in 1893, and played for Sussex from 1895 to 1920. From 1899 to 1903 he captained the county, and in those years was the leading batsman in England. In 1904 he returned to India, and played spasmodically after that.

Ranji revised batting technique. He played back rather than forward as was the style of the day, his most famous stroke being the leg glance, which was regarded as some sort of Eastern magic. In both 1899 and 1900 he scored over 3,000 runs, and for seven years he dominated the averages. He played for England from 1896 to 1902, and went on one tour of Australia. His highest score was 285 not out for Sussex against Somerset in 1901, and in Tests 175 against Australia in 1897/98.

He lost an eye in a shooting accident, went home to Nawanager and was a delegate to the League of Nations.

Prince Ranjitsinhji, who was often asked to pose like this as his leg glance was one of the most famous shots in all cricket history.

Records

Highest Team Total
All cricket: 1,107, Victoria v New South Wales (Melbourne), 1926/27
First-class: as above
Test: 903-7 dec, England v Australia (Oval), 1938

Lowest Team Total
All cricket: 0, Fakenham v Litcham (Fakenham), 1815 (this is the first-known instance, but it is not uncommon for sides to be dismissed without scoring in minor matches)
First-class: 6, Bs v England (Lord's), 1810
Test: 26, New Zealand v England (Auckland), 1954/55

Highest Individual Innings
All cricket: 628, A.E.J. Collins, Clark's House v North Town (Clifton), 1899
First-class: 499, Hanif Mohammad, Karachi v Bahawalpur (Karachi), 1958/59
Test: 365*, G. St. A. Sobers, West Indies v Pakistan (Kingston), 1957/58

Best Bowling in Innings (XI-a-side)
All cricket: 10-0, A. Dartnell, Broad Green v Thornton Heath (Norbury), 1867 (this is the first known instance; the feat has since been performed about 20 times)
First-class: 10-10, H. Verity, Yorkshire v Notts (Headingley), 1932

Test: 10-53, J.C. Laker, England v Australia (Old Trafford), 1956

Best Bowling in Match (XI-a-side)
All cricket: 20-16, A. Rimmer, 7th Grade v Cathedral GS (Christchurch, NZ), 1925/26
First-class: 19-90, J.C. Laker, England v Australia (Old Trafford), 1956
Test: as above.

Most Runs in Career
All cricket: Unknown, but W.G. Grace scored over 80,000
First-class: 61,760 (av 50.66), J.B. Hobbs (Surrey and England), 1905-34
Test: 9,367 (av 50.63), S.M. Gavaskar (India), 1970/71 to 1986

Most Wickets in Career
All cricket: Unknown
First-class: 4,204 (av 16.72), W. Rhodes (Yorkshire and England), 1898-30
Test: 357 (av 27.06), I.T. Botham (England), 1977-86

Most Hundreds in Career
All cricket: Unknown
First class: 199, J.B. Hobbs (Surrey and England), 1905-34
Test: 32, S.M. Gavaskar (India), 1970/71-86

*Ian Botham's 356th Test wicket, which broke Dennis Lillee's record.
Jeff Crowe is lbw in the Third Test at the Oval in 1986.*

*Wilfred Rhodes, the only man to have taken over 4,000 first-class wickets,
and whose long career led to many other records.*

Reference books

For cricket history up to 1878, a set of MCC Scores and Biographies compiled by Arthur Haygarth provides the student with virtually all the principal scores and the biographies of the cricketers in 14 volumes. A 15th volume dealt with post-1878 cricketers. From 1879 to date the one source which gives all English first-class matches is a set of Wisden's Almanacks.

The Association of Cricket Statisticians have published Guides to First-class Matches in all the main Test-playing countries; these Guides give the whereabouts of all first-class matches and include some 200 scores which are not easily found elsewhere. The Association, in conjunction with Newnes, has also published the 'Who's Who of Cricketers', which contains biographies of every cricketer ever to appear in a first-class match in England.

Turning to the history of the game, there are three books which can be recommended on the overall history: 'A History of Cricket' by H.S. Altham and E.W. Swanton (Allen & Unwin); 'Cricket: A History' by Rowland Bowen (Eyre and Spottiswoode); and 'The Barclay's World of Cricket' by E.W. Swanton and John Woodcock (Collins).

Apart from these general histories, there are histories on each of the major countries and all the 17 first-class counties, as well as many of the other cricket clubs both large and small. The book which should be consulted is 'A Bibliography of Cricket' by E.W. Padwick (J.W. McKenzie); this is the most detailed and contains well over 10,000 cricket items.

Refuge Assurance Sunday League

Refuge Assurance took over the sponsorship of the John Player Special League in the 1987 season.
(see also Player League)

Rhodes, Wilfred

Born: 29 October 1877, Kirkheaton, Yorkshire
Died: 8 July 1973, Branksome, Dorset
Career: 1,110 *m*; 39,969 runs (av 30.58); 4,204 wkts (av 16.72)
Tests: 58 *m*; 2,325 runs (av 30.19); 127 wkts (av 26.96)
Rhodes is one of the game's great all-rounders, whose long career led to some amazing aggregates. He began his career for Yorkshire in 1898 as a slow left-arm bowler. By the time he retired in 1930 he had taken 4,204 wickets, no other bowler in history reaching 4,000. He took 100 wickets in a season 23 times, another record.

That was only half his talent, for having begun as a tail-end batsman, he eventually opened for England. He began his Test career at No. 11, but in 1911/12 at Melbourne put on 323 with Hobbs for the first wicket, England's highest.

Not unnaturally, Rhodes' total of 16 'doubles' is six more than his nearest rival, and unlikely to be beaten.

Rhodes' Test career lasted over 30 years (a record), and when he played his last Test, in the West Indies in 1929/30, he was 52 years 165 days old, the oldest Test player.

Bowling was his main strength, and his best performance 7 for 56 and 8 for 68 against Australia at Melbourne in 1903/04.

On retiring, Rhodes became coach at Harrow School and lived to be nearly 96.

Richards, Barry Anderson

Born: 21 July 1945, Durban, South Africa
Career: 339 *m*; 28,358 runs (av 54.74)
Tests: 4 *m*; 508 runs (av 72.57)
For a time in the early 1970s, Barry Richards was regarded as the best batsman in the world. He was a forceful opening batsman with all the strokes. After beginning with Natal in 1964/65, he made his Test debut in 1969/70, South Africa's last Test series. In four matches against Australia he averaged 72.57, then his Test career was at an end.

Richards became a sort of cricketing mercenary, playing mainly for Natal and Hampshire, although his most famous and highest innings was for South Australia against Western Australia in 1970/71, when he scored 356, 325 of them on the first day (against Lillee, McKenzie and Lock).

World Series Cricket was perfect for him, and he was one of the leading players, but unfortunately his genius was mostly seen in surroundings much below his own standard.

Richards, Isaac Vivian Alexander

Born: 7 March 1952, St Johns, Antigua
Career: 386 *m*; 28,533 runs (av 49.97); 177 wkts (av 43.41)
Tests: 82 *m*; 6,220 runs (av 54.56); 19 wkts (av 55.36)
From the second half of the 1970s Viv Richards has been the outstanding batsman in the world. He made his debut for the Leeward Islands in 1971/72, and joined Somerset in 1974, where he remained until 1986. In 1987 he began playing for Rishton in the Lancashire League.

He is a magnificent batsman, usually at No.3, whose eye and timing is so good that he hits the ball powerfully with comparatively little effort. He is particularly strong on the leg side, frequently playing across his legs in a way that would be dangerous for lesser batsmen. He also bowls occasional off-breaks, particularly in limited-overs games, where he has proved a sound fifth bowler for his country.

Richards had a tremendous year in 1976, scoring 1,710 runs in 11 Tests, 829 (average 118.42) in four Tests in England, which included his highest Test score, 291, at the Oval. His career highest is 322, for Somerset against Warwickshire in 1985; the runs came in under five hours, and he became the first West Indian to score 300 in a day.

Richards, however, reserves many of his great innings for limited-overs cricket. In one-day internationals, he is easily the world's heaviest scorer. In 1984 at Old Trafford, he scored 189 not out against England, the highest score in such matches, many of them coming in an unfinished last-wicket stand of 106. He made his Test debut for West Indies in 1974/75 and took over as captain in 1984/85.

Ritchie, Gregory Michael

Born: 23 January 1960, Stanthorpe, Australia
Career: 95 *m*; 6,174 runs (av 44.73)
Tests: 27 *m*; 1,636 runs (av 36.35)
An elegant right-hand batsman, Ritchie made his first-class debut for Queensland in 1980/81 and was capped by Australia two seasons later. He came to England on the 1985 tour and was the only new batsman to make an impression, being second to Border in the Test averages and hitting 146 in the Third Test at Trent Bridge, which remains his highest Test innings to date.

Roundarm

A style of bowling in which the ball is delivered with the hand not above shoulder height, but above the normal elbow height. Such type of bowling was commonly used between 1835 and 1864, being superseded in the latter year by the legalisation of overarm bowling.
(*see also* Overarm and Underarm)

A.E. Stoddart, who captained two tours to Australia, and was the most successful player of all at combining cricket with rugby union football.

Rugby Union

Six English Test cricketers have also represented England as Rugby Union internationals: A.N. Hornby (9 matches, 1877-82); F. Mitchell (6, 1895-96); M.J.K. Smith (1, 1956); R.H. Spooner (1, 1903); A.E. Stoddart (10, 1885-93); G.F. Vernon (5, 1878-81); S.M.J. Woods (13, 1890-95).

Lillywhite and Shrewsbury, who managed the 1887/88 cricket team to Australia, arranged for a team of rugby players to be sent out directly the cricket programme ended and then managed the first-ever English rugby side to tour New Zealand. The team also played some soccer matches and Australian Rules football. A.E. Stoddart was the only cricketer who stayed over to join the rugby tour.

Run

The 1744 Laws state: 'Each Umpire is ye sole judge of all . . . good or bad runs at his own wicket.' A 'run' is added to the score when each of the two batsmen (that is to say, any part of the batsman's person, or his bat, provided he is holding it) has crossed the popping crease at the other end of the pitch from which he was stationed when the bowler delivered the ball.

Run out

A mode of dismissal, which occurs when a batsman is attempting a run, but fails to arrive at the relevant popping crease before the ball breaks the wicket. The batsman is shown in the scorebook as 'run out' and the bowler is not credited with his wicket.

Runner

When a batsman is disabled in such a way that he is incapable of running between the wickets, he may request another player to do his running for him. Such a substitute player is known as a 'runner'. The runner must be equipped in the same way as the batsman for whom he is acting.

Run-up

The bowler's approach to the wicket prior to his delivery of the ball. In some cricket matches, the distance of the bowler's run-up is restricted.

Barry Richards in commanding form against the Australian tourists in 1975, when he captained Hampshire for the first time and scored 96 and 69 for once out.

*The world's best batsman in the 1980s. Vivian Richards batting in Barbados in
the Third Test against England in 1980/81. He scored 182 not out in the second innings.*

S

Score

1 The total number of runs together with the number of batsmen dismissed made by a team, normally denoted as: 345 for 7, or 345-7, in one innings. (In Australia shown as 7 for 345).
2 The total number of runs made by an individual batsman.
3 The action of making a run, or runs, off a delivery from the bowler.
4 The action of writing in the scorebook the details of play as it progresses, hence 'scorer' as the person who does the writing, though this may also refer to the batsman who made the score.

Scoreboard

A large board with movable numbers which indicate the score of the side which is batting. In its simplest form the board allows for the display of three sets of numbers. The top set show the present total number of runs; the middle set show the number of batsmen dismissed and the bottom set the number of runs made by the last batsman to be dismissed.

This basic idea has been expanded so that in its most elaborate form, the scoreboard can display the surnames of all the players in both teams, with, for the batting team, the number of runs made by each player as well as his mode of dismissal, and for the fielding team, the number of runs hit off each bowler and number of wickets taken by him.

Some major Test grounds have electronic scoreboards.

Scorebook

A book containing pages of printed grid lines on which the scorer writes down the details of play as the match progresses.

Scorecard

A sheet of thin card on which is printed the names of the members of each team appearing in a specific match with spaces beside each name so that the spectator can write down the dismissal details of each batsman. There is also usually a space under each team where the bowling analyses can be entered. It is sometimes referred to as a 'matchcard'.

The first known scorecard was issued by T. Pratt of Sevenoaks in 1776.

Scotland

The Scottish Cricket Union was formed in 1879, dissolved in 1883 and re-formed in 1908. The national side have been regarded as first-class since 1905, but in recent years only the three-day fixture with Ireland has been given first-class status. Scotland has competed, however, in the English Benson & Hedges competition since 1980, though with little success.

The majority of Test touring teams to England have also played matches in Scotland, at least until the advent of twin tours to England.

The year 1985 was officially the bi-centenary of cricket in Scotland, but the game did not become established until the 1820s and 'Scotland' played their first match in 1865.

Scottish County Championship

The Championship began in 1902 and has been staged continuously since, except during the two world wars. Aberdeenshire, who have played a leading part in the Championship since it commenced, won the 1986 title with ease. Apart from Aberdeen, the only other counties to appear in every year are Forfarshire, Stirlingshire and Perthshire; virtually every Scottish county, however, has at one time or another produced a county cricket team, though several have not possessed an official county cricket club. The first recorded inter-county match was between East Lothian and Stirling in 1851.

Selectors

The TCCB (q.v.) appoints a Test Selection sub-committee to choose English representative teams. The ballot by the TCCB in the spring of 1986 produced the following: P.B.H. May (Chairman), P.J. Sharpe, A.C. Smith and F.J. Titmus. Titmus was the only new face, replacing A.V. Bedser.

The first Test Selectors for English cricket were appointed in 1899 to select the Test sides for that season. The original selectors were Lord Hawke, W.G. Grace and H.W. Bainbridge.

Services cricket

The Royal Navy, the Army and the Royal Air Force have all at some time been considered as first-class teams.

There is a reference to crews of British ships playing cricket in Lisbon in 1736 and indeed the Navy was responsible for many pioneering matches at both familiar and unfamiliar venues throughout the world. Between 1912 and 1929 the Navy matches against the Army were considered first-class as were a few matches against the Royal Air Force. The Army played first-class matches from 1912 to 1939 and the Royal Air Force from 1927 to 1946.

The three services provided a first-class 'Combined Services' side until 1964 and the Combined Services XI still play occasional three-day matches.

Sharjah

Abdul Rehman Bukhatir made a dream come true when he created a cricket stadium out of the desert in the Gulf state of Sharjah, with Asif Iqbal as his chief adviser. The stadium held its first major international tournament in 1983/84, when India, Sri Lanka and Pakistan competed for the Asia Cup. Since then one-day limited-overs internationals have been held there with increasing success, and in April 1986 there was a total purse of £60,000 for the five-nation 'Australasian Cup'. The stadium had a new stand erected in 1986, bringing the capacity to 18,000.

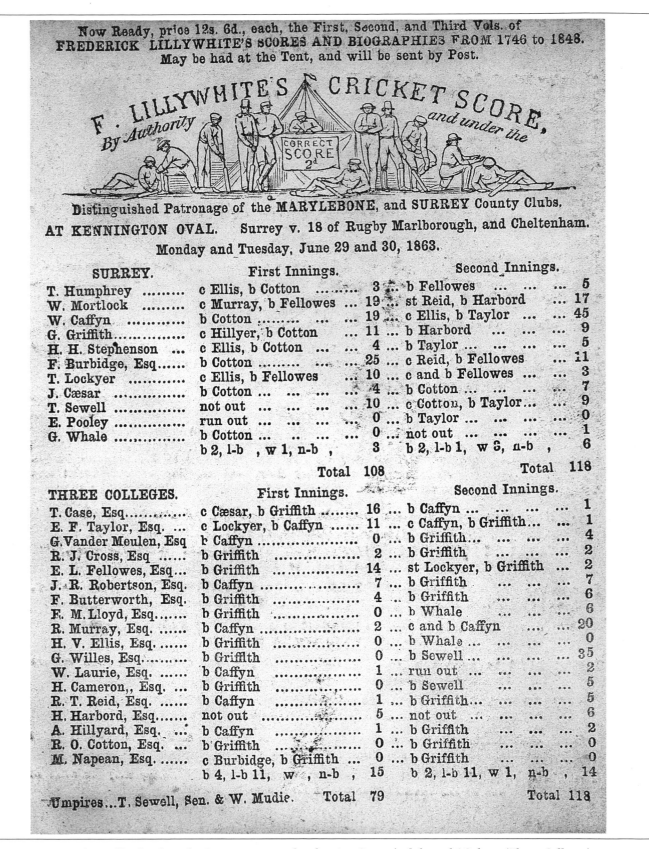

Now Ready, price 12s. 6d., each, the First, Second, and Third Vols. of
FREDERICK LILLYWHITE'S SCORES AND BIOGRAPHIES FROM 1746 to 1848.
May be had at the Tent, and will be sent by Post.

F. LILLYWHITE'S CRICKET SCORE,
By Authority and under the

CORRECT SCORE 2d.

Distinguished Patronage of the MARYLEBONE, and SURREY County Clubs.

AT KENNINGTON OVAL.   Surrey v. 18 of Rugby Marlborough, and Cheltenham.

Monday and Tuesday, June 29 and 30, 1863.

SURREY.	First Innings.		Second Innings.	
T. Humphrey	c Ellis, b Cotton	3	b Fellowes	5
W. Mortlock	c Murray, b Fellowes	19	st Reid, b Harbord	17
W. Caffyn	b Cotton	19	c Ellis, b Taylor	45
G. Griffith	c Hillyer, b Cotton	11	b Harbord	9
H. H. Stephenson	c Ellis, b Cotton	4	b Taylor	5
F. Burbidge, Esq	b Cotton	25	c Reid, b Fellowes	11
T. Lockyer	c Ellis, b Fellowes	10	c and b Fellowes	3
J. Cæsar	b Cotton	4	b Cotton	7
T. Sewell	not out	10	c Cotton, b Taylor	9
E. Pooley	run out	0	b Taylor	0
G. Whale	b Cotton	0	not out	1
	b 2, l-b , w 1, n-b ,	3	b 2, l-b 1, w 3, n-b ,	6
	Total	108	Total	118

THREE COLLEGES.	First Innings.		Second Innings.	
T. Case, Esq	c Cæsar, b Griffith	16	b Caffyn	1
E. F. Taylor, Esq.	c Lockyer, b Caffyn	11	c Caffyn, b Griffith	1
G. Vander Meulen, Esq	b Caffyn	0	b Griffith	4
R. J. Cross, Esq	b Griffith	2	b Griffith	2
E. L. Fellowes, Esq	b Griffith	14	st Lockyer, b Griffith	2
J. R. Robertson, Esq.	b Caffyn	7	b Griffith	7
F. Butterworth, Esq.	b Griffith	4	b Griffith	6
F. M. Lloyd, Esq.	b Griffith	0	b Whale	6
R. Murray, Esq.	b Caffyn	2	c and b Caffyn	20
H. V. Ellis, Esq.	b Griffith	0	b Whale	0
G. Willes, Esq.	b Griffith	0	b Sewell	35
W. Laurie, Esq.	b Caffyn	1	run out	2
H. Cameron, Esq.	b Griffith	0	b Sewell	5
R. T. Reid, Esq.	b Caffyn	1	b Griffith	5
H. Harbord, Esq.	not out	5	not out	6
A. Hillyard, Esq.	b Caffyn	1	b Griffith	2
R. O. Cotton, Esq.	b Griffith	0	b Griffith	0
M. Napean, Esq.	c Burbidge, b Griffith	0	b Griffith	0
	b 4, l-b 11, w , n-b ,	15	b 2, l-b 11, w 1, n-b ,	14

Umpires...T. Sewell, Sen. & W. Mudie.   Total 79   Total 118

*One of F. Lillywhite's early Surrey score-cards, showing Surrey's defeat of 18 from 'Three Colleges'.
Note the strength of the Surrey side. This was 14 years before the first Test Match, but Caffyn,
Stephenson, Lockyer and Julius Caesar had all been on England's first tour, to America
four years earlier, and Stephenson, Mortlock, Griffith, Sewell and Caffyn had been on the first tour
to Australia in 1861/62.*

Ravi Shastri hitting out against England at Bombay in 1984.
He is one of India's talented all-rounders of the second half of the 1980s.

Shastri, Ravishankar Jayadritha

Born: 27 May 1962, Bombay, India
Career: 100 *m*; 4,653 runs (av 38.45); 273 wkts (av 30.50)
Tests: 43 *m*; 1,998 runs (av 34.44); 98 wkts (av 38.40)
A slow left-arm spinner, he made his first-class debut in 1979/80, when he was flown out to New Zealand to replace the injured D.R. Joshi in the middle of the 1979/80 tour. In his first match – the Wellington Test – he took three wickets in four balls. His talents, however, are not confined to bowling; a brilliant right-hand batsman, he equalled the world record in 1984/85 when he hit six sixes off an over from Tilak Raj, whilst scoring the fastest double hundred in Indian cricket in 113 minutes off 123 balls, with his 13 sixes creating another Indian record. He toured England in 1982 and 1986.

Sheffield Shield

Lord Sheffield, a notable 19th-century patron of English cricket and of Sussex cricket in particular, financed a tour to Australia in 1891/92, the team being captained by W.G. Grace. During the visit Lord Sheffield donated 150 guineas to promote cricket in Australia and the Australian Cricket Council used this gift to start a competition between the colonies. The first season of the 'Sheffield Shield' was 1892/93, with three sides competing: Victoria, South Australia and New South Wales. Each colony played each of the others twice and Victoria won all four of their matches, thus taking the Shield.

In 1926/27 Queensland joined the competition, but in their first year played only five matches, not having a return with South Australia. Thereafter each of the four sides played six matches per season.

The next entrant into the competition was Western Australia, who took part for the first time in 1947/48 and caused a major upset by winning the title, though they played each of the other sides only once. It was not until 1956/57 that Western Australia began two matches each season against the other four sides, and thus from 1947/48 until that summer the competition was on a percentage system.

The most recent team in the competition are Tasmania, who joined in 1977/78, and like Western Australia earlier, opposed the other teams once only. In 1982/83, however, Tasmania also played two matches against each opponent and thus the competition now consists of 10 matches per team.

The Shield has been won most often by New South Wales, who claimed their 38th title in 1985/86, when Victoria had won 24 and South Australia 12. Western Australia have been very strong in recent years and already have ten titles to their name. The surprising fact is that Queensland have never taken the Shield, though often in second place. Tasmania have yet to make much of a mark in the competition.

Shell Shield

The Shell Shield for Caribbean Regional Cricket Tournament was instituted in 1965/66 under the sponsorship of Shell. In the late 1980s the following teams compete in this competition: Barbados, Guyana, Jamaica, Leeward Islands, Trinidad & Tobago, and Windward Islands. Each team plays one match against each of the opposing sides and the winners are the team which come top of the resultant league. The winning teams have been as follows:

1965/66 Barbados	1976/77 Barbados
1966/67 Barbados	1977/78 Barbados
1967/68 Jamaica	1978/79 Barbados
1968/69 Trinidad	1979/80 Barbados
1969/70 Trinidad	1980/81 Combined Is
1970/71 Trinidad	1981/82 Barbados
1971/72 Guyana	1982/83 Guyana
1973/74 Barbados	1983/84 Barbados
1974/75 Guyana	1984/85 Trinidad & Tobago
1975/76 Barbados, Trinidad	1985/86 Barbados

In some seasons the leading players in the West Indies have not taken part in the Shield, but in 1985/86 players had to appear in at least two matches to be eligible to represent West Indies in Test Matches and this improved the standing of the matches.

Shell Trophy

New Zealand's major first-class competition involves Auckland, Canterbury, Central Districts, Northern Districts, Otago and Wellington. Each team plays eight matches in a league. This has been in operation since 1979/80. From 1975/76 to 1978/79 there was a league system and a knock-out cup, the Shell Cup going to the winners of the league and the Trophy to the knock-out winners. The Shell Cup is now awarded to the winners of the limited-overs competition.

The winners of the first-class competitions have been:
1975/76 Canterbury (Cup), Canterbury (Trophy)
1976/77 Northern Districts (Cup), Otago (Trophy)
1977/78 Canterbury (Cup), Auckland (Trophy)
1978/79 Otago (Cup), Otago (Trophy)
1979/80 Northern Districts
1980/81 Auckland
1981/82 Wellington
1982/83 Wellington
1983/84 Canterbury
1984/85 Wellington
1985/86 Otago

Shooter

A delivery from the bowler, which when it hits the ground runs straight along instead of bouncing. A very difficult delivery for the batsman, but one that is not commonly found on a properly prepared pitch.

Shortest cricketers

English cricketers seem to be growing taller at the same rate as policemen are getting younger. It is believed that the shortest ever county cricketer was T.W. Gunn of Surrey who was 5 feet 1½ inches. He appeared from 1863 to 1869 in first-class matches. Players under 5 feet 6 inches are very rare in post-Second World War English county cricket, though M.S. Ahluwalia of the 1980s Cambridge University side is reported to be 5 feet 4½ inches.

Short-leg

A position in the field, a few yards from the batsman on the leg side and described more precisely by an additional adjective: 'backward short-leg' or 'forward short-leg'. The short-legs form a semi-circle close in on the leg side, between silly mid-on and the wicketkeeper.

Shropshire

The present club dates back only to 1951 and the county did not join the Minor Counties Championship until 1957. The title was won for the first time in 1973. The win was due to a magnificent team effort under the captaincy of G.V. Othen, and with D.N.F. Slade as the leading all-rounder.

Shropshire cricket is not all of recent vintage, since the county can boast proudly that they were the first to publish a cricket annual with the full scores of their matches – that was in 1865. This early county club seems to have begun about 1829 and dissolved in 1905, when it became the Gentlemen of Shropshire CC. Until after the Second World War, the cricketers of Shropshire ignored the Minor Counties Championship as being too competitive; they preferred to play in only friendly matches.

Sightscreen

A large white screen of timber or canvas set on the boundary directly in line between the batsman and the bowler's hand at the time of the delivery of the ball. Sightscreens are provided on most grounds in order to give the batsman a better chance of seeing the ball, especially when the normal background is dark, or where there is traffic moving.

In night matches, the screen is black and the ball white.

Singapore

For cricket purposes Singapore used to combine with Penang and Malacca as the Straits Settlements, and as such the main match each year was against the Federated Malay States. The Singapore Cricket Association was formed in 1949 and now plays in the Malaysian Cricket Association Championship. It was as part of the Malaysian CA that Singapore joined the ICC in 1967, but since 1974 Singapore have been a separate entity and as such have taken part in all three ICC Trophy competitions, though with limited success.

When the British left Singapore in the 1970s this considerably weakened cricket, reducing the number of teams by half, but some progress toward improving the standard has been made in recent years.

Single wicket

The common form of cricket is strictly speaking 'double wicket', but in the 19th century 'single wicket' matches were common. In these the batsman receives the ball continuously from the same end until he is dismissed, and at the bowling end there is normally only a single stump. Each team consists of one man, or up to six men.

This type of cricket is now found, with rare exceptions, played only by schoolchildren in an informal manner.

Slindon

In the early 1740s, the Sussex village of Slindon could field a team which was the equal of any in England as the following

newspaper notice shows: 'On Monday, 6th September. Will be played in the Artillery Ground the greatest match at cricket that has been played for many years, between the famous parish of Slindon in Sussex and eleven picked gentlemen of London. And as 'tis expected there will be the greatest number of people that ever was known on the like occasion, it's to be hoped – nay, desired – that gentlemen will not crowd in, by reason of a very large sum of money is laid that one of the Sussex gentlemen gets 40 notches himself.' This was in 1742 and the batsman expected to get 40 notches was Richard Newland, the Slindon captain, then considered the best batsman in England.

The Slindon team was most probably sponsored by the Duke of Richmond, who resided at nearby Goodwood House.

Slip

A position in the field adjacent to the wicketkeeper on the off-side. There are sometimes up to three slips, the first being nearest to the wicketkeeper.

Slow bowlers

Slow bowlers may not capture the imagination in the way fast bowlers do, but there are few more interesting sights than to watch the seemingly (from the boundary) innocuous slow deliveries diddle out the most experienced of batsmen. The most outstanding examples in post-war English cricket came in 1950 with the sudden arrival of Sonny Ramadhin and Alf Valentine. The West Indian pair had the English players all at sea. Of course in 1956 came England's turn in the shape of Jim Laker and the Australians were mesmerised.

In the 1960s, India seemed to be breeding spin bowlers at the same rate as the West Indies were producing the fast variety. Bedi, Chandrasekhar, Venkat and Prasanna all commanded respect.

The one ingredient that is totally lost in modern cricket is the art of slow underarm bowling. The craft of William Clarke and later of Simpson-Hayward vanished almost entirely by the First World War and completely by the Second. The leg-break and googly merchants seem to have finally been its death knell; those who might have practised the skill being more interested in the developments of Bosanquet and his followers, notably the South Africans Vogler and Faulkner. The Australians proved even more interested in the leg-break. Bradman considered Bill O'Reilly as the greatest of slow bowlers and he had taken over from Mailey and Clarrie Grimmett, who were equally great in their day. In the post-Second World War era Australia possessed so many leg-break experts that they flowed over into English county cricket, Dooland being the outstanding example. Richie Benaud, now the voice of Australian cricket, was one of the last famous Australian leg-break bowlers. England had one on his own in Doug Wright of Kent, whose delivery was surprisingly quick. It is now considered more economical to employ a left-arm spinner and the leg-break vogue in England seems to have passed.

The 'natural' break is off-spin and the first outstanding right-hand overarm slow bowler to arise in this field was Alfred Shaw 'the Emperor of Bowlers'. His career spanned over 30 years with Notts, England and Sussex. Yorkshire, which county came to the top in the 1890s, relied much more on left-arm slow bowlers. Ted Peate was the first in a most talented line, to be followed by Bobby Peel, Wilfred Rhodes, Hedley Verity and Johnny Wardle, all of whom played for England. Colin Blythe of Kent battled with Rhodes for the title of England's outstanding left-arm spinner of the Edwardian era. After the First World War, Kent relied more on the leg-breaks of 'Tich' Freeman. Though he was not greatly successful at Test level, Freeman still remains the only bowler to take 300 wickets in a first-class season.

Apart from their clutch of leg-break experts, South Africa's most outstanding spinner has been Hugh Tayfield. In the 1950s his off-breaks brought a shoal of wickets and in his day he came close to rivalling the great Jim Laker. A great off-break bowler of a little later was the West Indian Lance Gibbs, who from 1958 to 1976 took 309 Test wickets, at the time a record.

Although most of the slow bowlers mentioned have had long careers, much more extensive than their fast colleagues, there are a few exceptions, two of which merit attention. Jack Iverson, the Australian, sprang briefly to fame in 1950/51, as the mystery bowler. He possessed an unusual grip, which confused English batsmen, the leg break and googly being hard to distinguish. D.W. Carr, an English amateur, was brought out of club cricket in his late 30s and played for Kent and once for England, as a googly bowler, at a time when such bowlers were rare. His only Test brought him seven wickets, but at fair cost.

The outstanding spin bowlers in Test cricket in the mid-1980s are the Middlesex pair of Phil Edmonds and John Emburey, the former being left-arm. Australia are short of slow talent and West Indies have Roger Harper, who also appears for Northants. Abdul Qadir keeps the leg-break tradition alive in Pakistan, as does Laxman Sivarama-krishnan in India.

(*see also* Fast bowlers, Medium-pace bowlers, and individual entries for cricketers)

Small, Gladstone Cleophas

Born: 18 October 1961, St George, Barbados
Career: 148 *m*; 399 wkts (av 29.67)
Tests: 4 *m*; 16 wkts (av 19.62)

Small came to live in England when a boy, and becoming a good right-arm fast-medium bowler, made his debut for Warwickshire in 1980. He made his debut for England in the Second Test against New Zealand in 1986. He went on the tour of Australia in 1986/87, and returned to the side in the Fourth Test when Dilley was injured, capturing seven wickets and being named Man of the Match as England made sure of winning the series.

Sobers, Garfield St Aubrun

Born: 28 July 1936, Bridgetown, Barbados
Career: 383 *m*; 28,315 runs (av 54.87); 1,043 wkts (av 27.74)
Tests: 93 *m*; 8,032 runs (av 57.78); 235 wkts (av 34.03)

Gary Sobers is said by many to be the greatest all-rounder cricket has seen. He began principally as a slow left-arm bowler for Barbados in 1952/53, developed an aptitude for newball pace bowling when with South Australia in the early 1960s, and eventually could bowl any variety of swing or spin, and frequently bowled in three styles in one match. However, he developed so rapidly as a batsman that soon he was also the best batsman in the world. Added to this he was a brilliant fieldsman.

His Test career started in 1953/54, and his first really remarkable series came in 1957/58 against Pakistan, when he scored 365 not out, the highest-ever Test score, at Kingston. In the series he made 824 runs, average 137.33.

Sobers took over the captaincy of West Indies in 1964/65. He was to be captain 39 times, a record until passed by Lloyd. His Test performance in England in 1966 was outstanding: 722 runs, average 103.14, and 20 wickets, average 27.25.

In 1968 he joined Notts for seven seasons, lifting the county up the table. At Swansea in 1968 against Glamorgan, he hit each ball of an over for six, the first time such a feat had been performed. In 1970 he was captain of the Rest of the World team that played England.

He is one of the select band of cricketers to pass 2,000 runs and 200 wickets in Tests – Sobers' total of 8,032 Test runs was a record, since passed only by Boycott and Gavaskar. Towards the end of his career he was troubled by a knee injury, which finally persuaded him to retire in 1974. He was knighted in 1975.

Societies

Societies which are based on cricket but are not themselves cricket clubs have grown in number since the mid-1950s and in 1987 there were perhaps 50, most of which are based in the British Isles and belong to the Council of Cricket Societies. Membership of these societies is normally open to anyone on payment of an annual subscription, the amount of which varies depending on the facilities provided by the society. The three senior societies are the Cricket Society (founded 1948), the Northern Cricket Society (founded 1948) and the Wombwell Cricket Lovers (founded 1951).

The Cricket Society was previously the Society of Cricket Statisticians, which held its first meeting in November 1945, having been founded by Antony Weigall. In 1973 the Association of Cricket Statisticians was formed to research further into cricket history and statistics and now publishes 12 books each year. The membership of the Cricket Society is about 2,000, that of the Association of Cricket Statisticians about 1,300 and other societies have memberships from a few dozen to 1,000.

Softball cricket

Sponsored by Wrigley's, the softball cricket tournament began in 1981 as a method to encourage young school children to take up cricket, and by 1986 some 2,000 schools were involved in this tournament, the important feature being that it is not necessary to have a proper cricket ground in order to play softball cricket.

Somerset

A county of surprises, Somerset's reputation as a club composed chiefly of amateurs, whose qualifications rested entirely on the premise that they once changed trains at Taunton, is exaggerated, but they did find a place in the eleven on sundry occasions spread over 16 years for R.C. Robertson-Glasgow, who was noted more for his sense of humour, as well as his brilliant cricket essays, than his play.

Somerset gingerly dipped their toe in the Championship in

Gary Sobers was one of the most versatile of cricketers, regarded by many as the greatest all-rounder.

1882, but withdrew in 1885. In 1891 they cocked a snook at the county authorities by forcing their way back into the Championship by simply arranging fixtures with the official first-class counties and then daring authority to say that their matches would not count in the Championship table. The Somerset captain was H.T. Hewett, a most competent batsman, but in 1893 he took umbrage over the committee's interference with his leadership and at the age of 29 retired from county cricket.

Between the wars the hitters arrived, most prominent among whom were Arthur Wellard and Harold Gimblett. With the resumption of Championship cricket in 1946, Somerset came fourth, their best season thus far, despite a very variable eleven – no fewer than 14 amateurs flitted in and out of the side during the year.

In the 1950s the county had the misfortune to take the wooden spoon in four successive years, but the 1960s saw a distinct improvement. Bill Alley, who joined the county at an age when most professionals were thinking of retirement, spent 12 seasons at Taunton. This former Australian boxing professional put punch into the team, and in 1963 they came third in the Championship. It was not however until 1979 that Somerset took a title, and in that memorable year they gained two. Viv Richards hit a brilliant hundred then Joel Garner took six Northants wickets for 29 and Somerset won the Gillette Cup. The following day they performed the double by carrying off the John Player League. The combination of Garner and Richards and the explosive Botham provided Somerset with two trophies after 104 years of waiting.

Successes in the one-day competitions continued in the 1980s. The Benson & Hedges Cup was won in both 1981 and 1982, and in 1983 the NatWest (formerly Gillette) Trophy was won again. Test commitments however deprived the county of the West Indians in 1984 and of Botham for almost half the County Championship games each season, so despite the presence of three mega-stars, Somerset have yet to win the Championship itself. With the non-retention of Richards and Garner at the end of the 1986 season, and the departure of Botham in sympathy with his West Indian friends, Somerset began a period of rebuilding.

South Africa

Due to political controversy, South Africa have not played official Test cricket since 1969/70. Cricket followers can only speculate on what might have been, had South Africa's team been allowed to compete on the world stage since then. Possessing such cricketers as the Pollock brothers, Barry Richards, Kepler Wessels, Clive Rice, Mike Procter and Eddie Barlow, South Africa could field a side which would have given a good account of itself against England and Australia, if not the West Indies. Instead there have been a series of 'rebel' tours to South Africa by England, West Indies, Australia and Sri Lanka, during which the South African representative team have more than held their own.

The start of first-class and Test cricket in South Africa is a rather curious and certainly unsatisfactory one. The first English side to tour South Africa went out in 1889/90. It was a modest combination gathered together by a retired army officer who had served in South Africa. Nineteen matches were played, 17 being against odds and two being 11-a-side against a fairly representative South African team. Whilst it is not too far-fetched to describe these matches as 'first-class'

*Clive Rice of Notts hits out in the Benson & Hedges Cup
semi-final against Lancashire in 1984.*

and indeed they make a suitable starting point for 'first-class' cricket in South Africa, they have been raised to the status of Test Matches and are traditionally regarded as South Africa's first Test games. The stupidity of this ranking becomes immediately apparent when it is discovered that five years later, the first South African team toured England and their major games were not even granted 'first-class' status.

In the same season as this first 'Test Match', South Africa's present first-class competition – the Currie Cup (q.v.) – was founded. In 1951/52 this competition was divided into two sections, both of which are considered 'first-class'.

South African domestic cricket has been dominated by three sides, Western Province, Natal and Transvaal, with the last named being the most powerful in recent years. The major limited-overs competition is at present sponsored by Nissan and was founded in 1969/70 as the Gillette Cup.

It was one of South Africa's leading cricket patrons, Sir Abe Bailey, who was the driving force behind the idea of a grand 'Triangular Tournament' between England, Australia and South Africa (i.e. the three Test-playing countries) which was staged in England in 1912. Unfortunately bad weather and a second-rate Australian side caused the tournament to be a failure and only in recent times was the idea re-started. (see also the succeeding entry, also Australia v South Africa, England v South Africa and individual entries for cricketers and grounds)

South Africa v New Zealand

Results: Played 17; South Africa won 9; New Zealand won 2; Drawn 6

Of the five series between the two countries, South Africa won the first three, the fourth was tied and the last resulted in three drawn games.

The teams met for the first time in New Zealand after South Africa had toured Australia and lost all five Tests in 1931/32. The First Test took place at Lancaster Park, Christchurch. The feature of the batting was an opening stand of 196 by Jim Christy and Bruce Mitchell made in only 120 minutes. Both batsmen scored centuries and benefited from some poor fielding. When New Zealand batted they were baffled by the leg-spin of Quintin McMillan and Weir was the only home batsman to flourish (in the second innings he was undefeated with 74 out of 146). South Africa won with an innings to spare. The Second Test at Wellington showed New Zealand in a slightly better light, but even two good innings by H.G. Vivian (100 and 73) failed to prevent South Africa winning by eight wickets.

Although it was more than 20 years before the next series, the result was little different, in that South Africa were totally in control. The side that came to New Zealand in 1952/53 were the remarkable team under Jack Cheetham, which had unexpectedly tied a series against Australia.

In the First Test at Wellington, Jackie McGlew hit an unbeaten 255 and South Africa declared at 524 for 8. New Zealand failed to reach 200 in either innings. There was some very painful batting on both sides in the Second Test and South Africa spent over 500 minutes making 377 in the first innings. Once New Zealand managed to avoid the follow-on, a draw became the obvious result and interest in the match's later stages was minimal.

The following season New Zealand made their first tour to South Africa. Geoff Rabone captained the tourists, who struggled in their early matches against the Currie Cup sides and were predictably beaten in the First Test by an innings, Hugh Tayfield taking nine wickets and Roy McLean making a hundred. The Second Test at Ellis Park, Johannesburg, was the scene of some vicious bowling by Neil Adcock. Both Lawrie Miller and Bert Sutcliffe were forced to retire in mid-innings to receive hospital treatment, the latter returning to the crease later with a turban bandage and saving the follow-on with a whirlwind innings of 80 not out. The *Cape Times* noted after the game: 'All the glory was for the vanquished [New Zealanders]. Fiery bowlers on a fiery pitch failed to wither the dauntless spirit of a side of lesser cricket talent, perhaps, but not of smaller hearts.'

New Zealand in fact had the best of the Third Test, making 505 with John Reid reaching 135 and young Beck being run out at 99. South Africa scored only 326 and the follow-on was enforced, but by this time only three hours remained and the game was drawn. Tayfield and Adcock demolished the visitors in the fourth match, not a single New Zealander reaching 50, and though South Africa only managed a first innings lead of 11 in the final game, they still won by five wickets, giving the Springboks the series 4-0.

The fourth series also took place in South Africa. Captained by John Reid New Zealand were no longer regarded as complete novices and came to the First Test with two first-class wins under their belts. The opening Test at Durban was low scoring, only McGlew making a century, and New Zealand began their final innings needing 197 to win, but lost by 30 runs. The Second Test was drawn, then New Zealand recorded their first Test victory in the third match at Cape Town.

In this historic match New Zealand, through John Reid and Zin Harris, obtained a first-innings lead of nearly 200, but did not enforce the follow-on. Having made 212 in their second innings Reid declared, setting South Africa 475 minutes to make 408. New Zealand eventually won with about 30 minutes to spare by a margin of 72 runs.

New Zealand never recovered from a poor first innings in the Fourth Test and lost decisively, but in the Fifth they gained a good advantage from batting first and went on to win by 40 runs and thus square the series.

The last series between the two sides – in New Zealand in 1963/64 – was marred by slow scoring, echoing the pitches which did nothing to encourage either the batsmen or the bowlers. All three matches were drawn. Eddie Barlow hit most runs in the series and Peter Pollock was the most successful bowler.

South Australia

For many years the colony played the role of the third man, as the two giants, Victoria and New South Wales, squabbled intermittently between themselves. The South Australian Cricket Association was founded in 1871 and the first first-class match played in November 1877 against Tasmania, whilst the team were founder members of the Sheffield Shield.

For a long time South Australia was a one-man band, but that man was almost an orchestra by himself. The great George Giffen played from the very first season until 1903/04. On nine occasions he managed the match 'double' of 100 runs and 10 wickets, a number not remotely challenged by any other Australian and indeed in the whole history of the game exceeded only by W.G. Grace.

Clem Hill arrived in the 1890s to give Giffen a hand and other later players include Clarrie Grimmett and Don Bradman. The Chappell brothers came in more recent years, but tragically for South Australia, Greg defected to Queensland. The Sheffield Shield has been won 12 times and South Australia have the pleasure of playing at Adelaide which is regarded as the most agreeable of Australian state grounds.

Spin
The rotary motion imparted to the ball by the bowler in order to make a delivery move to leg or to the off when it hits the ground, hence 'spin bowler' and 'spinning finger', being the finger which gives the ball its revolving movement.

Spofforth, Frederick Robert
Born: 9 September 1853, Balmain, NSW, Australia
Died: 4 June 1926, Long Ditton, Surrey, England
Career: 155 m; 853 wkts (av 14.95)
Spofforth was about the first international fast bowler to strike fear into opponents' hearts: he was nicknamed 'the Demon Bowler'. After making his debut for New South Wales in 1874, he played in the second Test Match ever in 1876/77, but it was in 1878, at Lord's, that he first shook Englishmen, taking 6 for 4, including a hat-trick, and 5 for 16 to beat MCC, captained by W.G. Grace, in a day. In 1878/79, back in Australia in the third Test ever, he took the first Test hat-trick, and his 6 for 48 and 7 for 62 resulted in a ten-wicket defeat for the Poms.

Spofforth was 6 feet 2 inches, and leapt into his delivery stride, thus bringing the ball down from a great height. At first, he relied entirely on speed; later he reduced his pace and developed more guile. Perhaps his greatest match was the first Test ever played in England, at the Oval in 1882. England needed 85 in the second innings to win, but were dismissed for 77. Spofforth's figures were 7 for 46 and 7 for 44. It was this match which provoked the obituary for English cricket and the 'Ashes' (q.v.).

Spofforth was successful on all his five tours to England, and in 1888 emigrated and played for Derbyshire, who were not then first-class.

F.R. Spofforth, the 'Demon Bowler', who had five outstanding tours of England, taking 207 wickets in 1884.

Square
1 The area of the cricket field, usually about square, from which a rectangle can be selected to form the pitch for a given match. There is usually room for six or more pitches on a square, the groundsman preparing them in rotation so that no one section of the square becomes too worn.
2 At right angles to the batsman and bowler, hence 'square-leg' is a fielding position on the leg side (similar to point but on the opposite side); also 'square hit', being a stroke made in the direction of square-leg or point.

Sri Lanka
Having been elected a full member of the ICC, Sri Lanka made their bow in Test cricket in the 1981/82 season and in 1984 earned a well-deserved draw on their first Test appearance at Lord's.

The first cricket club was formed in Colombo in 1832. The major domestic match of the season in Ceylon, as it then was, from the 1880s to the 1930s was Europeans against Ceylonese, the former team generally being able to field three or four players with first-class county experience, of whom W.T. Greswell was the best-known. Many of the English teams *en route* for Australia stopped off at Colombo for a one-day match, as did several Australian sides touring England, but the main overseas visitors came from India and it was to India that many Ceylonese teams went.

It is generally considered that first-class matches involving Ceylon commence with the game between Ceylon and Bombay in Colombo in 1925/26, but even to the present day there has been no first-class domestic competition on the island.

The first Ceylon side to tour overseas and appear in first-class cricket visited India in 1932/33, and in 1952/53 the regular series of games between Madras and Ceylon began for the Gopalan Trophy. The games are played alternately in Madras and Colombo.

*Mike Procter, the great South African all-rounder, in the
delivery stride of his awkward action, bowling for Gloucestershire in 1977.*

Sri Lanka won the first ICC Trophy in 1979 and it was partially due to this victory that the country were given Test Match status. Sri Lanka have toured England, playing first-class matches in 1979, 1981 and 1984, and in 1986 sent over a Young Sri Lankan Team (under 19). This side won the two one-day internationals against Young England, but having drawn the first two 'Test' matches, lost the third, which was played at Trent Bridge, by six wickets.

The standard of cricket in Sri Lanka has risen very rapidly since the mid-1970s and the sport is extremely popular there. (*see also* Colombo, Australia v Sri Lanka, England v Sri Lanka, India v Sri Lanka, New Zealand v Sri Lanka and Pakistan v Sri Lanka)

Staffordshire

Unlike many minor county clubs, the present Staffordshire Club have had a continuous existence of over 100 years, being formed in 1871. The county are forever associated with the remarkable Sydney Barnes, who tried first-class county cricket twice, but then rejected it in favour of his native Staffordshire, though such was his talent that even as a minor counties man he still commanded a place in the England team. The county won the Championship in 1906, 1908, 1911, 1920, 1921 and 1927, all due to the bowling of Barnes. His biographer claims that Barnes took 6,229 wickets, average 8.33, in competitive cricket in his career.

Stamps

The first English set of postage stamps to appear with cricketing connotations was issued by the GPO in 1973 to commemorate the centenary of the County Championship, though as pointed out at the time it only commemorated the rules governing the qualification of players. The stamps depicted W.G. Grace, as drawn by the cartoonist Harry Furniss.

The Australian Post Office issued a set of stamps to

celebrate the centenary Test Match in 1977 and a similar event was celebrated in England by stamps in 1980. Gary Sobers has been featured on several stamps from the West Indies and the issue of cricketing stamps has become common since the mid-1970s. Marcus Williams is the recognised expert in this field.

Stance
The attitude of the batsman as he waits for the bowler to deliver the ball, hence 'two-eyed stance', when the batsman stands with the front of his body facing the bowler.

Statistics
The well-known remark that statistics can be made to prove anything, is as true of cricket statistics as of any other branch.

Cricket statistics are usually confined to Test or first-class cricket, principally because other classes of the game are not sufficiently well documented to enable the compilation of 'records' in any detail. Through the researches of many individuals and the publication by Bill Frindall of a definitive set of Test Match scorecards (*The Wisden Book of Test Cricket 1877–1984*, published by Queen Anne Press, 1985) statistical buffs are well catered for. This volume also contains a large selection of statistics by Bill Frindall. A detailed statistical book *England v Australia Test Match Records 1887–1985*, edited by David Frith, was published by Collins-Willow in 1986.

The problems of compiling definitive first-class records are becoming well known, due to the work of the Association of Cricket Statisticians. For too many years record compilers attempted to produce statistics on first-class cricket without first composing and publishing a list of first-class matches. Ideally the same process ought to be used as with Test Matches, i.e. a book or books containing the definitive version of every match should precede the issuing of the 'records'. Because of the number of matches this is not practicable, but the Association of Cricket Statisticians have come as near as possible to this by publishing Guides giving the whereabouts of every first-class match and the necessary amendments to errors in those matches, for the Test-playing countries. Philip Bailey is considered the leading authority on first-class cricket statistics.

(*see also* Introduction)

Stroke
The action of the batsman hitting the ball, particularly when this results in runs being scored; in contrast 'strokeless' indicates making no strokes which result in runs.

Stump
1. A wooden turned rod, usually made of ash, three of which are set in the ground to form a 'wicket'. The stump is 28 inches long, plus a spike at one end which is driven into the ground, the other end being grooved to take the bail(s).
2. The act of dismissing a batsman, when he moves outside the popping crease, whilst attempting to hit a delivery from the bowler. Only the wicketkeeper can 'stump' a batsman, the former having to break the wicket whilst the ball is in his hand, or by throwing the ball to break the wicket, hence 'stumped'. In the scorebook the batsman is showed as 'st'.

Substitute
A man who comes on to act as a fielder in place of an injured member of the given team. The opposing captain can object to the substitute acting as wicketkeeper. As a general rule substitutes cannot bat or bowl, but they are occasionally permitted to do so, when the player for whom they are acting is totally disabled within a short time of the match commencing and will obviously be unable to take any part in the proceedings.

In the score details, when a substitute takes a catch, he is usually shown abbreviated as 'sub'.

Suffolk
Although Suffolk played Norfolk as early as 1764 and the Bury St Edmunds Club in the 1820s was one of the strongest in England, the county did not have an official county club until 1864 and that collapsed within ten years; another began in 1876 but again survived less than a decade. The 'Country Vicar' who wrote articles regularly over many years for cricket publications launched the Suffolk County Cricket Association and entered a team in the Minor Counties Championship between 1904 and 1914. The county did not return to the Championship until 1934 and have won the title twice. In 1946, under the captaincy of A.G. Powell, the two professionals G.C. Perkins and W. Duckham bowled the club to victory. Their second Championship in 1977, under R.E. Cunnell, was due to R.N.S. Hobbs' leg spin and the batting of D.G. Bevan.

Sunday cricket
In England some club sides played friendly Sunday matches in the years between the two world wars, but it was not until during the Second World War that club cricket on Sundays became relatively common. The first inter-county first-class match involving Sunday play took place at Ilford, when Essex played Somerset on Saturday, Sunday and Monday, 14, 15 and 16 May 1966. It was at that time illegal to charge admission, but 6,000 spectators paid nearly £500 through scorecard sales and collections. In Australia, the first first-class match played on a Sunday was between Western Australia and Queensland in 1964/65.

The first Test Match in England including Sunday play was at Trent Bridge in June 1981.

Sundries
The term used in Australia for what are elsewhere known as 'extras' (q.v.).

Surrey
Surrey have been regarded as one of the strongest counties ever since inter-county cricket took on a recognisable form. The two outstanding periods in Surrey's history were in the latter part of the 19th century when they were County Champions under John Shuter for six successive seasons, and the 1950s when Stuart Surridge and Peter May led the team to seven successive titles, a run unequalled in the competition.

The rather odd aspect of this formidable record is that Jack Hobbs, regarded by his contemporaries as the greatest

The Surrey club in 1952, after winning the first of a record seven successive championships.
Standing, left to right: A. Sandham (coach), G.A.R. Lock, A.F. Brazier,
R.C.E. Pratt, T.H. Clark, G.J. Whittaker, E.A. Bedser, J.C. Laker,

P.J. Loader, G.N.G. Kirby, A.J.W. McIntyre, D.F. Cox, H. Strudwick (scorer),
S. Tait (masseur). Sitting: D.G.W. Fletcher, A.V. Bedser, L.B. Fishlock,
W.S. Surridge (captain), P.B.H. May, J.F. Parker. B. Constable.

English batsman, was a member of a Surrey title side only once, despite a career spanning 30 years – and even the one success was somewhat suspect, being in 1914, when the last matches of the season were cancelled due to the war.

The great side of the early 1890s possessed an all-round quality of quite brilliant proportions. The bowling was chiefly in the hands of Lohmann, described by C.B. Fry as the most difficult medium-pace bowler he had faced, but now largely forgotten. Assisting Lohmann were a trio imported from Notts, Bowley, Sharpe and Lockwood. Then in 1892 came Tom Richardson, but Surrey's grip slackened under pressure from the increasing power of Yorkshire.

The 1950s attack was spearheaded by Alec Bedser, Jim Laker and Tony Lock, the last two providing the spin attack and Bedser being aided by Loader with the new ball. The whole attack was materially assisted by some brilliant close fielding – Surridge and Lock being outstanding.

Peter May was the star batsman throughout the 1950s title wins, with Barrington and Stewart maturing during the decade; the runs for the 1890s had come principally from the 'Guvnor' (Bobby Abel) and the two unrelated Reads, the amateur, W.W. and the professional, Maurice.

Since the 1950s, the Championship has been regained just once – in 1971, when Arnold and Pocock bowled out the opposition. Two one-day titles have come the county's way. In 1974 the Benson & Hedges Cup was won mainly by some astute batting and captaincy from John Edrich. In 1982, Surrey completely outplayed Warwickshire to win the final of the NatWest Trophy by nine wickets with 26.2 overs in hand. Alan Butcher hit an unbeaten 86, though the left-arm seamer, David Thomas, with 3 for 26, gained the Man of The Match Award.

Brief though this essay is, a line or two must be devoted to C.W. Alcock, perhaps cricket's greatest administrator. Alcock was secretary of Surrey from 1872 until his death in 1907. He was responsible for the first Test ever played in England and also organised the fixtures for many of the touring teams to England. He founded and edited a weekly cricket magazine and for 29 years edited Lillywhite's Annual. Behind the scenes he created the great Surrey side of the 1890s. He was also secretary of the Football Association.

Sussex

Seven times in modern cricket history (since 1864) Sussex have come second in the Championship table, yet they have never succeeded in capturing the major county title. In the last 30 years of the 19th century, when the opposition won the toss at Hove, the bottom half of the batting order went down to the beach for the day, whilst the rest took the Sussex attack apart. Lord Sheffield brought in the old England captain, Shaw, as coach, but the latter despaired of turning the locals into county cricketers and ended by importing players, and, though in his mid-fifties, he was forced into playing for the county himself.

Near the turn of the century Ranji arrived. Sussex had previously enrolled the services of the Australian captain, Murdoch, with little success, but with the Indian Prince as their leader and C.B. Fry as his lieutenant, Sussex came second in 1902 and again in 1903. These two exceptional batsmen toyed with most county attacks, but to clinch the title Sussex required two equally talented bowlers. These, however, were not forthcoming.

In the 1930s, Sussex again challenged for the crown. This time they came second in three successive seasons: 1932, 1933 and 1934. They owed their rise this time to two pairs of brothers, John and Jim Langridge and Harry and Jim Parks, together with the steadiness of Maurice Tate, but this impressive combination could not quite knock Yorkshire off the top.

The immediate post-Second World War years were undistinguished, but in 1953 they popped up in second place again. Led by David Sheppard, who topped the batting averages, and was assisted during the holidays by Winchester schoolmaster Hubert Doggart, they had three notable pros, Suttle, Parks (son of the 1930s Jim) and young George Cox. The capable quartet of Thomson, James, Oakman and Marlar made up an attack for all weathers.

It was the flamboyant Ted Dexter ten years later who gained Sussex their first title as the first winners of the Gillette Cup, though it was a bowlers' match. The Sussex bowlers repeated their success the following summer, dismissing Warwickshire in the final for a mere 127, Thomson taking 4 for 23. The Cup came Sussex's way in 1978 and in 1986, when Paul Parker's batting had much to do with their victory. In between times, Sussex managed to come second yet again in the Championship of 1981. Parker topped the batting average that year, but the county owed much to the fast bowling of the South African, Le Roux, and the splendid all-round cricket of Pakistan's Imran Khan. Sussex therefore still await their first Championship title and until that happens the county's greatest days remain in the long distant past – the 30 years before 1856. The revolutionary round-arm bowlers – Broadbridge and William Lillywhite – came from Sussex in the 1820s and were followed in the 1840s by the 'Little Wonder', John Wisden (of the Almanack).

Sutcliffe, Bert
Born: 17 November 1923, Auckland, New Zealand
Career: 232 m; 17,283 runs (av 47.22)
Tests: 42 m; 2,727 runs (av 40.10)
Bert Sutcliffe, a left-hand opening batsman, was New Zealand's best player throughout the 1950s. He began playing for Auckland during the Second World War; later he switched to Otago and then Northern Districts. He hit 197 and 128 in the same match against the MCC tourists at Dunedin in 1946/47, and 58 at Christchurch in the only Test Match, his first.

In England on the 1949 tour, he averaged 60.42 in the Tests. His highest Test score came in 1955/56, against India at Delhi, when he made 230 not out. In domestic cricket he hit 355 and 385 for Otago, the latter being the highest first-class score by a left-hander. A stroke-player of great artistry, he became an excellent coach when he retired.

Sutcliffe, Herbert
Born: 24 November 1894, Harrogate, Yorkshire
Died: 22 January 1978, Crosshills, Yorkshire
Career: 754 m; 50,670 runs (av 52.02)
Tests: 54 m; 4,555 runs (av 60.73)
Sutcliffe was both fortunate and unfortunate to be associated in the most famous opening partnership of all time, Hobbs and Sutcliffe: fortunate for obvious reasons, unfortunate because he has always been regarded as secondary to his

Bert Sutcliffe ducking a bouncer in the 1949 Oval Test Match. He was New Zealand's leading batsman for nearly 20 years, but was not on the winning side in 42 Tests.

illustrious partner, despite having the higher Test average.

Sutcliffe made his Yorkshire debut in 1919, in the first season after the First World War, and played for them until 1945, when there were only 11 first-class matches after the Second World War ended.

Sutcliffe was noted for his immaculate grooming at the wicket; also for his imperturbability. Good on all wickets, he excelled on difficult ones, and the more often he was beaten the more determined he became. His best seasons were 1931 and 1932, when he passed 3,000 runs. In the latter season he made his highest score, 313, when he and Holmes put on 555 for Yorkshire against Essex at Leyton, for over 50 years a world record, for the first wicket.

He made his Test debut in 1924, and made 15 century opening stands with the older Hobbs, perhaps the most famous being the 172 on a difficult pitch at the Oval in 1926, which virtually won the Ashes. He never failed on three tours to Australia – in fact he hardly ever failed at all, and of batsmen who have scored over 2,500 Test runs, only Bradman has a higher average.

Sweep

A batsman's stroke, during which he goes down on one knee and almost literally sweeps the ball to leg with a horizontal bat.

Sydney

Administered by a Board of Trustees, the Sydney Cricket Ground, home of the New South Wales Cricket Association, was opened in 1877 and the first first-class match was played there in 1877/78. Prior to this, cricket was played on the Domain and then in the 1860s on the Albert Ground, but due to a dispute, the New South Wales Association were moved to the present site.

The first Test Match staged there was between Australia and England in 1881/82. The best-known feature of the ground is 'The Hill', which is surmounted by the scoreboard. There was much controversy in 1978 when six large towers were erected to bring floodlighting to the ground, but these are now an accepted part of the arena.

Herbert Sutcliffe, posing in the nets, as immaculate as ever.

T

Tallest cricketers

In recent years the tallest cricketers appearing regularly in County Championship cricket have been Joel Garner of Somerset and Dallas Moir of Derbyshire, both standing at 6 feet 8 inches, but still below A.T.C. Allom of Surrey (1960) at 6 feet 10½ inches.

Tasmania

In the middle of the 19th century Tasmania possessed a useful cricket side, but as the game improved on the mainland of Australia, the island colony stagnated. Victoria opposed Tasmania in February 1851 in the first inter-colonial match in Australia and therefore the beginning of first-class cricket there. Through the years Tasmania played Victoria at intervals, but matches against the other Cricket Associations were infrequent.

What little strength Tasmania had was further dissipated by being divided between Hobart and Launceston: the Southern Tasmanian Cricket Association was formed in 1866, but did not develop into the Tasmanian CA until 1906.

Only in 1977/78 were Tasmania admitted to the Sheffield Shield and in the first years the side's leading figure was the Lancastrian, Jack Simmons. In 1978/79, Tasmania won their first prize – the Gillette Cup – beating Western Australia in the final by 47 runs.

Tate, Maurice William

Born: 30 May 1895, Brighton, Sussex
Died: 18 May 1956, Wadhurst, Sussex
Career: 679 m; 21,717 runs (av 25.01); 2,784 wkts (av 18.16)
Tests: 39 m; 1,198 runs (av 25.48); 155 wkts (av 26.16)

Maurice Tate made his debut for Sussex in 1912, bowling off-breaks. Ten years later he switched to medium-fast seam bowling and immediately became the best of his type in the world – indeed he was a pioneer of seam bowling. It was frequently said of Tate that when the ball pitched it increased in pace. Scientists might dispute this, but it is the impression that the batsmen received.

Tate made his Test debut in 1924, and was England's most successful bowler on two tours of Australia. He was also no mean middle-order batsman (he occasionally opened) who hit 203 against Northants in 1921, his 23 centuries including one for England against South Africa in 1929.

Tate was a genuine all-rounder: of four players to score 1,000 runs and take 200 wickets in a season, he performed it most often (three times), and he is one of nine players who scored 20,000 runs and took 2,000 wickets in a career.

Team

The body of players which make up one side in a game. The

Laws state that a team can consist of any number of players, though they recommend 11, which number is required for first-class matches. There have, however, been matches recorded with 56 players on one side and on a number of occasions one player has challenged and beaten 11. Until the Second World War, 12-a-side matches were seen fairly regularly.

Test and County Cricket Board

The Test and County Cricket Board (TCCB) held its first meeting in December 1968, and consists of representatives of each of the first-class counties, the MCC, Minor Counties Cricket Association, Oxford University CC, Cambridge University CC, Irish Cricket Union and Scottish Cricket Union. The body governs Test and first-class cricket in the British Isles and normally has two meetings annually. There are however 11 TCCB sub-committees which deal with the various subjects involving the Board in detail.
(*see also* Administration)

Test Matches

The first-known use of 'Test Match' referring to cricket appears in Hammersley's 'Victorian Cricketer's Guide' published in Melbourne in 1862. On page 159, during a review of the 1861/62 season, the following is noted: 'Of the thirteen matches [by the English touring team], five only can be termed "test matches"; the three played at Melbourne and the two at Sydney.'

The phrase 'Test Match' to describe international matches between England and Australia came into general usage during the 1880s. The match between Australia and Lillywhite's Team of 1876/77 in Melbourne in March 1877 is regarded as the first Test Match (the 1861/62 matches were against odds).

By the start of the 20th century historians were divided as to precisely which matches were regarded as 'Test Matches', but the list published by C.P. Moody in 'Australian Cricket and Cricketers' in Melbourne in 1894 has come to be considered the 'official' list.
(*see also* individual entries for Test-playing countries and for each series)

Third man

A position in the field behind the slip fielders on the off side, which can vary between 'deep' and 'short' and also 'fine' or 'square'.

Throwing

Since the legalisation of overarm bowling in 1864, there have been two periods during which throwing, i.e. the straightening of the bowling arm at the elbow during the delivery swing, has caused major problems for umpires and administrators. The first outbreak occurred in the 1880s with the Lancashire bowler, Jack Crossland, as the most quoted offender.

Kent and Nottinghamshire broke off fixtures with Lancashire, and Crossland was removed from county cricket,

Maurice Tate of Sussex, whose success as a fast-medium bowler obscures the fact that he also scored over 20,000 runs and was a genuine all-rounder.

The Centenary Test Match at Melbourne in 1977, and the Man of the Match, Derek Randall, hooking Lillee for four runs, watched by Brearley.

although not by being no-balled, but because he was not after all qualified for Lancashire. George Nash, also of Lancashire, was the other main culprit in the 1880s and he was quietly dropped.

The problem however did not disappear and a fresh spate of throwing occurred in the 1890s. This time the umpires, notably Jim Phillips, acted and a number of English bowlers as well as several Australians were no-balled. This action combined with an agreement by the English county captains not to use certain bowlers brought the matter to a close.

There were isolated instances of players being no-balled for throwing in the inter-war period, but none of these occurred in England. The problem arose again in the 1950s and reached a climax with the South African fast bowler G.M. Griffin, who was no-balled 11 times by the umpire, F.S. Lee, during the 1960 England v South Africa Test at Lord's in 1960, and after the match, was again no-balled in an exhibition game and forced to complete an over bowling underarm. In Australia, Ian Meckiff came in for similar

treatment in the Test against South Africa at Brisbane in 1963/64, being no-balled four times in one over by the umpire, C.J. Egar, and Meckiff actually announced his premature retirement from first-class cricket after that game.

Although there have been other examples of bowlers being no-balled for throwing since the mid-1960s, this difficult area of legislation seems now to be working satisfactorily.

In the days before 1864, bowlers were occasionally no-balled for delivering the ball with too high an arm, but umpires tended to ignore the Law in this matter and sooner or later the Law was altered to legalise what had been happening for some years: as underarm evolved into roundarm, then the latter evolved into overarm.

Tie

The result of a match in which both sides have made the same number of runs. In County Championship cricket for a game to be a tie, the side batting last has to lose all its wickets; if the

English sides have toured India since 1889/90. This is a one-day game at Pune in 1984/85.

match ends with the side batting last having wickets in hand, then the game counts as a draw.

Tours

A great feature of the cricket calendar is the visit to England of a major team from overseas and the same is true of English cricket sides travelling abroad and indeed the visit of any country's players to a foreign soil.

With the great enthusiasm that exists for centenary and bicentenary celebrations, perhaps 1989 will be marked in an appropriate manner as the bicentenary of the first cancelled tour! It was in 1789 that the Duke of Dorset's planned cricket expedition to France was abandoned due to the Revolution. England finally managed to send a team outside the British Isles 70 years later, when George Parr's professionals went to North America.

Apart from the semi-serious visit by the Aborigines in 1868, it was not until 1878 that the Australians came to Britain and, making so much money, they returned at two-year intervals until 1890. Not that the flow of cash was entirely one way; the English teams of the 1870s and 1880s went almost as frequently to Australia, until they finally killed the golden goose by sending two rival parties in the same season.

The United States, Canada, India and in the 1890s South

Fred Trueman bowling for Yorkshire against Middlesex at Scarborough in 1965, his last season as a Test fast bowler.

Africa sent teams to England, but they were mainly amateur sides and attracted little public attention, therefore no money was to be made – indeed they had to pay their own way.

Aside from the principal England team, the number of amateur combinations which embarked on cricketing holidays abroad grew as travel facilities became easier. Before the Second World War these sides were often content with trips to Portugal, Denmark, the Netherlands and other not too distant parts, but now schoolboy cricketers seem to rush off to India or Australia almost without noticing it, and to attempt to compile a definitive list of every English cricketing team touring overseas would be a terrible task, as in fact would the compilation of teams coming to the British Isles.

The schedule for Test-playing tours has grown since the Second World War to the extent that the leading English cricketers rarely have a winter's break from the game. To satisfy the other Test-playing countries this is inevitable, but scarcely desirable.

Trent Bridge
Situated in the Nottingham suburb of West Bridgford, the ground was laid out behind the Trent Bridge Inn in 1838 by William Clarke, captain of the Nottingham team. The first county match (against Sussex) took place on the ground in 1840, previous games having been staged on The Forest.

The pavilion, erected in 1886, was the first of the grand late Victorian edifices which grace the current English Test grounds. Like the Oval, the ground was also in regular use for important soccer matches, and until 1910 was the home of Notts County FC. In 1897 and 1909 England staged soccer internationals there, while the first Test in Nottingham took place in 1899 against Australia. The main stands were erected between the wars, but a recent addition has been the Larwood and Voce stand.

During the First World War the pavilion was used as a hospital and in the Second as an army post office. The ground is the headquarters of Nottinghamshire County Cricket Club and the present seating capacity is about 15,000, though the record attendance for a single day's play is reported to be 35,000.

Trueman, Frederick Sewards
Born: 6 February 1931, Stainton, Yorkshire
Career: 603 m; 9,231 runs (av 15.56); 2,304 wkts (av 18.29)
Tests: 67 m; 981 runs (av 13.18); 307 wkts (av 21.57)
Trueman was a fiery fast bowler who made his first appearance for Yorkshire in 1949, and a sensational Test debut in 1952, when he and Bedser had India 0 for 4 wickets in their second innings at Headingley. His 8 for 31 at Old Trafford in that series was his best Test bowling.

For ten years or so Trueman was the most feared fast bowler in England. Very strong, broad in the beam and with a classic sideways-on action, he always bowled wholeheartedly and with belligerence. He had a reputation for outspokenness that appealed to the ordinary fan but probably cost a few Test appearances.

His best season was 1960 with 175 wickets, average 13.98. In the Fifth Test at the Oval in 1964, Neil Hawke of Australia was his 300th Test victim – he was the first to reach this figure.

After retirement he became a regular member of the BBC Test Match Special commentary team.

Trumper, Victor Thomas
Born: 2 November 1877, Darlinghurst, NSW, Australia
Died: 28 June 1915, Darlinghurst, NSW, Australia
Career: 255 m; 16,939 runs (av 44.57)
Tests: 48 m; 3,163 runs (av 39.04)
Trumper's poor figures for a 'great' belie his stature: he is generally regarded as the greatest Australian batsman of his era, and some would say any era. It was the style and grace of his batting which appealed. He was a giant in the golden age of cricket, and nobody had a more appropriate name: the victory and triumph went hand in hand with modesty.

'Trumper jumping out to drive' is one of cricket's most famous photographs. It was taken in England, where he toured four times, making his highest career score, 300 not out, against Sussex at Hove in 1899. In season 1902 he carried all before him. His most famous innings was at Old Trafford on a soft wicket. With the sun coming out, the English bowlers were told to keep him quiet until lunch, when the pitch would become sticky. Trumper scored 104 before lunch, and Australia won by three runs.

Trumper died of Bright's disease when only 38.

Turner, Glenn Maitland
Born: 26 May 1947, Dunedin, New Zealand
Career: 455 m; 34,346 runs (av 49.70)
Tests: 41 m; 2,991 runs (av 44.64)
Turner was the best New Zealand batsman of the 1970s. He began his career with Otago in 1964/65 as a very defensive opener, who once scored only three runs in a pre-lunch session, but later, after he had joined Worcestershire in 1967, he radically altered his style, developing the attacking strokes while still remaining sound.

Turner achieved some interesting feats in county cricket. He became the first batsman to score a century against all 17 first-class counties. In 1973 he scored 1,000 runs before the end of May which has not been achieved again in the 13 years since. In 1981 he scored 141 of Worcestershire's 169 against Glamorgan: 83.4 per cent of an innings is a first-class record. He scored his 100th century with 128 before lunch against Warwickshire in 1982, and went on to 311 not out – had Worcestershire not declared he might have beaten the record score ever made in one day, 345.

In Test Matches, he also achieved some remarkable feats. Against England at Lord's in 1969 he carried his bat for 43 out of 131, the youngest player to do this in Tests. In 1971/72 in the West Indies, he carried his bat for 223 out of 386, the highest score by a player achieving this feat. In the same series he scored 259, New Zealand's highest Test score. In 1973/74 against Australia he became the first New Zealander to score a century in each innings of a Test.

He captained his country, but was not always at one with the authorities, and missed some Tests. He retired in 1982/83.

Twelfth man
It is common practice in 11-a-side matches to select 12 players and then decide on the final 11 on the morning of the

The Trent Bridge cricket ground, with England playing the West Indies in the First Test of 1980.

match. The discarded player acts as a substitute fielder if required and as general 'dogsbody'. One celebrated twelfth man was S.G. Barnes, the Australian Test cricketer, who was unexpectedly dropped from the Australian side and ended up as twelfth man for New South Wales v South Australia at Adelaide. He brought the drinks out to the fielders dressed in a morning suit with carnation, scent spray, portable radio and cigars.

Glenn Turner, New Zealand's outstanding batsman of the 1970s, holds many records in Test and county cricket. He is batting in the Third Test at Headingley in 1973.

V TRUMPER

The legendary Victor Trumper, on one of his tours to England. He was the outstanding Australian batsman of the golden age of cricket.

U

Umpire

One of two officials who are appointed to see that the game is played according to the Laws (and any other regulations governing the match in question) and to give their decisions on any points submitted to them by the players.

One umpire stands at square-leg (*see* Square) and the other at the bowler's end in a line so that he can give a decision on a question relating to lbw.

Underarm

A style of bowling in which the hand is below the elbow at the moment of delivering the ball. Until 1835 only underarm bowling was permitted by the Laws, but nowadays such bowling is usually only seen in children's games.
(*see also* Overarm and Roundarm)

Universities Athletic Union

Cricket is played at nearly 40 Universities (as well as Oxford and Cambridge) in England and Wales and most of these are affiliated to the Universities Athletic Union, which governs all sports at University level. The UAU organise a cricket competition between the Universities and since the mid-1960s this competition has been dominated by Durham, Exeter, Loughborough, Manchester and Southampton. The first competition was staged in 1927 when Manchester were the winners. The UAU also select a representative XI which plays matches mainly in the early part of the season.

USA

Regarded nowadays as minnows in the cricketing world, it is difficult to realise that a team raised from Philadelphia used to come to England and play on equal terms with the first-class counties. The Gentlemen of Philadelphia toured England five times between 1884 and 1908 and on their last three trips were granted first-class status.

The United States played Canada as early as 1844 and it was to North America that the first English team travelled in 1859. The strong centres of cricket in the United States in the pre-1914 era were Philadelphia and New York, and English professionals went out to various clubs each season as players and coaches. The professionals were capable of fielding a fair team and for some years, an annual Gentlemen v Players match was organised. The most celebrated American cricketer was J.B. King, who topped the English first-class bowling averages in 1908, when he was a member of the Philadelphian touring side.

As the notable Philadelphian cricketers of the turn of the century retired no new talented players came to take their place and the standard of cricket in Philadelphia gently declined. Various English sides went out in the inter-war period but they failed to revive the game and the slide was not finally arrested until John Marder began his crusade in the 1950s, and in 1968 a team from the United States toured England playing mainly county second elevens. The United States had became an Associate member of the ICC in 1965 and have competed in the three ICC Trophy competitions, being most successful in 1986 when seven out of eight matches were won and the team missed going into the semi-finals only on run rate.

V

Vengsarkar, Dilip Balwant

Born: 6 April 1956, Rajapur, India
Career: 190 *m*; 12,583 runs (av 48.58)
Tests: 85 *m*; 4,985 runs (av 40.20)
An attractive right-hand batsman, who used to open, but now goes in lower down, he made both his first-class and Test debuts in 1975/76. He made his impact as a world-class batsman whilst on the 1977/78 tour to Australia, and did exceptionally well on his first visit to England in 1979 – in the 1979 calendar year he hit over 1,000 runs in Test cricket. Another feat which he has accomplished is that of hitting three hundreds in successive Tests at Lord's.

Verity, Hedley

Born: 18 May 1905, Headingley, Leeds
Died: 31 July 1943, Caserta, Italy
Career: 378 *m*; 5,603 runs (av 18.07); 1,956 wkts (av 14.90)
Tests: 40 *m*; 669 runs (av 20.90); 144 wkts (av 24.37)
Verity, because of the strength of Yorkshire, did not make his debut for them until 1930, but throughout the 1930s was the best slow left-arm bowler in England. He did not take long to make his mark: 10 for 36 in an innings against Warwickshire in 1931, followed by 10 for 10, the best innings analysis in all first-class cricket, in 1932 against Notts. Seven times during

Dilip Vengsarkar was the outstanding Indian batsman on the 1986 tour of England. He is seen batting in the First Test, when he became the first overseas batsman to score three Test centuries at Lord's.

English village cricket. An idyllic setting at Swan Green, Lyndhurst, in Hampshire's New Forest.

the 1930s he took nine wickets in an innings, in nine of those ten seasons he took 110 wickets

Verity was a little quicker than the usual slow left-armer. He was also a useful lower-order right-hand batsman, who opened once in a Test in Australia, helping Barnett to stands of 53 and 45.

His Test career began in 1931, and his most famous day came in 1934, when, against the strong Australians, including Bradman, he took 14 wickets for 80 in one day to give England victory by an innings. He was in his prime when war broke out, and he died of wounds in an Italian prisoner-of-war camp.

Victoria

Although the colony of Victoria played their first first-class match against Tasmania in February 1851, the first Victorian Cricket Association was not formed until 1864 and was then of little consequence, being hardly more than an appendage to the Melbourne Cricket Club, which ran the Melbourne Ground and organised a number of the early tours to and from England. The great 'Australian row' of 1912 changed the status of the MCC and VCA, since when the latter has controlled its state cricket.

In the early days of the Sheffield Shield the great rivalry was between Victoria and New South Wales, but Victoria's best period in Shield cricket came between the wars with a batting line up of Bill Ponsford, Bill Woodfull and Jack Ryder, and the bowling of Leslie Fleetwood-Smith, Bert Ironmonger and Ernie McCormick.

Keith Miller, Lindsay Hassett and Bill Lawry were other notable Victorians, as was the famous wicketkeeper, J.McC. Blackham.

Village cricket

A knock-out competition was founded in 1972 for village cricket clubs by John Haig and Co. Nearly 800 villages competed. Sponsors since then have been *The Cricketer* and Samuel Whitbread, and are now Norsk Hydro. The 1986 final was won by Forge Valley from Scarborough. The most exciting final was in 1985 when the Scottish team, Freuchie, and Rowledge each scored 134 runs, but the former was awarded the title having lost fewer wickets. The finals of the Village Cricket Championship, except for the season of 1974, have all been staged at Lord's, and matches are limited to 40 overs per side.

159

Clyde Walcott cuts a ball past Barrington at slip for West Indies against Surrey in 1957. McIntyre is the wicketkeeper.

W

Walcott, Clyde Leopold
Born: 17 January 1926, Bridgetown, Barbados
Career: 146 *m*; 11,820 runs (av 56.55); 174 *ct*; 33 *st*
Tests: 44 *m*; 3,798 runs (av 56.68); 53 *ct*; 11 *st*
Walcott, at 6 feet 2 inches, was the biggest, burliest and hardest-hitting of the 'three Ws' (Weekes and Worrell were the others) who dominated West Indian batting in the 1950s. He made his debut for Barbados when 16, and four years later made his highest score, 314 not out, when he and Worrell added 574 unfinished for the fourth wicket against Trinidad.

His Test debut followed in 1947/48, when his wicketkeeping was an asset – later in his career he moved to slip and took up fast-medium bowling. His batting relied on powerful drives and cuts with an occasional crashing hook. He made 15 Test centuries, the highest, 220, coming against England at Bridgetown in 1953/54. A leg injury suffered when scoring 90 in the First Test at Edgbaston in 1957 slowed up his career, which ended with British Guiana in 1963/64.

After retirement, he managed several West Indian Test sides.

Wandering clubs
The first established 'wandering' English cricket club were I Zingari, which were created in 1845, whilst second in importance are the Free Foresters, founded in 1856. Both these clubs have played first-class matches.

The wandering clubs had no ground of their own and most of them were composed of ex-public school or university cricketers. In the last 30 years of the 19th century the vogue for wandering clubs mushroomed and a list of some of them makes amusing reading: Knickerbockers, Accidentals, Inexpressibles, Dingle Wanderers, Anomalies, Gnats, Perfect Cures, Active Fleas, Perambulators, Et Ceteras, Limits, XYZ, Owls, Rouge et Noir, Jolly Dogs, Odds and Ends, Caterpillars, IOU, Waifs and Strays, Butterflies, Desperadoes, Eccentrics, Hic et Ubique, Gryphons, Nonentities, Grasshoppers, Casuals, Harum Scarum, I Vagabondi, Idle Boys, Variegated Annuals, Rose of Denmark, Unmitigated Duffers, Fossils, Cock-a-doodle-doo, Pelicans, Don Quixotes, Cochin Chinas, Bohemians, Fly by Nights, The Calves, Will-o'-the-Wisps, Lavender Kids, Spiders, Anythingarians, The Witches, The Wretches, Omnum Gatherums, Incapables, Rovers, The Other Johnnies.

Warwickshire
For the first 40 or more years of the County Championship, the competition was monopolised by the 'Big Six'; even the expansion in 1895 seemed to make little difference to the divide between the haves and the have-nots. In 1911, however, Warwickshire unexpectedly broke the ring. In 1910 the county languished in 14th place with four victories; the following summer they were first with 13 victories. Warwickshire owed almost all to a 22-year-old amateur all-rounder who very nearly retired before the season began. He had accepted the county captaincy for 1911, then had second thoughts, resigned, did not play in the opening match, which Surrey won in a day and a half, then the committee persuaded F.R. Foster to change his mind. He did so, took 116 wickets at 19.15 to top the bowling, scored 1,383 runs at 44.61 to top the batting, and brought the Championship title to Edgbaston.

Two world wars went by before Warwickshire achieved such eminence a second time. In 1951 the rise was not so meteoric – three fairly lucrative summers preceded the Championship win. The Warwickshire side were, however, unusual in that they were almost entirely professional: one amateur made one appearance during the whole campaign of 28 matches. The committee had broken with tradition in 1949 by appointing a professional captain, Tom Dollery. They had three notable bowlers – the spinner Eric Hollies, and two fast men, the New Zealander Tom Pritchard and Charlie Grove. The batting was fairly evenly shared between seven of the principal eleven: the captain, the opening pair of Spooner and Gardner, Hitchcock, Ord, Wolton and Townsend. Unlike 1911 it was very much a team effort, which fact was underlined by the absence from the England Test side of 1951 of any Warwickshire player.

Warwickshire's third title came in 1972, under the wicketkeeper-bowler, A.C. Smith, with the aid of Dennis Amiss and no fewer than four West Indians, Kanhai, Kallicharran, Gibbs and Murray. The Caribbean contingent, however, had had nothing to do with the Gillette Cup victory of 1966, Cartwright, Bob Barber and Amiss being the architects of Worcestershire's defeat in the final, but when the success was repeated in 1968, Kanhai had arrived.

The county have also claimed the John Player title once, in 1980, when the sparkling batting of Amiss had as much as anything to do with their win – the fielding was also particularly athletic that year. Since then things have not gone the county's way.

Weekes, Everton de Courcy
Born: 26 February 1925, Bridgetown, Barbados
Career: 152 *m*; 12,010 runs (av 55.34)
Tests: 48 *m*; 4,455 runs (av 58.61)
Weekes was probably marginally the best batsman of the Weekes-Worrell-Walcott triumvirate which revived West Indian cricket in the 1950s.

Weekes (whose Christian name is in honour of the football club) made his debut for Barbados in 1944/45 and played his first Test against England in 1947/48. He scored 141 in the last Test of the series, then in India made centuries in his next four Test innings to create a record of five in succession. He was run out for 90 in the sixth. His Test average on that tour was 111.28 – on his next visit in 1952/53, when he made his highest Test score, 208, it was a mere 102.28.

Weekes was the shortest of the 'three Ws', and extremely agile and quick on his feet. He was also powerful, and scored with hard shots all round the wicket. On retirement he became a coach, and international bridge player.

Everton Weekes, who after the Second World War became the leading West Indian batsman, taking over the mantle of George Headley.

Wellington

The Basin Reserve, Wellington, was first used for cricket in 1867/68 and the first first-class match took place there in 1873/74 when Wellington played Auckland. Home of the Wellington Cricket Association, it first saw Test cricket in 1929/30, when England opposed New Zealand. Major alterations were carried out on the ground in 1979 and this included the construction of the R.A. Vance Stand. Because of these alterations, the 1978/79 Test, scheduled for Wellington, was transferred to Napier.

West Indies

The first-known cricket club in the West Indies existed in Barbados in 1806 and the first first-class match took place in Bridgetown, Barbados, in 1864/65, between Barbados and Demerara. A tournament between Demerara, Barbados and Trinidad was first staged in 1892/93 and was held in each colony in turn, though not always annually, until 1938/39. Owing to distance, Jamaica, who also possessed a good side, did not compete and most of their important matches were thus against touring sides.

Seven English sides went out to the West Indies prior to the First World War and played first-class matches, and the first West Indies team visited England in 1900; they returned a second time in 1906 and were granted first-class status, but won only three of their 13 important matches.

Test Match status arrived in 1928 when the West Indies visited England for the fourth time, but during the inter-war period they gained a reputation for being much better cricketers at home than they were overseas.

In view of the present reputation of the West Indian fast bowlers, it is strange to realise that their reputation as a side which could compete with the strongest in the world was made initially through the spin bowling of Sonny Ramadhin and Alf Valentine, who confused the English batsmen of 1950. These two unknown youngsters of course received great support from a trio of batsmen, 'the three Ws', Weekes, Worrell and Walcott. No sooner had this combination begun to fade than Gary Sobers emerged and quickly gained a reputation as the world's greatest all-rounder.

The former British colonies became independent states in 1960, but despite differing political views, four – British Guiana (formerly Demerara and now Guyana), Trinidad & Tobago, Jamaica and Barbados – remained as a single cricketing entity and have been joined as 'first-class' teams by the Leeward and Windward Islands, so that six sides now compete in the 'Caribbean Regional Cricket Tournament' which is sponsored by Shell and was founded in 1965/66. The same six sides also compete in a domestic limited-overs competition, which began in 1975/76 and is now the Geddes Grant/Harrison Line Trophy.

During the 1980s the West Indian side under Clive Lloyd and latterly Viv Richards have dominated the international scene and had a sequence of 27 Tests without defeat. The West Indies won the first World Cup in 1975 and retained the title when the second Cup was held in 1979, but were surprisingly beaten by India in the 1983 series. Possessing the most outstanding batsman of the 1980s, Viv Richards, and a formidable array of fast bowlers, it looked as if it could be some little time before they were toppled from their lofty pinnacle.

(*see also* the succeeding entries, also Australia v West Indies and England v West Indies, also individual entries under cricketers, competitions and grounds)

West Indies v India

Results: Played 54; West Indies won 22; India won 5; Drawn 27

The West Indies have dominated this series, which began in 1948/49 with John Goddard's team in India. It is remarkable to read in the reports of this first meeting that neither side possessed bowlers of sufficient speed to worry the batsmen, and as the spin bowlers found little help from the docile wickets, four of the five Tests were drawn. West Indies batted first in the opening game in Delhi and no fewer than four of their batsmen, Clyde Walcott, Gerry Gomez, Everton Weekes and Roy Christiani hit hundreds. India ran up a total of 454, but still had to follow on and the game then petered out. West Indies continued the run glut at Bombay, declaring with their total of 629 for 6; once more India followed on, before centuries from Modi and Hazare produced a second draw. At Eden Gardens, Calcutta, Everton Weekes took the opportunity of making centuries in both innings, thereby recording his

New Zealand playing England at Wellington in 1983/84.
John Wright is caught Cook bowled Botham in a drawn match.

*The West Indies tourists to England in 1939. Standing, left to right: W. Ferguson (scorer),
G.E. Gomez, J.B. Stollmeyer, L.G. Hylton, T. Johnson, C.B. Clarke, H.P. Bayley, E.A.V. Williams.
Sitting: G.A. Headley, I. Barrow, R.S. Grant (captain), J.M. Kidney (manager), J.H. Cameron,
L.N. Constantine, E.A. Martindale. Front: K.H. Weekes, J.E.D. Sealey, V.H. Stollmeyer.*

*The fifth Test between the West Indies and England in 1967/68, and Tom Graveney is out, caught by
wicketkeeper Murray after turning a ball from Lance Gibbs to leg and seeing it ricochet off Gary Sobers.*

England batsman Dexter has his off stump knocked completely from the ground by a ball from Watson of the West Indies in the Third Test at Kingston, Jamaica, in 1959/60.

fifth successive Test innings of over 100, not that this quite incredible feat really helped West Indies, as heavy scoring by India meant a third draw.

Weekes made only 90 (before being run out) in the Fourth Test, when West Indies began with an opening stand of 239 between Rae and Stollmeyer. This time the Indian batting failed. Jones and Trim managed to extract life from the wicket and India lost by an innings.

The final match in Bombay provided the only exciting climax of the tour. India were set 361 to win in 395 minutes. Hazare hit a fine hundred, but when the final over began 11 runs were needed and the last two men were at the wicket (Sen was absent hurt). Only five runs were added and so India ended still lacking six.

Everton Weekes hit 779 runs and averaged 111.28, whilst Hazare, with 543 runs at 67.87, was India's leading batsman. The less said about the bowling figures the better.

The next series, which took place in the West Indies in 1952/53, ended in the same result, with four draws and a single win by West Indies. Again Everton Weekes was the leading figure, his record of 716 runs, average 102.28, being little changed from the last series. Polly Umrigar was India's best run scorer. The one definite result came at Bridgetown, when Ramadhin took 5 for 26 and dismissed India for 129.

West Indies won the 1958/59 series by three matches to nil, Roy Gilchrist and Wes Hall being too fearsome for the Indians. Sobers, Solomon, Butcher and Kanhai on the other hand found few terrors in the home attack, for whom the leg-spinner Gupte toiled with too little reward.

When India went to the West Indies in February 1962, they had just beaten England by two matches to nil and were therefore entitled to a degree of confidence. They were, however, dismissed for 203 and 98 in the opening Test in Port of Spain, the main damage being done by Wes Hall. Hall was again responsible for his side's success in the Second Test, when he took nine wickets.

Shaken by these two defeats, the tourists travelled to Barbados to meet the island side before playing the Bridgetown Test. It was in the former match that the dreadful accident befell the Indian captain, Nariman Contractor. He had his skull fractured by a rising ball from Charlie Griffith and was rushed to hospital where he underwent brain surgery.

The 21-year-old Nawab of Pataudi was given the captaincy for the remainder of the tour, but the Indians lost all three of the Tests.

The two series in which India came out on top were in 1970/71 in the West Indies and 1978/79 in India. In the first of these, Gavaskar's batting was outstanding. With four centuries in the series, he totalled 774 runs at an average of 154.80. The one definite result of the series came at Port of Spain. India's spinners, Bedi, Venkat and Prasanna managed to subdue the home batsmen and West Indies were dismissed for 214 and 261. India won the game by seven wickets with Gavaskar being undefeated on 67.

India's other successful series was due to the defection of the majority of West Indian Test cricketers, who opted for Packer's WSC. So the second string West Indians did well to lose only one of the six Tests, and that by the relatively close margin of three wickets. Gavaskar was again the main Indian batsman, with over 700 runs and an average of 91.50, but it was Viswanath who scored the vital hundred in the victory at Madras.

Clive Lloyd has led West Indies in the two series since then and has won both by a clear margin, with India failing to win a single match on either occasion.

West Indies v New Zealand
Results: Played 21; West Indies won 7; New Zealand won 3; Drawn 11

All six series between the two sides are of post-Second World War vintage. New Zealand have captured the rubber once, in 1979/80, when the West Indies under Clive Lloyd toured. This series, which consisted of three matches, was made most unpleasant by the West Indian attitude to certain umpiring decisions. In the First Test at Dunedin, Holding appealed for a catch against Parker and when the umpire indicated 'not out', the West Indian bowler kicked down the stumps. The West Indian manager described the umpires in a television interview as atrocious and Holding's action as understandable. New Zealand won the game by one wicket, due to Richard Hadlee, who took 11 for 102, as well as scoring 50 in the first innings.

Hadlee and Cairns dismissed West Indies cheaply in the Second Test and New Zealand. weathering a barrage of bouncers, built up a commanding lead of 232. During the tea interval on the second day it appeared that the West Indies had decided to give up the match, since they declined to take the field after the statutory 20-minute break. The reason for this was the West Indian objection to Umpire Goodall. After some discussion, however, the West Indies were persuaded to continue and the remainder of the day's play was completed; the West Indies left the field to the jeers of the crowd.

On the fourth day Umpire Goodall was deliberately charged into by Croft. Three hundreds, by Haynes, Rowe and King in the West Indian second innings meant that the game was drawn. The final match was also drawn, though New Zealand again had the advantage after the first innings. Rain cut down the playing time and bad light brought a thoroughly ill-tempered series to an end.

New Zealand have toured the West Indies twice. The first trip was under Graham Dowling in 1971/72 and was only arranged after the proposed South African tour to New Zealand had been cancelled.

The First Test took place at Sabina Park and the home side enjoyed easy runs on a perfect wicket, Lawrence Rowe making 214 and Roy Fredericks 163, before Sobers declared. Glenn Turner replied with another double century and thus the match drifted to a draw. This set the pattern and indeed all five matches were drawn. Bruce Taylor nearly caused an upset in the Fourth Test when he took 7 for 74 and dismissed West Indies for 133. This they immediately repaired by hitting 564 for 8 in their second innings. Glenn Turner managed another double century in the Fourth Test, when New Zealand put on 387 before their first wicket fell.

There was some possibility of a West Indian win in the final match, but an unbroken stand of 65 for the eighth wicket by Taylor and Wadsworth held until stumps. Turner hit 672 runs in the series, averaging 96.00 and Bev Congdon, who acted as captain in the three last Tests, Dowling having injured his back, also flourished with 531 runs, average 88.50. Brian Taylor with 27 wickets was easily the best bowler on either side.

Geoff Howarth led New Zealand on the only other visit to the Caribbean, in 1984/85. The first two Tests were both drawn, but West Indies, under Viv Richards, broke the deadlock at Bridgetown. Marshall and Garner took full advantage of a rain-affected pitch to dismiss the tourists for 94. Richards then made a century for West Indies and Marshall took a further seven wickets in the second innings to allow victory by ten wickets.

West Indies gained another ten-wicket win in the Fourth and final Test in Kingston. For New Zealand the batting highlight of the match was a stand of 210 for the second wicket by Howarth and Jeff Crowe. Malcolm Marshall was the bowler of the series with 27 wickets at an average of 18.00.

West Indies v Pakistan

Results: Played 19; West Indies won 7; Pakistan won 4; Drawn 8

Only five series of matches have taken place of which West Indies have won three, Pakistan have won one and one has been tied.

The first series has its niche in cricket history with the record innings of 365 not out which the 21-year-old Gary Sobers hit in the Third Test at Kingston. Although Pakistan scored 328 in the first innings they were completely overwhelmed by the West Indies, who replied with 790 for 3 declared. Aside from Sobers' massive innings, Conrad Hunte made 260 and Sobers and Hunte added 446 for the second wicket. It should, however, be pointed out that Pakistan's bowler Mahmood Hussain bowled just five balls of the opening over and then retired with a strained thigh muscle, that the captain, A.H. Kardar, bowled 37 overs in spite of a broken finger on his bowling hand, and that Nasim-ul-Ghani, after sending down 14 overs, fractured his thumb. Pakistan were dismissed in their second innings for 288, but batted two men short.

West Indies had already won the Second Test and went on to win the Fourth. Pakistan then salvaged their pride by winning the Fifth Test by an innings. Fazal Mahmood took six wickets in the first innings and Nasim-ul-Ghani six in the second as West Indies were dismissed for 268 and 227. Wazir Mohammad was Pakistan's highest scorer in this match with 189, though it was Hanif Mohammad who broke many Pakistan records when he made 337 in the first drawn Test. His innings lasted 16 hours and 13 minutes, the longest recorded to that date.

The following season the West Indies went to Pakistan for a series which the latter won by two matches to one. The great Fazal captained Pakistan in this series and did more than anyone else to beat the West Indies. Pakistan won the first match by ten wickets, Fazal having seven victims; in the second game he claimed 12 for 100 (West Indies were dismissed for 76) and Pakistan won by 41 runs.

Kanhai hit a double hundred in the Third Test, which West Indies won by an innings; the game marked the debut of 15-year-old Mushtaq Mohammad, whose all-round cricket was to play such a part in the future: he captained Pakistan nearly 20 years later in the fourth series against the West Indies.

Clive Lloyd led the West Indies in the three other series and lost only one game out of the 11 played, so West Indies have had matters very much their own way for, to Pakistani eyes, too long.

In 1985/86, West Indies made a tour of Pakistan in which only one-day internationals were played, West Indies winning three matches to two.

Western Australia

Until the railway arrived in 1917 it was a major task to travel to Perth and this prevented the Cricket Association, which had been formed in 1885, organising much cricket with other colonies, though South Australia were opposed in March 1893, in the first first-class match involving Western Australia. It was not until 1947/48 that the Association entered the Sheffield Shield and then Keith Carmody led the debutants to the title. The 1970s under John Inverarity were great years for Western Australia with Dennis Lillee, Bob Massie and Terry Alderman providing a very strong attack and the success has continued into the 1980s. The state has dominated the domestic limited-overs competition, being winners five times.

Wicket

1 The target, comprising three upright stumps and two bails, at which the bowler aims when delivering the ball.
2 A batsman, who has been dismissed.
3 A 'wicket' partnership is the amount of runs added to the team's total by two batsmen, without a player being dismissed.
4 The ground between the two sets of stumps; in this meaning 'wicket' is used synonymously with 'pitch'.

Wicketkeeper

The fieldsman who stands behind the stumps at the batting end of the pitch to receive the delivery from the bowler if the batsman fails to strike it, or to catch the batsman out if the latter snicks the ball.

Wicketkeepers

Of all the skills in cricket, wicketkeeping is the one which goes unnoticed when it is good, but is the first to be criticised when something goes awry. If one reads the report of a day's play in the press and there is not a mention of the wicketkeeper, he's had a good day. The talented keeper makes the job look so simple, that there is nothing on which to comment. He knows his bowlers and when the ball passes the wicket he is in the correct position to receive it, no need for the last second acrobatic dive, or the spectacular save. K.S. Ranjitsinhji sums up the wicketkeeper's role in 'The Jubilee Book of Cricket': 'It is as if the bowler were at one end of a telegraph wire and the wicketkeeper at the other. There is a continual current of thought and action passing and repassing between them. At least this is what ought to be. The wicketkeeper may almost be described as part of the bowler; if the other fielders ought to bowl in spirit with the bowler, the wicketkeeper ought to do so ten times over.'

J.McC. Blackham is regarded as the greatest wicketkeeper during the first two decades of Test cricket and even in 1932, when he died, he is stated as being the finest wicketkeeper of all time. W.G. Grace, writing in 1890, was certainly of that opinion: 'He is marvellously quick, taking shooters and yorkers between the wicket and the pads with comparative ease. The quality of the bowling makes no difference to him, for he is equally at home with fast and slow.'

In the inter-war period another Australian takes the crown. Frank Chester, the most famous umpire of his generation, notes: 'I think my judgment is correct when I elect Oldfield as the greatest [wicketkeeper] of all time. Proof of his class is that after a long career his hands and fingers were as undamaged as when he started. His positional sense was so highly developed that he had no need to resort to acrobatics.' Don Bradman agrees with Chester: 'I could not do otherwise than class Oldfield as the finest wicketkeeper I have seen.'

Of the post-Second World War era, Alan Knott is regarded as the leading wicketkeeper. J.M. Brearley, the England captain, notes: 'In my view he was also the best wicketkeeper of his time.'

In selecting this trio of wicketkeepers, who are regarded so highly by their contemporaries, it is not with the intention of denigrating the expertise of a great many others, who in partnership with a particular bowler, or in a particular season or Test series were outstanding. Herbert Strudwick in conjunction with Bill Hitch, Godfrey Evans in Australia in 1946/47, Rodney Marsh with Lillee and Thomson, Ames with Freeman of Kent, MacGregor and Woods, H.B. Cameron in 1935, are just a few.

(*see also* individual entries for cricketers)

Wide

A delivery from the bowler which is so far away from the batsman's stumps that he is unable in the opinion of the umpire to reach the ball. The umpire then signals a 'wide', which is added to the score as an 'extra', but since 1985 has also been noted as 'run conceded' by the bowler.

Wills Cup

The major one-day limited-overs competition in Pakistan, instituted in 1980/81 and involving the leading Qaid-I-Azam Trophy teams. The PIA won the first three tournaments.

Wills Trophy

The principal one-day limited overs competition for leading Ranji Trophy sides in India, instituted in 1977/78.

Wiltshire

A founder member of the Minor Counties Championship, Wiltshire have taken part since 1897. The great days of the club were in the Edwardian era and they won the Championship in 1902 and 1909. In the former season they possessed a trio of formidable professional bowlers, W. Overton, W. Smith and T. Smart, all of whom took more than 50 wickets and the first two also made useful runs. In their second summer of success they played ten matches and won nine. Mitchell took 90 wickets at 12.53 each and C.S. Awdry and his brother R.W. Awdry scored most runs. The Awdry family continued to play a large part in Wiltshire cricket in the inter-war period,

The first English women's team to tour Australia and New Zealand and play a series of Test Matches. The 1934/35 tourists are, standing left to right: D. Turner, M. Child, M. Richards, M. Hide, J. Liebert, M. Taylor, G. Morgan, Sitting: D. Spear, C. Valentine, M. Maclagan, E. Snowball, B. Archdale (captain), B. Green (manager), J.E. Partridge, M. Burletson. Molly Hide was probably the best-known pre-war woman player.

notably the two sons of C.S. Awdry. In post-Second World War years J.H. Merryweather was for long the backbone of the county.

Wisden Trophy
To commemorate the 100th edition of Wisden Cricketers' Almanack in 1963, the proprietors of the annual instituted the Wisden Trophy to be played for in perpetuity by England and West Indies. The first series for the trophy was staged in England in 1963.
(*see also* England v West Indies)

Women's cricket
In the 18th and 19th centuries cricket played by women was regarded as little more than of curiosity value. The English Women's Cricket Association was formed in 1926 and that in Australia in 1931.

The first women's cricket series between Australia and England was staged in Australia in 1934/35, with England winning by two matches to nil under the captaincy of Betty Archdale. The English team went on to New Zealand and won the only Test.

Only one major tour to England took place before the Second World War, Australia sending a side in 1937, the rubber being tied one match each. England's leading pre-war player was Betty Snowball.

International matches by England have been frequent though not annual events since the Second World War. England's most accomplished wielder of the bat is probably Rachael Hayhoe Flint, who averaged over 60 in her Test career. Enid Bakewell is the outstanding all-rounder having achieved the 'double' of 1,000 runs and 100 wickets during the 1968/69 English tour to Australia and New Zealand.

Australian captain W.M. Woodfull.

Betty Wilson of Australia achieved the match 'double' of 100 runs and 10 wickets in a Test Match in 1957/58.

Woodfull, William Maldon
Born: 22 August 1897, Maldon, Victoria, Australia
Died: 11 August 1965, near Tweed Heads, New South Wales, Australia
Career: 174 m; 13,388 runs (av 64.99)
Tests: 35 m; 2,300 runs (av 46.00)
Woodfull, a schoolmaster by profession, made his debut for Victoria in 1921/22 and his Test debut in England on the 1926 tour. He and Ponsford became a prolific opening pair for

Frank Woolley, the graceful Kent left-hander, whose long career produced some record figures, including over 1,000 catches, the most of any player not a wicketkeeper.

169

Victoria. A sound batsman with little backlift, his studious approach to the game made him a respected captain of both state and country until his retirement in 1934. He led Australia on Ashes-winning tours of England in 1930 and 1934 and was at the heart of the 'bodyline' controversy in 1932/33 when he was one of the principal 'victims' and also the captain who spoke out against 'unsportsmanlike' tactics. He died after collapsing while playing golf.

Woolley, Frank Edward

Born: 27 May 1887, Tonbridge, Kent
Died: 18 October 1978, Halifax, Novia Scotia
Career: 978 *m*; 58,959 runs (av 40.77); 2,066 wkts (av 19.87)
Tests: 64 *m*; 3,283 runs (av 36.07); 83 wkts (av 33.91)
Woolley enjoyed a long career, and was one of the game's greatest all-rounders. His figures are impressive, but those who saw him claim that the artistry of his batting was above statistics. He was very tall and left-handed, and none of his nearly 60,000 runs came from anything but a graceful shot. His aggregate is second only to Hobbs'.

He made his debut for Kent in 1906, and played 764 matches for them until 1938. He scored 1,000 runs in a season no fewer than 28 times, a record equalled only by Grace. Eight times he completed the 'double', and no player can equal his record of four times scoring 2,000 runs and taking 100 wickets. When in his forties he more or less gave

up his left-arm bowling, which early in his career was medium and later slow, but he bowled enough to become one of nine players with a career aggregate of 20,000 runs and 2,000 wickets. He is also the only player, other than a wicketkeeper, to take 1,000 catches: his 1,018 is 144 ahead of Grace.

Woolley's Test career lasted from 1909 to 1934, but while good by normal standards, was not of the brilliance of his county career.

Worcestershire

Fostershire have progressed a long way since that famous brotherhood launched the county on their first-class way in 1899. The brothers were all trained at Malvern School and among their number was R.E. Foster, whose 287 was a world Test record in 1903/4, but whose career was to end all too early, cut short by diabetes, which led to his death aged 36.

The county enjoyed limited success before the First World War, and in 1914 were close to financial ruin. They were unable to compete in the first post-war summer of 1919, but re-entered the Championship in 1920. In the late 1920s Worcestershire spent three successive years at the foot of the table and their team comprised a variegated collection of both amateurs and professionals, few of whom could spare the time for more than a handful of matches. Briefly after the Second World War the team threatened to win the Championship. Howorth, Jenkins and Perks formed an effective

Champions for the second consecutive year in 1965, the Worcestershire team at Lord's was, standing, left to right: W.B. Powell (masseur), D.N.F. Slade, R.G.A. Headley, B.M. Brain, L.J. Coldwell, B.A. D'Oliveira, J.A. Ormrod, A. Ross-Slater (scorer); sitting: D.W. Richardson, J.A. Flavell, T.W. Graveney, M.J. Horton, R. Booth. The captain, D. Kenyon, was not playing in this match.

World Series Cricket at Sydney in 1979, Australia batting against the West Indies.

bowling force and the amateurs, R.E.S. Wyatt, C.H. Palmer and M.L.Y. Ainsworth helped E. Cooper to compile satisfactory run totals. In the 1950s Worcestershire fell back to almost their pre-war confusion until 1961, when two youngsters took off together – Ron Headley, the son of the famous George, as a batsman, and Norman Gifford, the Lancastrian, as a spinner. These two boosted the team mustered by Kenyon and with the two experienced seamers, Coldwell and Flavell, in top form, the county looked like taking the title. In the event they had to wait until 1964, by which time Tom Graveney had crossed the border from Gloucestershire. The success was repeated in 1965 and for the next ten summers the county were in the hunt for one of the trophies. They took the John Player League in 1971, as well as being beaten finalists in the Gillette and Benson & Hedges Cup. During this period the South African, Basil d'Oliveira, played an important role with both bat and ball. The first half of the 1980s did not produce any titles, but following the retirement in 1982 of their prolific New Zealand opening batsman, Glenn Turner, the county found another overseas player breaking records in 1986 – Graeme Hick from Zimbabwe. In the winter Ian Botham from Somerset and Graham Dilley from Kent were also added to the staff. They also had several other young men who could bring a title back to New Road within the next few years, including batsman-wicketkeeper Steve Rhodes, who was on the verge of an England place. Basil d'Oliveira's son Damian created a new record in 1985 when he hit a century in the Player League, thus emulating his father – the first father and son to perform the feat.

World Championship of Cricket

To celebrate 150 years of the founding of Victoria, this World Championship was arranged between the seven Test-playing countries in 1984/85. The countries were divided into two groups and then the two top teams in each group played in the semi-final. The final, which was a day/night match was won by India, who beat Pakistan by eight wickets. The Championship was sponsored by Benson & Hedges.

World Cup

see Prudential World Cup

World Series Cricket

This was the title given to the matches played in Australia by Kerry Packer's organisation, when the Australian authorities rejected his bid to televise the official Test Matches.

The World Series matches were divided into three types, the Super-Tests, which were five-day games, and two types of one-day limited-overs matches.

The ICC reacted by banning all the players who signed for the World Series from Test and county cricket. The courts however ruled this ban void.

The series lasted two seasons, 1977/78 and 1978/79, and included matches in the West Indies and New Zealand. On 24 April 1979 the Australian Board of Control gave Mr Packer's television company exclusive rights to Tests for three years. This agreement ended the World Series Cricket, which however brought several major changes to the game, notably floodlit matches.

A cricketer who excelled in all departments, Frank Worrell's lasting triumph was his captaincy of West Indies, particularly in Australia in 1960/61.

Worrell, Frank Mortimer Magline

Born: 1 August 1924, Bridgetown, Barbados
Died: 13 March 1967, Kingston, Jamaica
Career: 208 m; 15,025 runs (av 54.24); 349 wkts (av 28.98)
Tests: 51 m; 3,860 runs (av 49.48); 69 wkts (av 38.72)
Worrell was the most elegant and orthodox of the Weekes-Worrell-Walcott trio of West Indian giants. He was the slimmest, the rapier to their bludgeons – he excelled in the late cut. Perhaps his outstanding achievement as a cricketer, however, was in his captaincy.

He made his debut in 1941/42 for Barbados – after five seasons he switched to Jamaica. When 19, he made his highest score, 308 not out, sharing an unbeaten stand of 502 with Goddard against Trinidad. Three years later he and Walcott added 574, also unbeaten, against the same team. He had begun his career as an all-rounder, being a slow left-arm bowler. Later he became medium-paced, and opened the bowling, and could deliver an occasional very fast one. A middle-order right-hand batsman, he sometimes converted to opener, and was always willing to play to suit his side.

His Test career began in 1947/48 and in 1950 he made his highest Test score, 261, against England at Trent Bridge.

For the 1960/61 series in Australia, Worrell was made captain of West Indies. The First Test was tied, and Worrell led his team in one of the most exciting of all series. From 1964 the matches between the two countries have been for the Frank Worrell Trophy (q.v.).

From 1948 Worrell played in the Lancashire League, and studied at Manchester University. On retirement in 1964 he became a Warden at the University of the West Indies and a senator in the Jamaican parliament, but in 1967 he died of leukemia.

Y

Yorker

A delivery by the bowler which lands near or in the block-hole (q.v.). By some authorities this is regarded as an ideal ball to be sent down by a fast bowler to a fresh batsman.

W.H. Anstead, the Surrey fast bowler, was an early exponent of the yorker. He bowled with brilliant success in 1870, but owing to his profession, had then to give up serious cricket.

Yorkshire

The greatest of the cricketing counties, Yorkshire have paid a heavy price, in terms of trophies, for their decision to turn their face against the unseemly scramble to lure overseas talent.

Although cricket began in the county in the second half of the 18th century it was not until the 1890s, under that benevolent patriarch, Lord Hawke, that Yorkshire began to pull away from the rest of the field. The Championship had been won in 1867, 1869 and 1870, but rivalry existed between the leading centres of cricket in the county, as well as between the professionals themselves. Following the example of their neighbours to the south, Notts, Yorkshire were captained by a professional and what amateurs there were, were of little importance. Lord Hawke changed all that, and his hand guided the county almost to his death in 1938.

Yorkshire's Championship success in 1893 was due to the bowling of Wainwright, Peel and Hirst. Peel's career was prematurely ended by Lord Hawke because of his drunkeness, but Yorkshire immediately found a new left-armer in Rhodes. Schofield Haigh rose to fame as a contemporary of Rhodes. The batting was equally strong – Hirst and Rhodes being outstanding all-rounders.

After the First World War Yorkshire won the Championship from 1922 for four successive years. In Holmes and Sutcliffe they had acquired a great pair of opening batsmen and in Macaulay yet another in their line of famous bowlers. Hedley Verity arose in 1930 just at the moment of Rhodes' retirement. Rhodes is the only bowler to claim over 4,000 wickets in his career, but Verity quickly produced his own record by taking ten wickets in an innings at a cost of only ten runs – against Notts in 1932.

The flow of great players continued. When Holmes went, Hutton arrived – and within a few seasons had claimed the Test batting record of 364 for England in the 1938 Oval match.

Yorkshire won the Championship in the last three seasons prior to the outbreak of the Second World War, in which Verity lost his life, and in 1946 they were again Champions, having unearthed Arthur Booth, yet another slow left-arm bowler. He topped the first-class averages in what was his only full season of county cricket.

Yorkshire in 1922, when the county won the first of four consecutive championships.

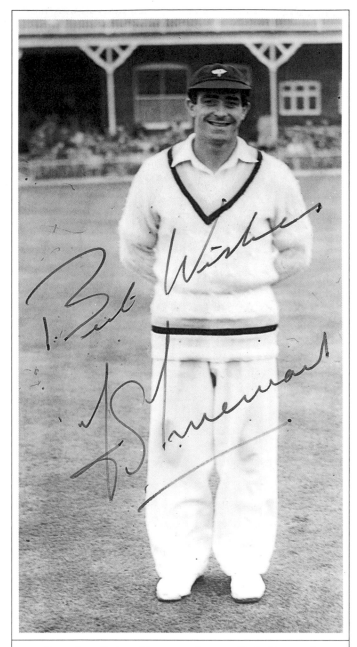

Once described as 'the most famous Yorkshireman', 1950s fast bowler Fred Trueman.

The great slow left-arm bowler of the 1930s who was killed in the Second World War, Hedley Verity.

During the 1950s, Yorkshire had to acknowledge the superiority of Surrey, but the Championship was won once more in 1959 and the following decade was one of renewed splendour with Illingworth and Close, initially assisted by Trueman and then by Boycott and Hampshire. The defection of Illingworth to Leicester in 1969 and Close to Somerset soon after, coupled with the strengthening of all the other counties through foreign mercenaries, spelt the end of the Yorkshire domination. Internal ructions further handicapped the county and the only recent success came with the John Player title in 1983.

Youngest cricketers

The youngest cricketer to appear in a first-class match in England is believed to be C.R. Young aged 15 years and 131 days, when appearing for Hampshire v Kent at Gravesend on 13 June 1867. The youngest in Australia is L.J. Junor, aged 15 years and 265 days, when appearing for Victoria v Western Australia in 1929/30. In India Alimuddin is stated to have been 12 years 73 days when appearing for Rajputana v Delhi in 1942/43.

The youngest Test cricketer is stated to be Mushtaq Mohammad, who was 15 years and 124 days when playing for Pakistan v West Indies at Lahore in 1958/59. The youngest for Australia is I.D. Craig, 17 years 239 days against South Africa in 1952/53 and for England D.B. Close, 18 years 149 days against New Zealand in 1949.

Yorkshire in 1933, completing a hat-trick of championships. Standing, from left: W. Ringrose (scorer), H. Verity, F. Dennis, W.E. Bowes, A.C. Rhodes, A. Mitchell, Heyhirst (masseur); sitting: W. Barber, G.G. Macaulay, P. Holmes, A.B. Sellers, H. Sutcliffe, M. Leyland, A. Wood.

Z

Zaheer Abbas

Born: 24 July 1947, Sialkot, Pakistan
Career: 447 *m*; 34,289 runs (av 52.11)
Tests: 78 *m*; 5,062 runs (av 44.79)

A stylish and prolific right-hand middle-order batsman, usually No. 3 or 4, Zaheer made his first-class debut in 1965/66 and his Test debut in 1969/70. He toured England with the Pakistan teams of 1971, 1974 and 1982, but most of his cricket has been played for Gloucestershire, for whom he made his debut in 1972. He has hit over 1,000 runs in an English season 11 times, his best summer being 1976 when he was the leading batsman in England with 2,554 runs (average 75.11); he also topped the English first-class averages in 1981 and 1982. He was the first Pakistani batsman to complete 100 first-class hundreds and by early 1987 had made 107. His highest innings is 274 for Pakistan v England at Edgbaston in 1974.

He batted in spectacles and later wore contact lenses. He captained Pakistan in 14 Tests.

Zimbabwe

The first cricket played in Rhodesia (as Zimbabwe was then called) was by British troops in 1890. As local-born players gained proficiency and formed teams and leagues, standards improved, and there were visits by MCC in 1930/31 and 1938/39, and Australia in 1936. In the 1930s Rhodesia began to play in the Currie Cup (q.v.) and after the Second World War were regular contestants. Many Rhodesian-born players (recently K.C. Bland) appeared in Test cricket for South Africa.

Touring teams from many parts of the world visited Rhodesia after the Second World War, but visits ceased for a time in 1965, when the country declared independence from Britain. The name Zimbabwe was adopted in 1979 and election to the International Cricket Conference was effected in 1981. The ICC Trophy (q.v.) was won in 1982 and 1986. The 1982 victory led to a place in the 1983 Prudential World Cup (q.v.), in which Zimbabwe played extremely well, actually beating Australia in their opening match.

An England B team toured Zimbabwe in 1985/86, followed by a team from New South Wales.

Statistics, Bibliography and Acknowledgements

In presenting the facts in this encyclopedia, we have endeavoured to provide the reader with a general knowledge of the principal elements which added together comprise a broad history of the game, as well as an overall picture of cricket in today's world. It is not a record book – *The Hamlyn A-Z of Cricket Records* (Hamlyn, revised edition 1985 by Peter Wynne-Thomas) already covers this field.

We hope that the information given will encourage further exploration of the sport's many facets – there are after all over 10,000 titles in cricket's bibliography, so there must be a book to throw further light on every aspect and to suit every taste. Despite all this literature and over 100 years of research by historians, some questions still remain unanswered. Somewhere hidden in an unassuming pile of old manuscripts there must be an original copy of the Laws of Cricket. Scholars all agree that the 1744 version was merely an update, yet no one has so far discovered an earlier edition.

Is it not amazing that the premier cricket club in the world, the MCC, have no records of their club's transactions for their first 30 to 40 years of existence? Did all their records really vanish when the Lord's pavilion burnt down, or, in the private papers of a descendant of one of the original presidents or committeemen, do some of the transactions remain to be uncovered? How did 11 come to be the ideal number for a cricket side, when 12 or 10 seem so much more suitable? Perhaps in a future edition of this work we will be able to publish the answer, because some reader has been motivated to dig in an unexplored field.

That, however, is enough of the unanswered questions. Before acknowledging the assistance we received whilst compiling this book, we must put in a word of explanation regarding the statistics used. After much research, for the first time a definitive list of first-class matches has been published by the Association of Cricket Statisticians. The records printed in this encyclopedia conform to this list and thus in some instances differ from the 'traditional' figures. Any reader who would like a detailed answer to a specific difference is invited to write to the compilers, who will be most pleased to provide the information.

We wish to thank Tony Woodhouse, David Harvey, Philip Bailey, Philip Thorn and John Cope for their advice on a variety of matters and also acknowledge the use of the following publications:

Wisden Cricketers' Almanack, various editions
'Who's Who of Cricketers' by P. Bailey, P. Thorn and P. Wynne-Thomas, Newnes, London, 1984
'Bibliography of Cricket' by E.W. Padwick, Library Association, London, 1983
The Cricketer, various issues
Wisden Cricket Monthly, various issues
ACS International Cricket Yearbook, 1986 and 1987 editions
The Journal of the Cricket Society, various issues
'Cricket' by W.G. Grace, Arrowsmith, Bristol, 1890
'The Language of Cricket' by W.J. Lewis, Oxford University Press, London, 1934
Cricket Quarterly, various issues
'Fresh Light on 18th Century Cricket' by G.B. Buckley, Cotterell, Birmingham, 1935
'Fresh Light on Pre-Victorian Cricket' by G.B. Buckley, Cotterell, Birmingham, 1937
'Cricket Scores, Notices, Etc' by H.T. Waghorn, Blackwood, London, 1899
'The Dawn of Cricket' by H.T. Waghorn, MCC, London, 1906
'The Laws of Cricket' by R.S. Rait Kerr, Longmans. London, 1950
'Cricket, A History' by R. Bowen, Eyre & Spottiswoode, London, 1970

In addition to these works, the many publications of the Association of Cricket Statisticians, the histories of the 17 first-class counties and their annual reports or yearbooks, the histories of the individual member countries of the ICC and the annuals published by those countries, were consulted to verify details on specific subjects.

Throughout the work (*) denotes not out, or unbroken partnerships. Records are complete to the end of the English 1986 season and players' biographies include the Australia v England 1986/87 Test Series.

Peter Arnold
Peter Wynne-Thomas
April 1987